THE EUROPEAN COMMUNITY
A Guide to the Maze

THE EUROPEAN COMMUNITY

A Guide to the Maze

THIRD EDITION

**Stanley A Budd
and Alun Jones**

KOGAN
PAGE

First published in Great Britain in
1985 by Inro Press, Edinburgh

Second edition published in 1987 by
Kogan Page Ltd, 120 Pentonville Road,
London N1 9JN

Third edition 1989
Reprinted 1990

*British Library Cataloguing in
Publication Data*
Budd, Stanley A (Stanley Alec), 1931–
  The European Community: a guide
  to the maze.—3rd ed.
  1. European Economic
  Community
  I. Title   II. Jones, Alun
  341.24′22

  ISBN 0-7494-0023-4

Typeset in 10/11 point Melior by
The Castlefield Press,
Wellingborough, Northants
Printed and bound in Great Britain by
Biddles Ltd, Guildford and King's Lynn

The opinions in this book are our own,
and should not be interpreted as being
those of the European Commission.

S.A.B.
A.J.

CONTENTS

PART VI
POLICIES IN PROCESS OF CHANGE

INTRODUCTION TO THE THIRD EDITION

'The Maze' was first drafted during Spring of 1985 and was finally completed in November of that year. Stanley Budd in the Introduction to that edition declared : 'It would be an enormous pleasure to find this book hopelessly out of date in a year or so, because sensible blueprints were at last becoming a reality'. He can be justifiably pleased. The second edition appeared in 1987 at a time of positive ferment in Europe. It was in May 1989 that I was approached by Kogan Page to produce a third edition to take into account the wide ranging developments in the European Community brought about by the Single European Act. I have incorporated these significant political initiatives in this new edition.

The message of this book is that the politically-inspired processes of change in Europe are occurring and moving at a rapid pace. A new political geography of Europe is in the throes of creation. However, many people, both young and old, continue to be ill-informed on the nature and scope of one of the principal actors in this wide-ranging political process – the European Community.

Updating 'The Maze' has not been an easy task since I have been at pains not to interrupt the flow of the work, though, at the same time, careful to remove items no longer of relevance in the EC of today. I fully agree with Stanley Budd's comment that 'the trivialisation of the European Community by the British media is far from trivial in the damage it causes.' However, it is for that reason that I have taken the liberty of removing the section on 'Myths and Misconceptions' which previously featured. The momentum of the European Community is now so great that even the attempted revitalisation of anti-European sentiment in some quarters seems to be unable to halt the tide of further European integration. The title of the text has also been changed in recognition not only of the popular usage of the term EC rather than EEC, but also to signify that the Community, even since 'The Maze' first appeared, has progressed into more than simply an economic grouping of countries.

Several people for various reasons deserve special thanks – Martin

Munro, Peter Wood, Bill Mead, and Jackie Grant. The staff of the European Commission in London also helped in providing up-to-date material for the text. Any errors or omissions are entirely my responsibility however.

Dr Alun Jones
Department of Geography
University College
London

Illness having prevented me from revising the book for this new edition, I am very grateful to Alun Jones for his trouble and work in preparing it at short notice.

S.A.B.

HOW TO USE THE BOOK

There are two sections. The first, on plain paper, looks at the Community and its various policies. Inevitably, entries are brief, oversimplified and no doubt sometimes partial. However, at the foot of each page is a reference to more detailed (and dispassionate!) material on the ground covered on that page.

Much of this is free from any Commission Office. Almost all of it can be consulted there, or at any European Documentation Centre. (The addresses of both are given in the last pages of the book.) References at the foot of pages in the main text refer to the coloured pages (Part VIII). This has its own separate index, and follows the same order as the main text.

ACRONYMS AND ABBREVIATIONS
See also Index

ACP	African, Caribbean and Pacific members of the Lomé Convention
BCC	Business Cooperation Centre
BEUC	European Bureau of Consumers' Unions
BICEPS	Bioformatics Collaborative European Programme and Strategy
BOTB	The British Overseas Trade Board
BRITE	Basic Research in Industrial Technologies for Europe
CADDIA	Cooperation in Automation for Data and Documentation for Import
CAP	Common Agricultural Policy
CCT/CET	Common Customs Tariff (between the EC and third countries)
CEDEFOP	European Centre for the Development of Vocational Training
CEN	European Committee for Standardisation
CENELEC	European Committee for Electrotechnical standardisation
CERD	European Committee for Research and Development
CFP	Common Fisheries Policy
CIT	Consultative Committee on Innovation and Technology
CODEST	European Development Committee for Science and Technology
COM or COMDOC	Commission Documents
COMETT	Community in Education and Training for Technology
COPA	Committee of Agricultural Organisations in the European Community
CORDI	Advisory Committee on Industrial Research and Development
COREPER	The Committee of Permanent Representatives
COST	Committee for European Cooperation in the Field of Scientific Research
CREST	Committee on Scientific and Technical Research

CRONOS	Community Statistical Office Computerised Economic Data Bank
CUBE	Concertation Unit for Biotechnology
DIANE	Direct Information Access Network for Europe
D-G	Directorate-General
DRIVE	Dedicated Road Safety Systems and Intelligent Vehicles in Europe
EAEC	European Atomic Energy Community (EURATOM).
EAGGF	(FEOGA – see below)
EBN	European Business and Innovation Centre Network
EC	European Community
ECDIN	Environmental Chemical Data and Information Network
ECOSOC	See ESC
ECSC	European Coal and Steel Community
ECU	European Currency Unit
ED	European Documentation (a series – see page A7)
EDC	European Documentation Centre
EDF	European Development Fund
EF	European File (a series – see page A6)
EFTA	European Free Trade Association
EIB	European Investment Bank
EMS	European Monetary System
EMU	Economic and Monetary Union
EP	European Parliament
ERASMUS	European Community Action Scheme for Mobility of University Students
ERDF	European Regional Development Fund (more usually RDF)
ESC	Economic and Social Committee
ESCAP	European Social and Community Action Programme
ESF	European Social Fund
ESPRIT	European Strategic Programme for Research and Development in Information Technology
ETUC	European Trades Union Confederation
EURAM	European Research in Advanced Materials
EURATOM	The European Atomic Energy Community (EAEC)
EUREKA	European Research Coordination Agency
EUROFER	European Confederation of the Iron and Steel Industry
EURONET-DIANE	Direct Information Access Network for Europe
EUROPMI	European Committee for Small and Medium-sized Industry
EUROSTAT	European Community Statistics

EUROTRA	Community Programme for a Machine Translation System of advanced design
EURYDICE	Education Information Network in the European Community
EVCA	European Venture Capital Association
FAST	Forecasting and Assessment in the field of Science and Technology
FEOGA	French acronym for EAGGF – European Agricultural Guidance and Guarantee Fund
GSP	Generalised System of Preferences
IBC	Integrated Broadband Communication
INSIS	International Information System
IRDAC	Industrial Research and Development Advisory Committee
ISDN	Integrated Services Digital Network (narrow band telecommunication)
IT	Information Technologies
ITTTF	Information Technology and Telecommunications Task Force
JET	Joint European Torus
JRC	Joint Research Centre (at Ispra, Italy)
MCAs	Monetary Compensatory Amounts
MFA	Multi-Fibre Arrangement
NAFO	North Atlantic Fisheries Organisation
NASCO	North Atlantic Salmon Conservation Organisation
NCI (or NIC)	New Community Instrument (also known as the Ortoli Facility)
OJ	Official Journal
OOPEC	Office for Official Publications of the European Communities
RACE	Research into Advanced Communications in Europe
RDF	See ERDF
SITPRO	Simplification of Trade Procedure
SMEs	Small and Medium-sized Enterprises
SPRINT	Strategic Programme for Innovation and Technology Transfer in Europe
STABEX	Stabilisation of Export Earnings (in the ACP countries)
STAR	Programme for access to advanced telecommunications in certain regions of the Community
STCELA	Standing Technological Conference of European Local Authorities
TED	Tenders Electronic Daily
UCITS	Undertakings for Collective Investment in Transferable Securities

UKREP	UK Permanent Representative (or Representation)
UNICE	Conference of Industries of the European Community
VALOREN	Development of certain regions of the Community by exploiting indigenous energy potential

PART I
THE EUROPEAN COMMUNITY AND ITS PURPOSES

Ask a thousand people in the streets of Britain what they feel about the European Community: their answers will reflect genuine bewilderment, tinged with hostility.

A great majority will readily acknowledge the value of the Community in building and keeping peace in Western Europe these past 40 years.

Around three-quarters of us support the principle of cooperation and integration, which is what the Community is supposed to be all about. How does this square with the furious arguments we read about whenever EC Ministers meet?

The notion of a Common Market is no longer of interest largely to economists and international traders. It is there to see in every shop window — a profusion of choice which has changed our shopping habits out of all recognition, even within the memory of a teenager. But what the devil has that got to do with 'harmonising' the noise of lawn-mowers, car exhaust systems, or the water we swim in at the seaside?

We know from our television screens that chronic and demeaning shortages of food still exist in Poland, Hungary and Russia, but not in France, Belgium and Britain, and no doubt the Common Agricultural Policy has something to do with that. So what, if it creates mountains of butter and cereals, while Africa starves?

There is nothing at all naive about such thoughts. Nor is it easy to reconcile these apparent contradictions. The fact is that the European Community, which began in a blaze of noble aspirations, and continued with a great programme of reconstruction and trust-building, finds itself very differently occupied today.

The Community (and in particular the European Commission, which is its think-tank, civil service, and keeper of the rules) is, in the 1980s, largely concerned with improving the prosperity of its citizens. Its role is to attempt to persuade governments to work together to attack unemployment; to try to tear down dishonest and bureaucratic barriers to trade; to reach joint agreements with Japan and the United States in exceptionally difficult times; and to confront Environment Ministers of 12 countries with the dreadful legacy they are amassing for our grandchildren. It must expose massive and continuing state aid to industries for which demand is

For detailed information see coloured pages A5, A10/11

dropping; try to convince Farm Ministers that they should put their careers at stake by recommending less, not more, money for farm support; and face member States with the true burden of their duty to the Third World. That, and a great deal more.

In short – preaching, nagging, exhorting, cajoling, exposing uncomfortable truths, and taking the flak when things go wrong, as an honest broker often does. This is not the way to be loved and understood.

THE BASIC FACTS

The phrase 'European Community' (or simply 'Community') is used throughout this book. 'European Communities' is perhaps more exact, since there are three, the UK having been a member of all of them since 1 January 1973:

The European Coal and Steel Community (ECSC);

The European Atomic Energy Community (EURATOM);

and

The European Community (now known simply as EC though previously termed EEC)

All three share the same institutions. The main ones are:

The Council of Ministers, which takes the Community's decisions;

The Commission — the Community's civil service;

The European Parliament, to which the Commission is answerable, and which increasingly wields influence upon the Community's activities;

The Court of Justice, which settles disputes concerning Community law.

How these intermesh to accomplish the aims of the Community is discussed in the following pages and Part IV.

The Community owes its being to the initiative of a number of European statesmen (Robert Schuman and Jean Monnet being the best known) who had the courage and vision to determine that the task of preventing another world war from breaking out in Europe was of paramount importance — not only to that continent itself but to mankind. Furthermore, it would require a new approach, since traditional diplomacy had failed twice in a generation.

The initial need, expressed in the Preamble to the ECSC Treaty as perfectly as it ever has been, was:

'to substitute for age-old rivalries the merging of essential

For detailed information see coloured pages A5, A10/11

interests; to create, by establishing an economic Community, the basis for a broader and deeper community among peoples long divided by bloody conflicts; and to lay the foundations for institutions which will give direction to a destiny henceforward shared.'

The ECSC came first, in 1951. Its aim was to lock together the coal and steel resources of Western Europe in such a way that these nation states could never again go to war against each other. It was signed by 'The Six' — France, Germany, Italy and the Benelux countries — and established the institutions which still exist.

The EEC came into being with the signature of the Treaty of Rome in 1957. It extended the principles tried and tested in the ECSC, brought into being a Common Market, and set a series of targets for the establishment of common economic policies. EURATOM was signed in the same year. It has as its purpose the safe development of nuclear energy for peaceful purposes.

These Treaties, too, were signed only by The Six. The UK, while publicly welcoming steps to recovery and unity in Europe, had great problems of her own — not least of which was the difficult transition from Empire to Commonwealth. She declined to join the Community at the time it was established, and thus played no part in its development during what, in retrospect, was not only its most dynamic period, but one during which the UK's influence could have been most positive and mutually rewarding.

During the 1960s the UK made two attempts to join the Community. She was kept out largely on the personal initiative of General de Gaulle of France, who argued, in essence, that her heart was not in it. Only in 1969, after de Gaulle's retirement, were negotiations for the enlargement of the Community to include the UK, Denmark, Ireland and Norway begun in earnest. Agreement was reached on terms of entry in 1971 (Norway later deciding not to enter).

The six became Nine on 1 January 1973, and (with the accession of Greece) Ten on 1 January 1981. It became a Community of Twelve on 1 January 1986, when Spain and Portugal joined. Membership of the EC is open to all democratic European countries. Turkey has made a request for membership and Austria did the same in July 1989.

* * * *

The European Community was established, first, to put an end to the futile squandering of lives in wars which began in Europe. Among the means of achieving this should be:

- the levelling out of inequalities between peoples and regions;
- securing employment, and building prosperity, within a Common Market;

For detailed information see coloured pages A5, A10/11

1958 = EUR 6

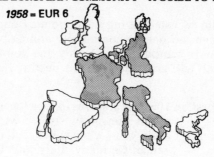

1973 = EUR 9

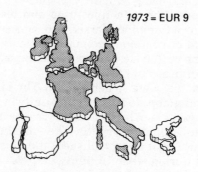

1981 = EUR 10

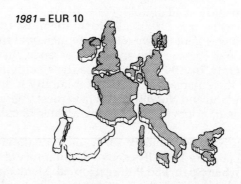

1986 = EUR 12

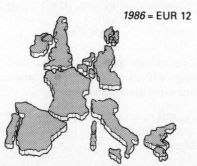

Figure 1 The growth of the European Community

- making the EC a fair trading partner and a more effective source of aid for the poorer countries of the world;
- pooling the energies of Europe's peoples in common technological and industrial progress, a common agricultural policy, closer political and economic links, a better environment, and a richer life.

Progress towards some of these objectives has been dramatic; on others slow and disappointing.

The prosperity of the original six members of the Community increased greatly after it was formed. During the ten years before the UK joined, their exports and their gross national product rose twice as fast as the UK's, their family consumption two and a half times as fast, and their investment five times as fast. The Community conducts well over 40 per cent of world trade. Its external tariffs are lower than were those of the UK before entry, and lower than those of the US or Japan. It is the biggest single market for the developing nations. Its aid record vis-a-vis the Third World, is better than anyone else's.

The Community's greatest achievement is less quantifiable. The nations of the world face, in the last decades of the twentieth century, problems at least as great as those of the previous 80-odd years. They face them, what is more, at a time when the breakdown of relations between continents, or even single nations, could have bloody consequences inconceivable to our grandparents.

The two world wars which broke out in Europe within a generation were caused, not only by real economic pressures, but by selfishness and stupidity; not only by political dishonesty but by the failure of traditional diplomacy; not only because of a lack of information and communication, but because we used words fraudulently. Treaties and agreements were broken, not only by deliberate act of bad faith, but because they were laden with complex protocols and understood imperfectly even by those who were involved in implementing them. Such international enforcement agencies as existed did not work.

The European Community is different from the supranational groupings of the past. The discussions which go on in Brussels may sometimes seem angry and repetitive, but by previous standards they are exceptionally well-informed. National Ministers, and the governments which they represent, still make all the important decisions. But they have the support of institutions of a new kind — planning, collecting information and opinion, drawing up blueprints, re-examining, reconciling — and doing all this from an independent standpoint. The Commission, the Parliament and the Court are responsible not to governments but to the peoples of Europe as a whole, and to the Community's democratic ideals. If the Council's agreements are often reached in ill-temper and in the small hours of the morning, they are eventually enshrined in many

For detailed information see coloured pages A5, A10/11

languages and in texts agreed, word for word, by all 12 nations. We often read of 'wine wars' between Italy and France, the anger of steel producers in Germany, furious demonstrations in Brussels by farmers and consumers from diametrically opposed points of view, or the difficulty of reconciling the views of the textile, shipbuilding, or motor vehicle industries of individual Community countries. It is worth reminding ourselves that there we are seeing, out in the open, the sort of economic and trading problems which would be there anyway (and might well be very much worse) if the Community did not exist. Solving such problems may seem a noisier and more lengthy business than it was fifty years ago. That is largely because the arguments are held in public. When agreements are reached, they are public too: more honourable, more likely to stick, less capable of misinterpretation and infinitely more open and democratic.

Memories die, but the facts are on record. Within the space of a single generation, and after a bloody war, the French and the Germans, the Italians and the Benelux countries, learned not only how to bury their differences and rebuild their shattered economies: they learned to trust each other more than they had done for a millennium. Those who worked for the Community during those good years have every reason for pride.

Today (many of them are still around) what they face is largely frustration. The Community remains, as it has always been, a non-stop negotiating machine, with detailed programmes and policies. It is charged with working to bring the peoples of member States together in a great range of fields — employment creation, energy, transport, the quality of life, relations with the Third World, scientific and technological cooperation, food and farming, free trade and fair competition, and much more. To move forward, it must reach a series of supranational agreements, eventually embodied in national laws.

Reaching those agreements has proved increasingly difficult. At a time of world recession, with many industries in grave trouble, the disciplines of Community partnership have become harder to tolerate.

It is, however, more than ever necessary to accept them. The Community is the world's largest trading group. Sitting between the two superpowers, its democratic solidarity is more than ever essential. With far more extensive links with the developing world than the US, the Soviet Union and Japan combined, it is the Community to which these countries properly look for justice and for help.

The importance of the Community as an entity has, for many years, been more readily acknowledged in the outside world than among the peoples of Western Europe themselves. As the world's largest trading bloc Community decisions have repercussions far

For detailed information see coloured pages A5,A10/11

outside its borders. The importance of what it has to say in the United Nations, in GATT, and in the East-West, and North-South dialogues, its public stances on the problems of the Middle East, Afghanistan or Latin America, derive from more than a simple aggregation of 320 million people: they represent the strength of a new form of democratic cooperation and integration, which demonstrably works. In trying to come to honest accommodation with the industries of Japan, the farmers and steelmakers of the United States, the shipbuilders of Korea or the exporters of the Third World, the Community's strength today must depend less on its competitive edge than on its moral power. To put it another way: if the member States of the Community had behaved, over the past twelve years, in the same way as they behaved individually during the similar recession of the 20s and 30s, the perilous plight of the world economy would assuredly be a great deal worse than it is today, and the danger of warfare immeasurably nearer.

★ ★ ★ ★

Those involved in Community affairs rather resent the use of the phrase 'the Common Market' to describe the worldwide and extensive range of activities in which it is concerned. Yet the Community's internal policies are at the heart of its role on the world stage. Only if the Community lives up to its own ideals, obeys its own internal rules, and *is seen to do so,* can it offer a standard of values which the rest of the world can respect.

The workings of the Common Market, and the monitoring of its trading rules, are the subject of Part III. But it is worth glancing here at their importance to the wider aims of the Community. Free trade and fair competition are essential not only for the economic health of the internal market, but to restrain protectionism elsewhere. Curbing bad practice within the Community is worse than useless if the offending companies merely export their practices to third countries and the Community sits back and lets them do it.

It we demand fair treatment for our own consumers in terms of truthful labelling and advertising, control of additives, healthy preparation and packaging, and all the rest, then other nations will be obliged to follow suit, because of the Community's importance in world trade. If peoples' rights (to education, to work, to travel freely, to equal treatment) are seen to be respected in the Community itself, then our right to expose breaches of such freedoms elsewhere becomes the more valid.

Which leads to the wider aims of the Community, and the conviction of those who want to see through-composed European unity: not merely economies locked together to stop Frenchmen, Germans and Britons from fighting each other, but so shaped as to give the fullest expression of shared ideals, mutual pride in centuries of cross-fertilised culture and history, a new explosion of creative genius based on cooperation as well as competition between

For detailed information see coloured pages A5, A10/12

peoples, and a joint approach to an exciting but increasingly unpredictable future. Such enthusiasts may be 'Eurofanatics', or they may look upon the Community as merely one avenue by which such aims may be pursued. But they believe that, at the least, it offers a new approach, and novel institutions which have stood up to fierce tests. There is also the pragmatic belief that the more 12 nations can agree together on a workaday basis (such as, say, how we implement standards of safety in industry) the more we are likely to find agreement on wider matters, such as monetary and economic union, competing fairly at an international level, and preserving peace.

The European Community's plans for closer political and economic integration between its member states were outlined in the Single European Act which was signed by all its members by 1987. The Act marks out a programme for the completion of a unified internal market in the EC by 1992. This will mean the unimpeded movement of EC citizens, goods and services, and capital.

THE UK IN THE COMMUNITY

The UK's membership of the Community has been on the whole an unhappy one. There are many reasons for this, but perhaps the most important is that we joined the Community far too late, and at the wrong time, and not on our terms. Since 1973 successive British governments have tried to alter this situation, though causing a considerable degree of acrimony with our European partners.

Had we been in from the beginning, the Community would assuredly have been a more acceptable place for the United Kingdom. Its common resources would be less massively devoted to agricultural support, and thus in better shape to face the very different problems of today. Our civil servants, businessmen, industrialists, representative bodies and the City (not to mention the media) would have integrated gradually into the system and helped to form it. As it was, on 1 January 1973 we found ourselves thrust into an institutional framework which we played little part in shaping and in which we felt distinctly uncomfortable.

In untroubled times this challenge would have been easily surmountable by what is, after all, one of the most adaptable nations on earth. Indeed, most of the first year of enlarged Community membership was a tribute to the patience, flexibility and understanding of all nine nations concerned. It is sometimes forgotten just how much difficult work was done in that brief time. The complex effects of British membership upon her relations with the United States of America, the Commonwealth, and her other trading partners were honourably and harmoniously dealt with. Norway, having at the last moment changed her mind about membership, was offered and accepted a new form of relationship

For detailed information see coloured pages, A5, A12

with the Community. The European Free Trade Association (EFTA – a former grouping of seven European countries not in the EC), having lost the UK, Denmark and Ireland, reforged links with the enlarged Community. Internally, blueprints for a whole range of policies — for the regions, for scientific and technological cooperation, for economic and monetary union, and a dozen more — were prepared, agreed by the Commission, and tabled for the Council of Ministers. A remarkable start.

But at the end of 1973 came the first 'oil shock'. Energy prices quadrupled, the recession began and individual States behaved with a selfishness which seemed in danger of splitting the Community apart. Grim lessons were learned, and in some respects the resilience of the Community's institutions, having survived these bitter days, has been toughened. But the intervening years have seen a worsening of the problems of Europe's industries, reflected in unemployment (today there are still almost 17 million people in the EC out of work). In the absence of some magical assessment of what might have happened to the United Kingdom outside the Community, the argument *post hoc ergo propter hoc* has proved all too potent in terms of public opinion.

The facts, however, insofar as they can be measured, indicate that the trend of British trade, already moving towards Europe and away from our traditional markets long before 1973, has continued and developed in a way which might not have been possible outside the tariff-free Market. Over 40 per cent of British exports now go to the Community, compared with 30 per cent in 1972. Germany is now our biggest customer. Our sales in the Community have risen since membership by 22 per cent per annum, compared with 21 per cent per annum for their exports to us.

In terms of manufactured goods the balance of payments seems to show a less cheerful story. But the key figure is the ratio of exports to imports. And since 1973, our ratio has held up very much better with the Community countries than with the rest of the world. There is little difference between our export/import ratio with the EC now as compared with 1973. In the same period the export/import ratio with Japan fell from 53 per cent to under 17 per cent.

During our first 10 years of membership, our exports of manufactured goods to the Community showed a consistent improvement. But during the same period the British share of the American import market for manufactured goods fell from 6.5 to 3.6 per cent, and in the case of Canada from 5.5 to 2.5 per cent.

In short, our manufacturing industry has been doing badly throughout the world, but better in the Community than in our other major markets.

And the benefits of membership must be taken into account. The impact of loans and grants from Europe upon the UK is well recorded in terms of hundreds of millions of pounds; to describe it, as some

For detailed information see coloured pages, A5, A12

anti-Marketeers still do, as 'just a little of our own money back' disregards the facts, as well as the purpose of Community aid. The industrial infrastructure projects which have blossomed in the regions of the UK are not some sort of stylish benison from Brussels, but an attempt to redistribute the resources of the Community in favour of the depressed areas, and a means of attracting inward investment and jobs. It has been estimated that some 2,500,000 jobs in the UK depend upon Community membership; many of them would not be there at all had we remained outside the 'home' market which now comprises 320 million people.

According to the Invest in Britain Bureau (part of the Department of Industry), Britain has attracted by far the largest share of direct overseas investment in the European Community. It has received more US investment than any other country, and more than half of all Japanese investment in the EC.

Since 1973 the UK as a whole has proved a very attractive springboard into Europe for investors from America, Canada, Japan and the other Community countries themselves. A great deal of this investment has gone to those very areas where Community loans and grants for infrastructure have made the most impact — Scotland, Wales, the north of England and Northern Ireland.

But whatever can be achieved at the Community level in the way of job creation and industrial opportunity will prove useless to Britain if our manufacturers and exporters do not take proper advantage of membership. So far, we have failed to do so. The question of how we can do better is outside the scope of this book, just as it is outwith the remit of the European Commission. (The latter's task is to facilitate trade and to help industries or regions which are in trouble; it is emphatically *not* its job to tell manufacturers and exporters in the UK, or anywhere else, how to win new markets in the Community.)

There are, however, many sources of help. One of the best is the magazine 'British Business', references to which appear throughout the book. There are helpful pamphlets and handbooks from the British Overseas Trade Board and a number of other departments and quangos. Many banks produce guidance for industrialists, businessmen and exporters — the series produced by the National Westminster Bank, Barclay's Bank and the Midland Bank being particularly valuable and up to date. The United Kingdom Permanent Representation in Brussels (see page 198) can give useful advice, as can the Commercial Councillors in individual British embassies to Community countries. Several books (in particular *Doing Business in the European Community*) are indispensable.

Three particularly valuable publications appeared recently:

- *The EEC: a Guide to Finance, Trade and Investment,* available from the Midland Bank, is crammed with information, not only on the subjects which the title would indicate, but on the role of the Community institutions, lobbying, the Community's external relations, and even the complexities of the CAP.

- The July 1986 issue of *British Business* published a supplement entitled 'DTI Guide', which is full of names, addresses and telephone numbers of those in government departments concerned with Community affairs, and contains a useful index.
- A COI reference pamphlet (no. 73/86) entitled *Britain in the European Community* is perhaps the most comprehensive official publication yet attempted on the Community and Britain's role in it, covering all important policies briefly and clearly from the government's standpoint, and containing a great deal of information for businessmen and traders.

For detailed information see coloured pages, A5, A9, A12

PART II
THE WAY THE EUROPEAN COMMUNITY WORKS

It would be tempting to suggest neat parallels:

Council of Ministers = Cabinet

European Parliament = House of Commons

European Court of Justice = Legal system

European Commission = Civil Service

Unfortunately, the parallels don't work. Indeed, any attempt to explain the institutions of the Community by relating them to Westminster/Whitehall is doomed to fail.

The Council of Ministers is indeed the nearest thing the Community has to a governance, and by far the most powerful of the institutions. No forward action of any kind, whether it be increasing food aid to Africa or fixing the quota for horse-mackerel, can be taken unless all 12 national governments have reached a consensus of opinion that it *should* happen; no major legislation can be achieved until all 12 governments agree to it in minute detail, over the same table, in the Council. But although the Council takes the Community's decisions, it does not initiate legislation. We should therefore look first at where policy-making begins. Generally speaking the Commission proposes and the Council disposes.

THE COMMISSION

The European Commission is perhaps the body which someone brought up in Britain finds most difficult to understand. We see our civil servants as an impartial, obedient corps, standing apart from the levers of power (although we have occasional doubts when we watch 'Yes, Prime Minister'!). We do not easily come to terms with Commission officials who argue very publicly, not only with their colleagues in the other Community institutions, but with national politicians and their policies.

The fact is that the Commission is a great deal more than the Community's civil service. It administers the Common Market, the Common Agricultural Policy, and the whole range of internal agreements already reached. But it is also the Community's 'think-tank'. It prepares a detailed agenda of work for the Council, and drafts its legislation. It conducts, on behalf of the Community as a

For detailed information see coloured pages, A5, A10

whole, complex trade relationships with the world at large (known as external relations agreements). The Commission President (currently Jacques Delors) plays a role, in European 'summit' meetings, on a par with the President or Prime Minister of a member State.

The Commission is based largely in Brussels, but has offices in Luxembourg, information offices in each of the member States, and delegations in many of the world's capitals. Contrary to popular opinion, it is far from being a large bureaucracy. (It has fewer employees in total than Wandsworth Borough Council.)

At the top of the organisation are 17 Commissioners — two from each large state and one from each of the smaller ones. The President, himself a Commissioner, is appointed by a process similar to papal chimney-smoke. Six Commissioners are titled Vice-President. The Commission has its own Secretariat; at its head, as Secretary General, until recently was M Emile Noël, whose booklet *Working Together* (available free from any Commission Office) is perhaps the best of a number of publications describing the working processes of the Commission and the Community as a whole.

The two Commissioners from the UK have to date represented the Conservative and Labour parties. Sir Leon Brittan and Bruce Millan are the current Commissioners from the United Kingdom. Their appointment has been agreed between the Prime Minister of the day and the leader of the Opposition, after consultation with other political leaders in Britain and elsewhere in the Community.

Each Commissioner takes an oath in which he pledges not to seek or accept instructions from national governments or political parties, but to serve the interests of the Community as a whole. Neither individual governments nor the Council can remove a member of the Commission from office, though it is possible for the European Parliament to sack the entire Commission.

Commissioners each hold one or more portfolios and bear primary responsibility for shaping Community policy proposals. They form a 'college': all 17 must themselves agree that a proposal is in a presentable state before it can be sent to the Council for the first stages in the decision-making process.

Thus, if the Commission proposes, say, new safety standards for the transport of radioactive waste, the Commissioner responsible for the environment will oversee the necessary draft proposals to be considered by the Council of Ministers. But in this he will work in the closest cooperation with several of his colleagues. And before the draft is submitted to the Council (and the Parliament) all Commissioners must agree that the proposals are sensible and that all the relevant factors are taken into account.

Commissioners are served both by the Directorates-General for which they are responsible, and by their own private offices, called Cabinets. There are some 20 Directorates-General (DGs) which,

For detailed information see coloured pages, A5, A10

together with the Secretariat-General, and a number of special bodies like the Legal Service, the Statistical Office, etc, compose the Commission's 'civil service'.

DG I covers External Relations;
DG II Economic and Financial Affairs;
DG III the Internal Market and Industry;
DG IV Competition;
DG V Employment, Social Affairs and Education;
DG VI Agriculture;
DG VII Transport;
DG VIII Development;
DG IX Personnel and Administration;
DG X Information Communication and Culture;
DG XI Environment, Consumer Protection and Nuclear Safety;
DG XII Science, Research and Development;
DG XIII Telecommunications, Information Market and Innovation;
DG XIV Fisheries;
DG XV Financial Institutions and Company Law;
DG XVI Regional Policy;
DG XVII Energy;
DG XVIII Credit and Investments;
DG XIX Budgets;
DG XX Financial Control;
DG XXI Customs Union and Indirect Taxation;
DG XXII Coordination of Structural Instruments.

A full list of these, and other Commission bodies, together with the names of senior officials, is given in the Commission Directory.

A Commissioner's cabinet is, in effect, his private office — but in the French, rather than the British sense. Its head, the chef de cabinet, wields considerable influence, preparing the ground for the weekly Commission meetings, and often standing in for the Commissioner himself. He and the deputy chef will almost invariably come from the same Community country as the Commissioner; those in junior posts may come from several other countries, but will normally be of the same political persuasion as the Commissioner (or none). Between them, members of the cabinet will cover all aspects of Community business.

Directors-General (who often have deputies and special assistants) are specialists in their field. The relative importance of Directors-General and chefs des cabinets varies from subject to subject and from Commissioner to Commissioner. Neither a chef nor a DG has an exact equivalent in the British civil service. Between them they cover the roles of Permanent Under-Secretaries, principal private secretaries, and political advisors, but who wears each hat is by no means always clear.

Commissioners are essentially political beings, usually with

For detailed information see coloured pages, A5, A10/12

established careers in their native governments. They are chosen for the informed influence which they can hope to exert, both in Brussels, Strasbourg and Luxembourg (the Community's institutional centres) and in national capitals. When arguing within the Commission it is expected that they should forcibly articulate the view from 'the country I know best'; but their collegiate role is essential to its proper functioning. (Any Commissioner who finds himself identifying too closely with his own national Government and its policies will very quickly be brought to book by his colleagues.) However, Commissioners taking too strong a line in favour of the EC may find themselves under pressure from their national governments. When Commissioners travel abroad they do so as representatives of the Community as a whole, not of the member state to which they happen to belong.

The President of the Commission, as well as being 'chairman of the board', plays a particularly important role at Community 'summits', where he ranks with Prime Ministers and Presidents of member States. When visiting third countries Commissioners will usually be accorded the status of a senior cabinet minister.

The staff of the Commission are recruited proportionally from all Community States, though there is some concern over the small number of British people working in the Community's institutions. Again, they must work for the interests of the Community as a whole, and not for their native countries (or indeed their individual interests or opinions, which they must frequently suppress). A rough balance by nationality is maintained inside the various DGs, which offers considerable protection against external or governmental pressure.

As well as being the power-house of Community work, the Commission (with the aid of the Court) must keep the Community's rulebook. In this task it has powers of its own. As the Community watchdog, the Commission must ensure that Community action is properly justified on the basis of those Treaties. In the case of the daily operation of major policies — the Common Market, the CAP, the rules of fair trade and competition, and other policies upon which agreements at 12-nation level have already been reached — the Commission has a direct role. (More of this in Part III.)

The Commission is also charged with trying to keep the Community moving forward towards its various goals. When a new Commission is appointed, one of its first tasks is to agree on a plan for the year ahead. This 'action programme', which is far more detailed than the Queen's Speech and less liable to change than any party manifesto, gives full and detailed advance notice of what the Commission hopes to achieve. It is regularly updated in a 'state of the Community' speech by the President, and progress made is recorded in a series of monthly and annual reports and a variety of detailed documents. (This, it should be repeated, is a programme of work.

For detailed information see coloured pages, A5, A10/12

Only the Council of Ministers can transform it into legislation.)

The massive process of consultation and preparation, which takes place before a policy proposal reaches the first published draft, is described in Part IV. Once a piece of suggested legislation has been prepared, it is the duty of the responsible Commissioner to present it to his colleagues. It must be examined by all of them, and adopted (if necessary by a majority vote) before being delivered formally to the Council of Ministers, who pass it to the European Parliament and the Economic and Social Committee for their opinions. It will then be published in the Official Journal of the Communities as a draft Regulation*, or Directive.

A *Regulation*, once adopted by the Council, will be binding in its entirety and applicable as it stands to all member states. If, for example, there is agreement in the Council on a new Regulation concerning permissible limits for driving hours, the agreement will be published in the Official Journal and will immediately become part of national law in the 12 member states.

A *Directive* is different. Though binding on member states as regards the results to be achieved, the form and method of achieving these results is left to the discretion of national authorities. For example, there are Directives on tax evasion whereby member States cooperate to prevent tax-dodgers from pursuing their wicked ways, and to catch them if they persist. All Community States are involved in this cooperation at national and international level; but it is up to individual nations to decide how they go about it.

Decisions are similar to Regulations, but may apply not to all Community States, but to one or more (or to individuals). The agreement by the Council to admit Greece to membership of the Community, for example, was a Decision, not a Regulation or Directive.

(There are also *Recommendations* and *Opinions*. These have no legal force; they are in effect merely advice to governments.)

Whatever form draft legislation may take, it cannot become law until Ministers representing all 12 Community governments agree on it. In the meantime, other bodies will make their views known.

THE EUROPEAN PARLIAMENT

The Parliament, like the Commission, can make no laws. It is essentially concerned with influence, not power, and must exercise every ounce of the former to win a vestige of the latter. Any extension of its present limited authority can be granted only with the unanimous agreement of the 12 Community governments, to date most reluctantly ceded. There is more on the Parliament's role in decision-making in Part IV and Part VI.

The 518 Members (MEPs) are elected every five years. The largest countries in the Community (the UK, France, West Germany, Italy)

* (Confusingly called a 'Decision' in the case of the ECSC.)

For detailed information see coloured pages, A5, A10/12

each have 81 seats. Of 81 from the UK, 45 are Labour, 32 Conservative, one is a member of the Scottish National Party and from Northern Ireland there is one Democratic Unionist Member, one Official Unionist Member and one from the Social Democratic and Labour Party. The Parliament is composed of political groups, not representatives of member states.

Although established as an 'Assembly' by the Treaties, the title 'European Parliament' has been used since 1962 and was formalised in 1986. Until 1979 it was appointed, not elected. In Britain alone 'first past the post' elections have so far been used, producing illogical results. (The Liberal/SDP Alliance, most consistently interested of all the parties in the Parliament, did not win a single seat in the 1984 elections despite obtaining 19.5 per cent of the vote and repeated this melancholy achievement in 1989.)

MEPs choose which of the various political groupings they wish to join. They may address the House as spokesmen for one of the various committees, as a representative of a political group, or in a personal capacity. Plenary sessions of Parliament are held in Strasbourg some 12 times a year, but in some ways committee work is more important. It is in private, rather than in public, that MEPs get on with their proper job, which is to think and work on behalf of the peoples of the Community as a whole, improve the workings of the decision-making process, expose injustice or bureaucratic stupidity, tackle the problems which face Western Europe across frontiers, involve themselves in the Community's worldwide relationships, and bring more realism, unity and cooperation into its work at a political level.

The Parliament has two strategic weapons: the ability to dismiss the entire Commission, and to influence the budget and the spending programme of the Community. The first of these powers has not so far been put to the test; it is a real threat and would probably be a useful dramatic gesture, but a somewhat ephemeral one, since the Commission would doubtless be reappointed next day by member governments. (The rather more positive weapon of sacking an individual Commissioner is not yet within the Parliament's powers.)

Authority over the Community budget has, however, been exercised many times. Parliament has achieved a certain amount of rejigging of Community spending to the advantage of social and regional policy, and is now having some success in correcting the imbalance caused largely by the price support mechanisms of the Common Agricultural Policy.

Virtually all members play an active part in one of the 18 committees, which cover Political Affairs; Agriculture, Fisheries and Food; the Budget; Economic, Monetary and Industrial Matters; Energy, Research and Technology; External Economic Relations; Legal Affairs and Citizens' Rights; Social Matters and Employment; Regional Policy and Planning; Transport; Environmental, Health

For detailed information see coloured pages, A5, A10/12

and Consumer Affairs; Youth, Culture, Education, Information and Sport; Overseas Development; Budgetary Control; Procedural Matters; Women's Rights; Institutional Affairs; and Members' Credentials.

When a Commission proposal is submitted to the Parliament *en route* to the Council, it is considered by one or more of these committees. They usually meet in Brussels, and take up a great deal of the MEP's time — about two weeks in each month. Many committees meet in outlying regions of the Community, so as to see problems on the ground. They have their own secretariats, and funds for commissioning expert evidence and research.

Reports prepared by specialist committees are usually published and discussed by the political groups before they are debated and voted upon in plenary session. Parliament then sends its opinions to the Council and the Commission.

It is during this process (examined in Part IV) that the Parliament has exerted most influence. The Commission takes the Parliament's opinions very seriously indeed, and has very often found them helpful in its perennial battle to strengthen the spirit of community and cooperation among the members of the Council of Ministers. Indeed, *pace* the manifestos of many MEPs, the Commission and the Parliament are natural allies against the all too real power of the Council.

Largely for reasons of national pride, the Parliament has yet to find a permanent home. Although most of its public sessions are in Strasbourg, its administrative headquarters are in Luxembourg and many of its meetings are in Brussels. There is a determination to end this situation despite pressures from the French and Luxembourg governments, by increasing the amount of the Parliament's work undertaken in Brussels.

Much has been made in the press and television of the costs of a Parliament which is largely a 'talking shop'. Two points might be made. The first is that 'talking shop' is what the word 'parliament' actually means, and that a member of the European Parliament has probably more ability to influence legislation than a back-bencher in Westminster. The second is that the whole of the Parliament's operations costs us, as citizens of the Community, about one penny per week.

The Parliament is pledged to adopt a uniform method of election, certainly some form of proportional representation; in Britain no agreement is in sight as to what this method will be.

Pamphlets on the Parliament and its procedures are available free from the London Office at 2 Queen Anne's Gate, London SW1H 9AA (01-222 0411). They give, *inter alia,* the addresses of all members and political groups, and the London offices of the groups with British members. There is a particularly good assessment of the work of the Parliament by George Clark, ex-political editor of *The Times,* and a

For detailed information see coloured pages, A5, A10/12

short film with an amusing commentary by Peter Ustinov.

THE ECONOMIC AND SOCIAL COMMITTEE

This is a purely consultative body, but like the Parliament it commands a great deal of expertise on most subjects with which the Community concerns itself. It has 189 members drawn from the 12 States, 24 from the UK. They are appointed for four years from lists supplied by member States, and are drawn from three groups; employers, workers, and 'various interests' — the last-named covering such subjects as agriculture, transport, small businesses, the professions, and consumer protection. Members are independent of individual governments, but are extremely valuable weather-cocks, since they are in a position to know how the national wind is blowing when new policies are being considered.

The Committee sees all important Commission proposals in draft, and delivers over 100 detailed Opinions on these every year. The full Committee meets eight times a year (with extra sessions if necessary) and observers are admitted. In addition there are working parties, each with its own bureau. At present there are nine: Agriculture; Transport and Communications; Energy and Nuclear questions; Economy and Finance; Industry, Commerce, Crafts and Services; Social Questions; External Relations; Regional Development; and Environment, Public Health and Consumer Affairs.

Both Parliament and Commission pay considerable attention to the Committee's views. But it is perhaps in its influence upon member Governments that the Economic and Social Committee can best influence policy. A list of UK Committee members and their addresses and responsibilities is available from any Community office. A free catalogue of publications is available from the Committee's Publications Division, Rue Ravenstein 2, B-1000, Brussels.

THE COUNCIL OF MINISTERS

The Council is incomparably the Community's most powerful institution, and its decision-making body. Its role has changed in a slow but seemingly inexorable way, particularly during the period of Britain's membership.

Writing only a few years ago, Emile Noël, the Secretary General of the Commission and a man with an unrivalled experience of the workings of the Community's institutions, felt able to declare:

> The teaming of the Commission and the Council in double harness is perhaps the most novel feature of the whole institutional system. The political authority which the Commission needs to partner the Council derives from the fact that it is answerable to Parliament alone.

For detailed information see coloured pages, A5, A10/12

'Double harness'... The 'political authority' of the Commission... The Council's 'partner'...

So it was certainly intended. The Community Treaties envisage a house with four pillars, none more or less strong and vital than the other three. Today, the paramountcy of the Council is not only beyond doubt; it has sometimes seemed in danger of submerging the identity of the Community itself.

Twelve national Ministers, each representing a member Government, take every single important Community decision. Rarely have they taken these decisions by any other means than complete unanimity. Far too often they have failed to reach any decisions at all. However, under the Single European Act it is hoped that the number of Council decisions taken by majority voting will increase.

In some cases this has been because the political difficulties were truly insuperable; but too often the machinery has broken down, and it is worth looking at why this should have come about.

Neither the Rome Treaty nor the Treaty of Accession is specific about the composition of the Council of Ministers. But at the beginning of 1973, after enlargement, tacit agreement was reached that the system should work like this:

(1) As often as possible, agreement on Community policies should be reached at the level of COREPER, the Committee of Permanent Representatives. This is the administrative arm of the Council. It is in two parts, one composed of the 12 'Ambassadors' to the Community, the other of their Deputies. Agreements on Community policy reached at COREPER level would be formally ratified by national Ministers in Council, as 'A' (agreed) points.

(2) When matters could not be agreed in COREPER they would come to sectoral Councils for debate. They would be dealt with by the responsible departmental Ministers (thus Fisheries Councils, Transport Councils, etc). It was the duty of these Ministers to reach agreement, even if they talked till dawn. They could invite the Commission to redraft proposals, summon expert help when necessary, occasionally make prolonged and tense telephone calls to Bonn, Paris or London, but *they decided*. Such Councils were (and are) held regularly — sometimes several times a week.

(3) The Council proper, consisting of Foreign Ministers, was to meet four times a year or so. It would offer top-level guidance, review progress over the previous months, and keep targets firmly in mind (and in the centre of the desks of departments involved). Only in emergency could departmental Ministers pass a problem up to the Council proper. This was the court of last resort; if Prime Ministers or Presidents came into the act (as, of course, they often did) it was at the other end of a hot line, through a scrambler, usually in the

For detailed information see coloured pages, A5, A10/12

small hours of the morning.

For most of 1973, the first year of enlarged membership, this worked well. But at the end of that year came the first oil shock. National interests were so predominant in the minds of ministers that agreements became harder and harder to achieve. Changes of government and other factors accelerated this process. Fewer and fewer decisions except of the most routine and minor kind were agreed at COREPER level. Departmental Ministers appeared at the conference table in Brussels to expound a formal bargaining position with almost no leeway, and which came as no surprise to anyone at the Council table, since it had been leaked to the press in advance. Agendas for the Council proper became longer, pricklier and more complicated, and decision-making groaned almost to a halt. The 'human face' of the Community began to look pretty sour.

COREPER members, instead of finding themselves positively and rewardingly involved in the process of European integration, found themselves having to put lengthy and formal statements in public, rather than working behind the scenes for private compromises. Commission officials saw their well-researched proposals thrown out by politicians who sometimes patently failed to understand them. Worse, they found these ideas being deliberately misconstrued by the media, sometimes with the connivance of national Government publicity machines, and made to look ridiculous.

In this inauspicious situation the European Council, the Community 'summit', was created.

The European Council had, until 1986, no legal standing in the Community Treaties. It was set up by Heads of State themselves in 1974, meets (in theory) three times a year, and has become yet another court of final appeal to which junior Ministers can pass the buck. Whether the blame for these developments lies with the Council, the Commission, the nature of the Treaties (or more probably all three) is a matter for speculation. But the end result is highly relevant, since it is responsible for many abounding misrepresentations and misconceptions about the nature of the Community.

European 'summits' have become laden with all the inflated expectations (and later anti-climaxes) implicit in that word. They are held in a glare of TV, press and radio publicity more appropriate to meetings concerned with preventing wars than to arguments about a penny a day per head in budget refunds. As a result, the essential nature of the Community, which Emile Noël exactly defined as the quite new interaction between Commission, Parliament and Council, has been diminished. Council meetings have appeared to be merely squabbling gatherings of national Ministers, busily defending their own national corners with their

For detailed information see coloured pages, A5, A10/12

eyes on newspaper headlines back home. And those headlines, as we shall see, have made the matter a great deal worse.

But, for good or ill, the Community's major decisions have too often had to be taken, not within the Council of Ministers (the proper body for such action under the Treaties) but within the European Council (which was invented by Governments themselves to come to terms with specific problems, but which has since come to assume both permanency and ultimate power).

The intolerable delay which this has imposed on the Community's decision-making system was finally tackled at the summit of February 1986, after intense discussion at inter-governmental level. The Single European Act (see Part IV and the section 'Policies in Process of Change') is a step in the right direction. Although its most important implications are probably at the level of political cooperation and the role of the European Parliament, it does, somewhat cautiously, amend the Treaty of Rome to increase the use of majority voting in the Council of Ministers.

Provision for majority voting is, of course, in-built in the original Treaties. Indeed, it has been regularly practised at Council meetings when one or two governments have felt the need to make a tacit protest by abstaining (or temporarily withholding agreement) on matters which might, were they to vote positively, run them into political trouble back home. The problem has been the 'veto', the 'Luxembourg compromise'.

The 'veto' on decision-making, as we note elsewhere, was intended to be used only when the vital national interests of a government were at stake. Unhappily, it has been used because of inadequate briefing, or for ephemeral political interests.

The implications of the Single European Act are that when a general policy (in particular, the completion of the internal market) has been agreed, then majority voting should become the rule rather than the exception. The major decisions must still be taken unanimously; the 'veto' will remain if 'vital national interests' seem under attack. But it should no longer be possible for a nation which happens to have a general election in the offing, or whose Foreign Minister has failed to master his brief, to hold up a decision which is agreed in principle, is clearly in the interests of the Community as a whole, and on which the others are agreed.

If it fails, it is difficult to see how the Community's institutions can continue to do the job demanded of them, particularly since the third enlargement of January 1986. There is more on this subject in the section entitled 'Policies in Process of Change'.

THE EUROPEAN COURT OF JUSTICE

If you object to the use of corporal punishment in schools, or seek international redress in domestic law, the European Court of Justice in Luxembourg is not your place. Try the Court of Human Rights in

Strasbourg, or the International Court at The Hague.

The Community Court can only rule on Community legislation. It gives final judgement on the interpretation of the Treaties and the ways in which they operate. If Community rules are working unfairly, it is open to governments, local authorities, companies or individuals to complain and seek redress. If the rules are being broken, the Commission (or the Parliament) can invoke the power of the Court to see that they are enforced. If a company proposes major reshaping of its trading or employment practices, and wishes to obtain a preliminary opinion upon whether its plan will fit in with Community legislation, it can do so.

The European Court consists of 13 Judges, and 6 Advocates-General whose task is to give detailed submissions on cases brought before the Court in order to help the Judges make their decisions. All are chosen 'from persons whose independence is beyond doubt and who possess the qualifications required for appointment to the highest Judicial offices in their respective countries'. The Court works in a similar way to appeal courts in member states. A full account of procedures is available free.

The Court was established under the Rome Treaty because of the new ideas implicit in a Common Market. Member states were required to accept increased competition in their domestic markets; to abandon trade barriers of various kinds (some hallowed by centuries of use); and to accept that once legislation had been agreed by their own governments it would be monitored by Brussels. Neither governments nor large industries found these restrictions congenial or easy; nor (by ignorance or design) did they invariably obey them. The first actions to reach the Court were almost all concerned with breaches of Community rules concerning free competition and fair trade. Most still are. But the Commission has made blunders in drafting new laws, and governments have made mistakes in implementing them. Thus actions have been brought by firms (and by governments) against the Commission, seeking to correct and repair possible injustice.

When Community legislation is passed by the Council of Ministers, it becomes part of national law, and it is the duty of governments to ensure that the law is kept. If a company or an individual fails to obey a new Directive, Decision or Regulation, it is for national law-keepers to bring them to book. The European Court may become involved only if this fails.

But only too often it is not companies, nor individuals, who break the Community rules on fair and free trade, but governments themselves. In such cases the first task is for the Commission: to establish the facts and decide on the action required.

Let us say that the Council has agreed on a Directive which, as from 1 January 1992, forbids member States from discriminating against computers made in another Community country. But six

For detailed information see coloured pages, A5, A12

months after that date, two States are still imposing massive taxes on each other's products (or funnelling them through one entry point with a single customs officer who insists on opening every package). The Commission's job is to find out whether this failure to implement the directive is deliberate and cynical, or a hiccup caused by oversight or a change of government. A reasonable time will be given for the offending governments to offer an explanation. If this does not arrive, or if it is unconvincing, the Commission may decide to take the matter to the European Court. The Court's decision is paramount in Community law in such cases.

If a government is found guilty, the Court can exert only moral pressure: you cannot fine a Government! On the whole, however, these sanctions have worked. For thirteen years no State failed to obey a ruling of the Court. More recently, alas, governments have become more adept in delaying their compliance with the law until the desired effect has been achieved. The process of appealing to the Court on infractions of Community law is often complicated and can rarely be short. By the time the ruling is made, the purpose of the infraction may have been achieved (the computer market is nearing saturation point), or a new infraction substituted for it (all computers containing a particular plastic are banned for 'safety' reasons). The new infraction will have to be investigated all over again; in the meantime the taxes, or the lonely customs officer, remain in position. All Community nations have been guilty of this sort of thing.

Companies which infringe Community law are a different matter. If they are found guilty, the Court has the power to impose fines, and has done so on many occasions. For examples of Court action, see the collection of leaflets called 'Do You Know Your Rights?'

Private individuals, firms, local authorities or others can appeal to the Court when they consider they have been unjustly served by Community legislation. There are no Court costs involved, though appellants must brief and pay for their own lawyers' fees. In the case of a private person who feels that he or she has been affected adversely by Community legislation, the easiest first step is to complain to the Commission, a simple procedure which can be initiated by a letter to any of the Commission's offices.

Judgements of the European Court are available for consultation in Commission Offices. Advice on the role of the Court and how to approach it can also be offered by the European Lawyers' Groups in England, Scotland, Wales and Northern Ireland. The implementation of the Single European Act is likely to overload the Court especially when rulings on various measures for the creation of the internal market have to be given. Consequently the EC has decided to establish a Court of First Instance where rulings on matters pertaining to the internal market can be made.

For detailed information see coloured pages, A5, A12

THE COURT OF AUDITORS

The independent Court of Auditors watches Community revenue and expenditure with a beady eye. It consists of 12 members, appointed for a six-year term, most of whom have had experience on their own national audit bodies.

Although working in close liaison with national Governments, the Court has considerable powers of search and entry, and can demand that national Governments and other bodies should provide any documentation or other information the Court considers necessary to carry out its task. It assists Parliament and the Council in exercising their powers of control over the budget and how it is used, and produces an annual report which is published in the Official Journal. All Community institutions (and national bodies) have the right to publish a reply to the Court's criticisms.

The Court has been particularly watchful over the operations of the CAP especially as regards the extent of fraudulent activities associated with export refunds for agricultural products. Many cases of fraud have been discovered by the Court when checking the Community's accounts. One well-known example is that of olive oil production in Sardinia, where the Court discovered that the area declared by farmers as being under olive trees was in fact larger than the actual area of the island itself!

For detailed information see coloured pages, A5, A12

PART III
THE UNCOMMON MARKET —
POLICIES AND PEOPLE

An important requirement for prosperity in the member countries of the EC is the creation of a completely integrated market in the Community. This is what the European Commission's programme to complete the internal market by 1992 seeks to do. Obviously the creation of the internal market will not solve all the Community's economic problems, though by removing the hundreds of physical, technical and fiscal barriers that divide the Community, a more favourable climate for economic prosperity will be achieved. Although the European Community is often referred to as 'the Common Market' a true common market does not exist. Many barriers to the free movement of people, goods and capital are to be found in the EC. These obstacles include varying national technical specifications, health and safety standards, environmental regulations, quality controls, and differences in VAT between member countries. The Commission has set itself the task of removing these so-called 'non-tariff' barriers by 1992.

At the heart of this task is the view that unless it can make full use of the potentially vast market of 320 million consumers that the EC of twelve countries consitute, then the European Community will lose ground and markets to its main competitors, the US and Japan.

In June 1985 the European Commission published a White Paper which traced the consequences of the removal of each non-tariff barrier, and the follow-up action that would be necessary to ensure that the removal of the different barriers worked in a coordinated way. The White Paper was adopted with commendable speed at the Milan Summit of 1985.

The timetable lays out stages for:

1. the removal of physical barriers (frontier controls, transport quotas, etc);
2. the abolition of technical barriers to trade, and the prevention of new ones arising; coupled with more freedom for workers and professionals, a common market for services (including financial institutions), freer capital movement and more industrial cooperation;
3. the removal of fiscal barriers, by bringing VAT rates closer together and tackling the problem of excise duties.

For detailed information see coloured pages, A5, A12/13

The costs of an uncommon market have been spelt out by the European Commission in the Cecchini Report of 1988.* These can be summed up as follows:

(a) high administrative costs incurred in dealing with different national bureaucratic requirements;
(b) higher transport costs because of formalities at borders;
(c) increased costs as a result of having to apply different national standards and so having smaller product runs;
(d) duplication of costs involved in separate research and development;
(e) the high costs of non-competitive and heavily regulated State activities, as exemplified by national public procurement policies;
(f) high costs and reduced choice for the consumer confined to his national market;
(g) the opportunity cost which prevents or at best discourages economic activity from spreading across frontiers to enjoy the full market potential.

TRADE BARRIERS AT WORK

Examples of some of these trade obstacles show the sort of problems that a prospective exporter can face in selling to another EC country. The brewing industry illustrates particularly well several types of barrier at work. Probably the best known example of a content/denomination regulation – a rule which prevents a product from using a generic name unless it conforms to certain content requirements – is the German beer purity law. The purity law, which was in fact censured by the European Court of Justice in 1987, has resulted in a highly fragmented German beer industry and a strongly protected market with imports about only 1 per cent of consumption.

The automobile industry which is a key sector of the European economy (employing some 7 per cent of the EC workforce) is characterised by a highly fragmented market in the Community. As the Cecchini Report noted 'the range of obstacles hindering the effective integration of the European car market provide a quintessential roll-call of Common Market disunity'. These obstacles include fiscal barriers, eg taxation levels on car sales differ in virtually all EC countries, ranging from 12 per cent in Luxembourg to some 200 per cent in Denmark and Greece; physical barriers, eg differences in communications standards between EC member countries which impede cooperation in vehicle development and production; and technical barriers, eg unique national vehicle equipment requirements such as side repeater flasher lights in Italy,

* Cecchini, P (1988) *The European Challenge 1992; The Benefits of a Single Market.* Gower Press, Aldershot.

For detailed information see coloured pages, A5, A12/13

yellow headlamp bulbs in France and dim-dip lighting in the UK. The Commission has estimated that the savings incurred by removing all the impediments to free trade in the car sector in the EC would be 2.6 billion ECU, or 5 per cent of the industry's unit costs.

Some 300 legislative proposals have been put forward in order to create an integrated market in the Community by 1992. There has, to date, been considerable debate over the implementation of some of these measures and compromise solutions have been sought. The situation for value added tax and excise duties provides one such example. The 4–9 per cent VAT rate is to be kept for certain necessities, though with the limited option of some zero rates, on goods such as food and children's clothing in the UK. This was in response to strong pressure from the British government. The plan for a single rate of excise duty for tobacco, alcohol and petrol has been abandoned.

There is a view held in some quarters in the UK that the European Commission is using the 1992 deadline in order to put through measures which are not directly necessary for the completion of the internal market. Health warnings on cigarette packets has been a recent (May 1989) bone of contention. While EC health ministers agreed to a directive on the labelling of tobacco products, the UK was the sole dissenting voice in voting against the directive and against plans to enforce the printing of maximum tar and nicotine levels on cigarette packets. The new rules, which will come into effect on 1 January 1993, require manufacturers to print 'Tobacco seriously damages health' on packet fronts and a second warning, chosen by governments from a list of sixteen, on the back. As far as the UK is concerned, the key difference between the warnings on the side of British packets and the new ones is that manufacturers will have to print them whether or not they agree with them.

For detailed information see coloured pages, A5, A12/13

PART IV

DECISION-MAKING AND HOW IT IS INFLUENCED

With an arsenal of things called Regulations, Decisions and Directives, the Community is not unnaturally thought of as a law-making body. Essentially, however, it is concerned with something rather different: persuading member States to coordinate, and if necessary change, their own laws for the better, by consensus. It stimulates all 12 States to take joint stances on an enormous range of issues, at home and internationally. And it tries to bring the peoples of the Community closer together in their trade, their work, and their lives. The Treaties establishing the Communities are not only a series of agreed rules, but of defined targets.

All Community institutions have a vital part in this. It is the task of the Commission to keep the Community moving forward, by prodding national governments into action. The job of the Parliament and the Economic and Social Committee is to examine Commission proposals in detail and, where they can, improve them and make them politically more acceptable. It is the role of the Council of Ministers to discuss and finally approve them, after such additional redrafting or other work as they consider necessary. Once agreement is reached in Council, the Commission resumes responsibility. It must ensure that the new agreement is honoured, with the help of the Parliament and recourse to the European Court if necessary. And it is the particular responsibility of the Court to ensure that injustice is exposed and remedied.

As Emile Noël points out in 'Uniting Europe', the Community is much more than an inter-governmental organisation. Its institutions have a legal standing, and powers of their own. It prepares an immensely detailed scheme of work for the Council. The current programme of the Commission runs to tens of thousands of words. Apart from religion, it touches upon pretty well every aspect of human endeavour.

The Community's proposals, when and if they become agreed law, will affect every industry, business and company in the Community; every worker, every housewife; every old age pensioner and every child. Since each decision made up by the Community involves compromise, some will love it, some will loathe it, and the vast majority will find it bearable, just as they do with any new legislation.

For detailed information see coloured pages, A5, A13

13 judges   6 advocates-general

Court of Justice

17

European Commission

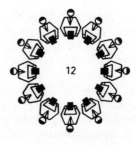

12

Council of Ministers

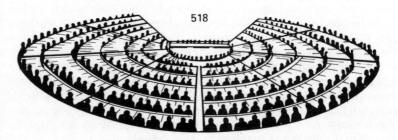

518

European Parliament

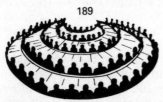

189

Economic and Social Committee
xxx
For coal and steel affairs:
Consultative Committee

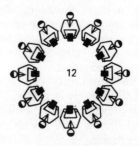

12

Court of Auditors

Figure 2 The institutions of the European Community

But there are crucial differences between Community and national legislation. Most Governments of the world prepare their laws in secrecy and present them as *fait accompli*. Until a national Chancellor of the Exchequer unveils his budget, it is a state secret. People have gone to prison for revealing its contents in advance. It is, to all intents and purposes, *law*. If it is defeated in the national parliament, there is a general election.

The Community Budget, on the other hand, is publicly and endlessly discussed, savaged, restored and usually savaged again before being adopted. So with all Community decision-making. It involves long and detailed opinion-gathering, the publication of an ever-changing string of 'green papers' for discussion, and above all opportunities for lobbying and for influencing the outcome unknown in national terms.

But it is up to those who have a view on proposed legislation to *use* these opportunities, and at the right moment.

THE QUESTION OF TIMING

A portrait painter who tried to improve his picture in the final stages by scraping out the full face and experimenting with a profile instead would be unlikely to succeed. Too much work has gone into the substructure. Yet even those who should know better appear to believe that the time to try to change a piece of proposed Community legislation is at the last moment.

In part, this misconception is based on the (accurate) assumption that nothing can actually happen in terms of new Community policies until national Ministers agree that it *should* happen. In part it is due to idleness on the part of those who should have been following the development of the proposal from its inception, and have failed to do so until it has exploded in the press after vigorous discussion in the Council.

The chance of influencing proposed legislation when it has got as far as a Council meeting is in all cases remote. Even when it is worth trying, only those who have been through the whole gruelling process of argument and horse-trading have any chance of being listened to. Newcomers to the process will be greeted with an exhausted shrug of the shoulders, and it matters little to whom they express their opinions.

★ ★ ★ ★

You are, let us say, the chairman of the finance committee of a district authority which has been discharging unprocessed sewage into a river for around a century. It is not a subject which you care to think about too often; a member of your staff follows it, doubtless with no wild enthusiasm.

But one day you see a 'special report' on television, indicating that

For detailed information see coloured pages, A5, A13

THE BASIC FACTS

The Council of Ministers takes the Community's decisions, acting on proposals submitted by the Commission. These may be far-reaching (monetary and international matters) or very specific.

On most occasions national Ministers have before them detailed reports from the European Parliament and the Economic and Social Committee to help them in their deliberations. Other, easier points on the agenda are usually agreed at a lower level.

If proposed legislation is particularly difficult, and individual Councils of junior Ministers cannot reach agreement, they may be passed up to the Council at Foreign Minister level, which meets several times a year. If agreement cannot be reached there, it must be considered by the European Council – the 'summit', usually meeting three times yearly, composed of Prime Ministers and Presidents plus the President of the Commission, and established in 1974.

Decision-making can only be based upon the Community Treaties. It would, for example, be improper for the Council to rule that the death penalty should be introduced throughout the Community for terrorist assassination, since no clause in the Treaties gives it power to act in such a matter of domestic law. But it *can* agree (and has done) on joint action to track down terrorists across frontiers, since this is trans-national action permissible under several Treaty provisions.

As we shall see, the decision-making process is distinguished by the extraordinary information-gathering which takes place before a proposal even reaches the Council, and by its openness. (Council meetings are in theory private, but there is an embarassing richness of 'leaking' to the press by spokesmen for individual States.)

A Commission proposal is traditionally first considered by the Council in a 'tour de table': all 12 States speak their piece, followed by debate. The President of the Council can exercise considerable

For detailed information see coloured pages, A5, A10, A13

influence; member States assume the Presidency in turn every six months. Throughout Council discussions, Commission and national experts are on hand to redraft proposals (often working all night).

The Council can reach agreement by weighted majority. For this, 54 votes are necessary out of a total of 76, the latter being apportioned thus: 10 to the UK, France, Germany and Italy, 8 to Spain, 5 to Belgium, Netherlands, Greece and Portugal, 3 to Denmark and Ireland and 2 to Luxembourg.

In practice, almost all decisions have in recent years been taken unanimously. The exception is when a nation feels that, although its interests will not be vitally harmed by an agreement, a token protest must be made. There may then be a majority decision – often with a formal reserve, entered by one or more States and usually lifted after a decent interval. The Single European Act provides for more majority voting in Council on specific measures within the framework of a policy already agreed (in particular, the White Paper on the internal market).

Council decisions are reached by a process of onrolling negotiation. National Ministers, at first expressing national views, gradually come together. One or more State finds itself increasingly isolated. Eventually it comes down to 11 against 1. Then the odd man out gives in, with good or ill grace, and agreement is reached – or the buck is passed upwards.

The European Court plays no direct part in this process. Its job is to rule on the fair and honest implementation of agreements once they are reached.

For detailed information see coloured pages, A5, A10, A13

if 'Eurocrats' get their way, your council will have to spend millions of pounds in building treatment plants or sewer outfalls. The whole question is on the point of discussion by Environmental Ministers in Brussels.

At this point, you panic. After giving your 'expert' on sewage a rocket, you compose a series of dramatic minutes and letters for your fellow councillors and local MPs. You give unattributable briefings to the local and national press, indicating the disaster ahead for your ratepayers if these meddlers in Brussels have their way. No doubt you will get impressive reportage. But you are too late. You are trying to get into the game when the bidding is over, the contract has been reached, and the first tricks have been played to.

Within hours of the TV report your newly-galvanised 'expert' on sewage will have talked to the real experts in the Department of the Environment, and read the wodge of Government circulars which have been on his files for years. He will have discovered that there are Community rules, long ago agreed, on the degree to which we are permitted by international law to pollute bathing beaches, interfere with marine life and fishing rights, or corrupt the high seas. These rules were argued out in the 1970s in great detail, by experts from every Community country. Environmental groups gave extensive evidence. The Parliament prepared a detailed report, spelling out the consequences for various industries, ratepayers, consumers, tourist boards, marine biologists. Other local authorities have built sewage treatment works with the help of huge grants from the Community. After endless painful consultation, the governments of all Community nations have come to a conclusion on what their Environment Ministers plan to say about the implementation of these agreements in the Council in Brussels. *And you are seriously hoping to change all that now!*

The time to influence the Community's decision-making is as early as possible in the process. There are four stages, although they overlap:

(a) when a new proposal for legislation is being drafted within the Commission and considered by experts and working parties;
(b) when the first draft becomes public;
(c) when the draft is being considered by the European Parliament and the Economic and Social Committee;
(d) when the revised draft is being considered again by the Commissioners and COREPER before being submitted to the Council.

A hypothetical example.

Let us say that the Commission believes the time is right for an attempt to get agreement on Community legislation on the *transport of oil by sea,* the object being to ensure that all 12 nations should move together towards common (and higher) standards of safety.

Such legislation would be right in terms of fair competition, but also for more important reasons. As things are going, an unimaginable catastrophe must happen one day as a giant tanker sheds its doleful cargo; the question is not *if* but *when,* and every government knows it. But for one country to 'go it alone' would be immensely expensive and difficult. An ideal case, in fact, for joint Community action, which would surely be followed by similar legislation in America and elsewhere, to the mutual benefit of the citizens of all lands and the denizens of sea and air.

The Commission therefore starts to prepare a draft Directive for consideration by the Council of Ministers.

STAGE 1

The task of coordinating the first draft is given to John P of the Commission's Directorate-General for Transport. He will write parts of it himself, and will work in the closest cahoots with the Directorates for Energy, the Environment, Competition, the Internal Market and Industrial Affairs. But others will have views, too — Fisheries, External Relations, Economic and Financial Affairs, Employment. Indeed, every Commissioner and more than half the Commission Directorates-General will contribute to the paper.

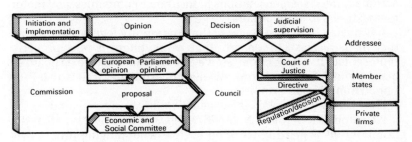

Figure 3 How a decision is taken in the European Community

For detailed information see coloured pages A5, A10, A12/13

All this, of course, is only within the Commission. Mr P and his colleagues must also canvass the widest possible opinion from member Governments, shipping and energy interests, ecologists, international organisations, trade unions, and a host of other bodies, all of whom will have relevant and strongly held opinions on the subject.

Usually this information will reach the Commission through one of the established links: COREPER; third countries with ambassadors in Brussels; and the International bodies (several hundred of them) which regularly lobby the Commission.

But there is nothing to prevent a pressure group, local authority, company or individual from making their views known direct. Indeed, the Commission positively encourages this at an early stage, and Mr P's digestion will suffer as he is lunched and dined *ad nauseam* by those with axes to grind.

When the first draft of our Directive on oil transport is prepared, it is passed to expert groups, from all Community countries. Meeting under Commission chairmanship, these experts attempt to reconcile differences and product a draft which all 12 nations can discuss in principle. They have no authority to commit their governments, but detailed knowledge of the subjects at hand, and a shrewd idea of what their political masters will wear.

Some of these meetings are formal and long established. Some are mixed in membership, representing civil services and the various associations involved. All will have easy access to the interest groups concerned.

In the case in point, there will be representatives of the oil and shipping interests of all 12 nations, plus a wide range of bodies whose interests could be affected by the proposed Directive, ranging from ecologists to nationalised industries, coastguards to plastic manufacturers, seamens' unions to insurance companies, and motor manfacturers to shipbuilders.

It is during these first stages of the Community legislation process that it is easiest to ensure that your interests are properly represented. It is the Commission's absolute duty to take on board as many points of view as it can reasonably assimilate. Write to Mr P, or phone him. His job is to listen.

How can you discover *when* such a draft is being prepared?

No problem in our hypothetical example. The fact that the Commission is starting work on such a wide-ranging proposal is certain to leak at the outset, and make news, carried worldwide. But not all proposed legislation is so dramatic. A proposal, say, to phase out the use of an ingredient in food packaging suspected of causing minor allergies may never get into the press at all at this stage. Yet it could, if agreed, be of critical importance to a small export firm using the material, and the company which supplies it. How can such firms ensure that they get their views across at the proper time?

For detailed information see coloured pages A5, A10/, A12/13

First, they should keep in touch with their own trade or professional association. Almost every industry and business in Britain has an appropriate lobby in Brussels. The staff of these organisations are continually in touch with Commission officials, and know exactly what legislation is planned and the stage it has reached. The most important of these liaison groups is the Union of Industries of the European Communities (UNICE), which represents the main industrial body in each Community country. (The CBI also has its own office.) But there are lobbies in Brussels representing everything from pastry-making to landscape architecture and from hearing-aid manufacture to seed-breeding. A full list is regularly published, and a slightly condensed version is in *The European Community — the practical guide.*

One of the best sources of information about decision-making in the Community at all its stages is the bulletin published ten times a year by the International Union of Local Authorities, *European Information Service.* References to this excellent document will recur throughout this book.

The annual reports and monthly *Bulletins* of the Community give, under subject headings, a forward look at work in progress.

MEPs will be up to date on the work of their own committees (they are, however, peripatetic and difficult to catch; write, rather than telephone).

The magazine *British Business* (again referred to throughout the book) prints, about twice a year, a complete list of actual and proposed legislation in the fields of trade and industry, including proposals in the early draft stage. Subjects covered in these surveys include motor vehicles, agricultural machinery, measuring devices, electrical equipment, textiles, dangerous substances, lifting apparatus, fuels, construction materials, protective clothing, cosmetics, toys, food additives, packaging, and a host of others.

Finally, for those who can afford the time and money there is a mass of material available in two superb newsletters published in Brussels. They are called 'Agence Europe' and 'European Report'.

* * * *

Stage I is the time to speak up when you have something to say about proposed legislation, and the Commission has an absolute duty to pay attention. But it is also true that the big guns will make the most noise. You will have to shout hard before anyone in Brussels will be able to hear you.

Fortunately, it is the British Government's duty to sound out British interests and make sure that Mr P and his colleagues in the Commission take them into account. The Government will shout for you, and is good at it. Stage I is therefore the best time to tackle your local MP, write to Government Departments, speak to the experts in the UK Permanent Representation, fire off letters to newspapers, and

For detailed information see coloured pages A5, A10, A12/13

make sure your views are known to your professional, business or trade association. This is probably the best time to lobby; Stage 2 is too noisy.

STAGE 2

This begins when the details of the new proposal are leaked to the press — usually partially, often dishonestly, and in our hypothetical case spectacularly. This is one of the aspects of the very open decision-making process of the Community which must be lived with: the other side of the coin of Commission accessibility.

Someone will get a copy of Mr P's draft, select the sensitive bits, present them out of context, and give the story to an agency. The tabloid headlines next day will read: 'NEW EEC LAW WILL PUT £1 ON THE GALLON', 'EUROCRATS MAKE NEW GRAB FOR BRITISH OIL', 'RUIN AHEAD FOR UK SHIPPERS THANKS TO MARKET MADMEN', etc, with variations in the appropriate language in France, Germany, Italy and elsewhere. MPs, leaders of local authorities, MEPs and representatives of industries and lobby groups will leap into print, often on the basis of inaccurate or loaded information. At best they will make points which they should have made through the channels open to them, long ago.

It is at this stage in Community work that the most inaccurate and damaging stories are carried by television and the press of Community countries. Bringing such stories back into touch with reality is difficult. They will run for days or weeks, the headlines being grabbed by the most outspoken of the protagonists. Nor will it be easy for the information officers of the Commission (or of government departments) to correct the facts, since Mr P's paper, which will probably not even have been seen by the whole Commission, is still technically classified.

Altogether, Stage 2 generates much hot air and little fact. It will, however, force Mr P's draft paper into the open, since MEPs, MPs and others will demand to see it. Those with a valid point to make should treat newspaper reports with considerable scepticism; get hold of what the draft *really* says as soon as it becomes available in Commission offices; read it with care; hold their peace while the fireworks sputter, and wait for Stage 3.

STAGE 3

The most important amendments to the Commission draft are likely to come about when the text is being considered by the Parliament. Now is the time to make use of your European MP. You can do this in three ways: by writing to the MEP in whose constituency you live, by writing to whoever serves on the appropriate committee, or by writing to one of the political groups.

Your MEP has no *power* over this sort of decision-making, but a

For detailed information see coloured pages A5, A10, A12/13

great deal of *influence*. This can be wielded during debate, in committee work (while the Parliament's comments are being prepared) and in lobbying Ministers, MPs and Government Departments in the UK and elsewhere. He can also use the Parliamentary Question system — a useful weapon, particularly in ensuring that the Commission has the fullest possible knowledge of local circumstances and problems.

Stage 3 is also a good time to work on Westminster. As soon as Commission proposals become public, they are deposited with scrutiny committees in both Houses for examination. The Lords committee, in particular, often produces a detailed report on proposed legislation. It takes evidence from experts, Ministers and civil servants, and maintains informal contacts with industrial and business groups. Lords reports are read by those who count. Get your word in if you can. Nobble a Lord.

STAGE 4

It is the task of COREPER to get Commission proposals into final shape for presentation to the Council for decision. The UK Permanent Representative (UKREP is the acronym) is 'our man' in COREPER. He and his staff coordinate the views of all relevant British interests, and give on-the-spot briefing to British ministers. The staff of UKREP is extensive, and has direct links with UK departments. Many of the experts who work in UKREP (two minutes walk from the Commission building in Brussels) are seconded from MAFF and the Departments of Trade, Industry and the Environment. They can get detailed and expert advice at short notice, and there is a shuttle service of civil servants between Brussels and London (not to mention Edinburgh, Cardiff and Belfast), all of whom touch down in UKREP at some point.

Exceptionally busy men and women. But they will do their best to help if you have important things to say about proposed legislation, and are ideally placed to direct you to the pressure points in the Commission or the appropriate UK Department.

Stage Four of the process is also usually your last chance to reinforce your case with the Commission. Commissioners, in particular, are expected to be expert on the political situation and the problems of the country they know best, and to be well informed on how the Ministers of that country are likely to play their hands at the negotiating table.

★ ★ ★ ★

A little healthy cynicism is in order when considering our (extensively amended) proposal for a Directive on the Transport of Oil at Sea as it first appears on the Council table. It will, for the best of reasons, include many suggestions which everyone knows will

For detailed information see coloured pages A5, A10, A12/13

have no chance of being agreed. For example, the first draft will no doubt suggest that oil tankers should be banned from the Channel; that Greek owners should pay the same wages to their employees as French or German companies and provide similar working conditions; and that no oil shipping should be allowed within 20 miles of coastal bird sanctuaries. No-one round the Council table, including those who wrote the draft paper, believes there is a snowball's chance in hell of getting such clauses through. Their task is to establish targets; who knows, one day they may be reached.

It is, however, wise for those who wish to lobby on behalf of their industry, their business, or their local authority, to discover the area of ground on which the Commission will stand firm; the areas on which it will move; and the areas which it will gracefully concede as a bargaining counter. Here, contacts in Brussels are, undeniably, of great value. There is no point in spending time and money undermining the wrong wall of the citadel – the one due to collapse at the first trumpet-blast.

SUMMARY

There are major differences between the shaping of national laws and of Community legislation.

In the first case, the object is to enable a government to carry out its declared policy, within the limits of its resources, no matter what the other parties involved may say. The duty of the opposition is almost always to oppose that policy. Drafting and enacting laws is a confidential process, and the individual back-bench MP at Westminster has surprisingly little to do with it. Consultation, fact-finding and opinion-taking are naturally conducted on a massive scale – but in private. Cabinet policy, once agreed, is enacted by simple Order, or the publication of a White Paper. If a Government fails to get its legislation through, it must go to the country.

In the Community, matters could scarcely be more different. There is no government, no cabinet, and little confidentiality. 'Back-benchers' in the European Parliament not only have easy access to those who draft legislation while they are drafting it: they can exact, in writing, a promise that the problems of their constituents are properly understood and taken into account. Constituents themselves can approach the Commission and get their points of view across, directly. Those who question aspects of proposed Community legislation may find their government not opposing them, but backing them to the hilt, and ready to use all its clout through the Council machinery. Any firm, local authority, trade or professional association, trade union, quango, or what-you-will, which feels it may be seriously affected by the Community legislation, has an absolute right to plead its case throughout the process of decision-making, with the backing of experts and pressure groups at a local, national or international level.

For detailed information see coloured pages A5, A10, A12/13

In short, opportunities for influencing decision-making in the Community are not only guaranteed: they are an essential part of the process itself.

But that influence must be exerted early: while drafts are being written, evidence gathered and opinions expressed. Put it off until there is an angry explosion in the press, with the biggest battalions firing their heaviest artillery, and you have almost certainly left it too late.

For detailed information see coloured pages A5, A10, A12/13

PART V
INDIVIDUAL POLICIES

The Community's range of activities is wide (see Figure 4). Though they all derive from the Treaties which established the institutions and mapped out their work, there is nothing immutable about them. Indeed, trying to adapt swiftly to changing circumstances, in the Community itself and the world at large, takes up an enormous amount of the energy and imagination of those who work in Brussels, Strasbourg and Luxembourg.

Bureaucrats are not traditionally fleet of foot or noted for changing their minds. But in democracies, at least, they have had to learn. Not least is this true in Brussels, where representatives of new Governments with radically different policies have a habit of appearing at the Council table and throwing carefully drafted compromise proposals into the waste-paper basket.

Another problem is having to draw up and agree on policies rooted in Treaties which, admirable though they are, were drafted in a different world: where fuel was cheap, acid rain had not been heard of, there was a waiting list for cars and ships, food shortages (not surpluses) were the problem to be tackled, and unemployment and inflation were things that happened elsewhere. The Community has in fact been described as an adult in children's clothing.

The need to look afresh at the Community's procedures, and the relative roles of the Council, Parliament and Commission is considered in the section entitled 'Policies in the Process of Change'.

What follows is a brief and doubtless subjective look at most current Community policies. Experts on specific subjects are certain to be disappointed by the inevitable over-simplification, though perhaps they may find more nourishment in the reference sections in Part VIII. I hope, at least, that they may be somewhat surprised at the degree to which their own subject interlocks with many others at the Community level.

EMPLOYMENT AND SOCIAL POLICY

There is little in the Community Treaties about job creation.

For detailed information see coloured pages A5, A13

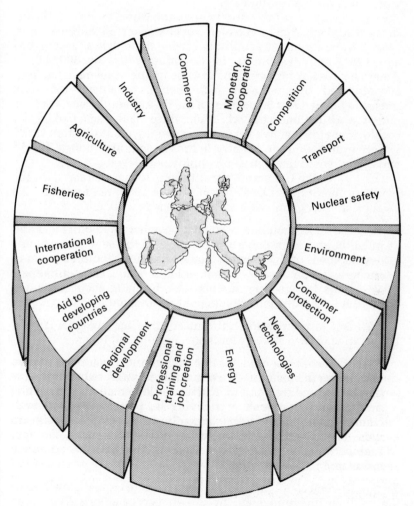

Figure 4 The activities of the European Community

Unemployment was not a problem in the fifties; it was low and dropping.

How different the situation today. Seventeen million people are out of work in the Community; employment has doubled since 1980. In particular regions, and among the young, the situation is even worse than the figures indicate.

Nor can we blame this entirely upon the world recession. During the past 20 years, America created work for nearly 34 million people; West Europe for only 3½ million. During the toughest years (1983 and 1984) employment in the Community fell by 800,000; in America it rose by four million. The rise in unemployment has been accompanied by an increasingly serious problem: long-term unemployment. Over 50 per cent of the EC's unemployed have been out of work for one year while one-third have been looking for employment for over two years. The unemployment situation varies widely from country to country in the Community, though Ireland and Spain record the highest unemployment levels.

The task of the Community institutions today, therefore, (in the words of the Stuttgart Declaration of June 1983, reinforced by the Commission programme for 1987–1990) is to work for:

'. . . an overall economic strategy to combat unemployment and inflation and to promote convergence of the state of economic development of the member States. Priority should be given to encouraging productive investment and raising competitiveness as a basis for creating durable jobs, bringing about sustained economic growth, and reducing unemployment.'

President Jacques Delors introduced the Commission's current cooperative growth strategy for more employment thus:

"The philosophy behind it is that each country would use its own margins for manoeuvre – lowering interest rates, reducing the tax burden, providing more incentives for job creation, stimulating productive investment, or reviving its policies on town-and-country planning and public amenities. This should allow us to press ahead with the restructuring of our economies, the fight against inflation, and get us back to the path of economic expansion and job creation."

Such a strategy could, he said, add one point to annual growth rates and reduce unemployment by 30–40 per cent over five years, creating new jobs at the rate of 700,000 to 800,000 a year. He emphasized, however, the parallel need for a better dialogue between employers and trade unions, the strengthening of the European Monetary System, closer cooperation in research and technology, and a comprehensive infrastructure programme for industry, Community-wide.

The problem about such a strategy is that the powers and resources

For detailed information see coloured pages A5, A13

of the Community's institutions are severely limited in their ability to implement it, partly because they started from a low base-line. As late as 1973, the Commission had only a tiny desk dealing with employment. It was largely concerned with discrimination against migrant workers and women, and had no money at all for job creation.

At the macroeconomic level there is little the Commission can do except study and advise from a European standpoint, offering Community objectives as a supplement (occasionally an alternative!) to the policies of national Treasuries. It commissions independent studies of various kinds, and in its Annual Economic Report suggests common guidelines for economic and fiscal policies.

A Commission programme to tackle unemployment internally was submitted in November 1986, and after discussions at the Summit was agreed (in a much watered-down form) by the Council on 11 December, with a recommendation that a start be made on it during 1987. It is an adaptation of an earlier plan put forward by the UK, Italy and Ireland, and its priorities are probably best summed up in the conclusions of the December Summit which, however general in tone, had at least the agreement of all 12 Heads of State. It reads in part:

> Economic and social progress and the constant improvement of the living and working conditions of the peoples of Europe are central goals of the Community. The growth of business and enterprise and all productive activities is essential to tackle the scourge of unemployment, particularly long-term and youth employment.
>
> To create the conditions for this, the Community must work to break down the remaining barriers to trade between Member States, reduce red tape, and open up opportunities so that European enterprise can flourish in all Member States.
>
> The European Council stressed the importance of growing convergence of economic policy in all the Member States over the last four years. This had led to reduced inflation, now estimated by the Commission to be likely to fall to 3% in 1987, the lowest Community average for 20 years. Reduction in unemployment and convergence in living standards were less satisfactory.

The Summit communiqué after somewhat curtly suggesting that 'a reduction in interest rates is desirable', went on to urge Finance and Employment Ministers to establish 'non-inflationary and substantial growth in employment', including measures to:

- promote long-term prosperity and job creation through the completion of the internal market;
- achieve sustained employment growth;

For detailed information see coloured pages A5, A13

- lighten regulations hampering business;
- help small and medium-sized enterprises to make a dynamic contribution to the creation of prosperity and jobs;
- encourage productive investment.

Welcome, if anodyne. However, in the section entitled 'An Action Programme for Employment Growth', the Summit communiqué, after recommending better training and the promotion of the creation of self-employment and SMEs, stepped tentatively on to new ground, recognising

> the importance of Community action designed to improve the workings of the labour market, including ways of increasing part-time and other flexible working patterns, providing better access to training for disadvantaged groups, and encouraging employment for such groups in inner city areas.

A few days later, goaded into action, the Employment Ministers approved all this. The communiqué also asked the Commission to develop the 'social dialogue' between workers and managers, called for more worker mobility, and promised to keep tabs on the whole Programme by demanding six-monthly reports on its progress. In May 1989 the European Commission published preliminary proposals for its charter of fundamental social rights, which represents the main social dimension of the internal market. The draft charter deals with the following rights: improvement of conditions of life and work; right to free movement of salaried and self-employed workers; work and termination; right to social protection; right to freedom of association and collective bargaining; right to professional formation; right to information; consultation and participation by workers; right to health and safety in the work place. These are likely to result in considerable debate at ministerial level. Indeed, the UK government has already voiced its opposition to the participation by workers in management decisions.

DIRECT COMMUNITY HELP

The Regional Development Fund, established to redistribute the Community's resources in favour of the poorer regions, is less than 15 years old. The job creation activities of the Social Fund are more recent still. (Both are dealt with in Part VII.) What they can achieve in terms of money and staff work is still limited.

Community funds have been of considerable value to governments, local authorities, and industries. By improving the infrastructure, the amenities and the environment of areas where the traditional industries are in decline, they have helped (in a way disproportionate to the sums of money involved) to attract what little investment there has been to the regions which need it most.

Such investment has, however, often been external, and has

For detailed information see coloured pages A13, A22

created 'external' jobs. They are a great deal better than none at all; but at the Community scale it is essential to tackle unemployment from within.

There is fairly general agreement that the best hope of breaking free from the industrial recession may lie at present with small firms. Certainly, small and medium-sized enterprises are crucial to the industrial and business health of the Community. 95% of the firms in Western Europe employ fewer than 500 people; if every such firm were to create just one or two new jobs, Europe's dole queue would reach manageable proportions overnight.

Much has been done to encourage cooperation between small firms, and to reward innovation and enterprise. But in the past it has proved extremely difficult to get Community financial help to those who needed it most.

Recently, however, Community funds have become accessible to small businessmen — and just as important, far better known. Employment Grant Schemes, Local Employment Initiatives, and the very cheap services (financial advice, legal help, accountancy, translation, etc.) for SMEs pioneered as 'Better Business Services' in 1983 in Scotland and now, termed 'Business Improvement Services', available in England and Wales (with a similar scheme in Northern Ireland) have worked very well.

Elise News, an occasional magazine available from 35 rue Vilain XIII, 1050 Brussels, is published to exchange information on these Local Employment Initiatives, as they are called. It is free. Other material is listed in the following section.

There is also a growing number of enterprise trusts eager to help the small firm. Often funded jointly by private companies, local authorities, and the Community, these can often not only offer financial help but training courses, help with development and marketing, and advice on exporting. A Background Report (B7/85) entitled 'Encouraging the Small Business', available from any Commission Office, lists the many recent developments in Community help for SMEs, and gives useful contact points for further information.

Community employment policy, limited though it is by the pitiful funds at its command, has had some success in the regions of the UK, both in creating the right infrastructure for investment and job creation, and in assisting small businesses directly. As we shall see in the next chapter and in Part VII, there are also growing opportunities for help in the new technologies, and in the whole field of training and retraining. But other aspects of employment (and far more controversial ones) should be looked at briefly here: such matters as work-sharing, flexible retirement, shorter working hours, and a new approach to leisure.

In June 1988 the Council agreed to the reform of the Community's structural funds (including the Regional Development Fund and the

For detailed information see coloured pages A13, A22

Social Fund). This came into operation in January 1989. There are five major objectives: promoting the development and structural adjustment of the less-developed regions of the Community; converting the regions seriously affected by industrial decline; combating long-term unemployment; encouraging the integration of young people into employment; encouraging the development of rural areas. The Commission has estimated that the budget required for the structural funds will need to be doubled in real terms by 1993.

RADICAL SOLUTIONS?

None of the Community's Ministers for Employment can admit it publicly, but all know in their hearts that a return to 'the good old days' is now impossible. There was a time when a man could feel he had a right to work at the same job in the same neighbourhood, for around 40 hours a week, for 40 or 50 years.

Gone, forever.

Nor, unless we change our ways, can we go on paying ourselves more and increasing our living standards year by year. Over recent years unit labour costs in the Community have increased; they have fallen in the US and in Japan. During 1986, Japan led the world in competitiveness, with the US second, Germany fourth, and Britain, France and Italy in 15th, 16th and 18th places respectively. In Japan and America increases in earnings have been offset by rising productivity. In Britain and Italy they have not.

The Community as a whole has failed to come to terms with changes in industry and employment with regard to mobility of labour, and adaptability (by both sides of industry) to change. This has been harmful in two particular ways: first, unwillingness to move from one area to another has concentrated unemployment in certain areas to an unacceptable degree; second, industries (and especially multi-nationals) have too often taken the easy way of 'exporting unemployment' – closing marginal plants in the periphery where they are desperately needed and withdrawing them to the rich and richly-equipped heartlands of the Community.

The Community has tried to intervene by the provision and encouragement of large-scale programmes of training, and by the 'disincentive' aspect of regional policy – in some ways at least as important as the fund mechanisms – ensuring that excessive State aids are not given to attract investment into the 'easy' regions at the expense of areas which most need them.

But these, even where they work, are palliatives. The Commission seeks to persuade national Governments to face up to the painful cure; to look, now, at the possibilities of making the available work go round more people. Here, to put it mildly, progress is going to be difficult.

After much discussion with both sides of industry and national experts, the Commission has produced a series of draft 'guidelines'.

For detailed information see coloured pages A13, A14

They are on the greenest of paper, and UK opinion on them is strongly divided.

On *overtime*, the Commission suggests voluntary restraint, with paid leave in compensation for overtime worked above an agreed threshold. Provision for *flexible retirement* should be made, by gradually giving workers the right to choose when they should retire. There should be a new deal for *part-time workers.* There should be a start on a common framework on *working hours,* covering the number of hours worked weekly, or annually, or both. Abuses caused by short-term contracts for *temporary workers* should be curbed, and their social protection strengthened. There should be more active 'training for leisure', and more opportunities for *voluntary work,* particularly in the social field.

The first two of these proposals, on overtime and flexible retirement, have barely been debated in public.

During 1984 the Council considered the draft plan for shortening working hours. Without setting target dates or being specific about methods, this invited member States to examine ways in which working time could be reduced without affecting competitiveness or increasing unit labour costs. Nine Community countries were ready to accept the proposal; Britain could not.

There has been equal antipathy in the UK to the Commission's draft plans for strengthening regulations governing part-time and temporary workers. Of the Community's 9 million part-timers, nearly half are in the UK, and 83% of these are women. The Commission works from the premise that many part-time workers are exploited, and the majority *feel* exploited. The aim is to guarantee them the same rights to training, promotion, and (pro rata) salary and social security, as full-timers. The UK Government's view (Hansard, 16 November 1983) is that the draft Directive as it stands would introduce 'undesirable rigidities' into the labour market and decrease job opportunities. (One problem has been to define the number of hours worked per week. In Britain a worker may put in 30 hours per week and still be classified as part-time.)

The Commission's draft plans on temporary work were published in May 1982, and were the subject of a detailed report by the Parliament's Social Affairs Committee. The intention is to give temporary workers the same rights as permanent workers; to protect permanent workers by reducing the misuse of temporary work; and to ensure that only sound and reputable companies (and not builders' 'lumps', cowboy transport companies and the like) should supply temporary workers, especially across national frontiers.

This draft plan found favour with the Economic and Social Committee, but not with British businessmen, who opposed it strongly, arguing that it might harm efficiency, reduce opportunities for temporary workers, yet not guarantee that opportunities for permanent work would be enhanced. The House of Lords committee

For detailed information see coloured pages A13/14

added its view that employment businesses in the UK were relatively well-regulated, and thus 'substantially different from their counterparts elsewhere in the Community'.

It is difficult to find much optimism in Commission circles that any of these radical suggestions for tackling unemployment will find a ready welcome – particularly in Britain. The plans will, however, be planked firmly on Minister's desks at regular intervals – now with a hint of backing from the summit. A number of Commission-sponsored reports on such problems as working hours, part-time labour and adaptation to technological change were produced during 1985 and 1986. Some are listed on the blue pages.

SOCIAL POLICY

Growth and prosperity (it hardly needs saying) do not necessarily bring a happier life. Nor have recent economic developments spread either the rewards or the suffering equally. It was not much fun being a migrant worker in Germany in the 1950s; nor is it today. The attitude of some companies towards employing handicapped workers is less enlightened now than it was in the late 1940s. Working women still face discrimination which has found ways of bending even long-established national laws.

The Community has, however, some hard achievement to its credit in all of these fields. Equal pay for *women* had been enshrined in the laws of all ten nations since 1976, with right of appeal to the European Court (several times successfully exercised). Since 1978 equal treatment in access to employment, training, promotion and working conditions is in theory guaranteed and there can be no discrimination in social security or access to it. Draft legislation seeks to abolish any kind of discrimination which still exists in civil, commercial and tax laws and to tackle a rash of non-legal obstacles to women's rights, such as traditional segregation of roles, lack of information and training etc.

During 1986 women won two notable victories in the European Court, one concerning discrimination in terms of retirement age, the other on allowances for looking after invalid relatives. A new Medium Term programme, which runs until 1990, will concentrate on consolidating existing rights, improving information, exploring new ways of creating jobs for women and training them in the new technologies, looking at the special problems of Spain and Portugal, and helping the most vulnerable or disadvantaged categories of women, such as single parents. (A suggestion that men should have the right to 'paternity leave' and so enjoy with their wives the first, fascinating months of a baby's life were, however, greeted with such strident hilarity in the British press that they seem to have disappeared, at least temporarily, from the scene.)

The problem of *migrant workers* is different in scale and kind for the Community countries in continental Europe as compared with

For detailed information see coloured pages A13/14

the UK. The Social Fund has, however, helped in the education of Vietnamese refugees in Britain, and in encouraging language training (both in English and indigenous languages) among Commonwealth immigrants.

Anyone advising on Community funds has the depressing task, every other day, of telling those with good ideas for helping *the handicapped* that there is nothing the Community can do for them. The importance to our society of caring for the old and the mentally handicapped is critical, and growing: but the Social Fund has no money to offer. It has, perforce, had to limit its financial aid to vocational rehabilitation – getting the handicapped into a job, back to work after an accident, or making life at work easier. The two major programmes so far mounted have concentrated on new ideas for training and employing the handicapped, making the exchange of good ideas easier, and helping to devise new ways of improving the quality of life for the handicapped worker (and his or her family). Above all, the Commission has contributed to campaigns aimed at convincing employers that giving jobs to the handicapped is not only right in itself but can repay the investment in purely practical terms.

Future plans include financial support to increase the mobility of handicapped people; to devise and improve materials used in teaching, health care and daily life; the duty-free importation of items for handicapped people manufactured outside the Community, and the development of new equipment for use at work and in the home.

During 1986 the Commission submitted to the Council a Model Code, promoting vocational training and employment for the disabled, measures of positive discrimination on their behalf, and the elimination of negative discrimination in laws or bureaucratic practice against those seeking access to training or work. It also suggests incentives to employers to cover any special costs involved in employing the handicapped. The Code (and many other Community documents) are now available in Braille and in cassette form for the blind.

The Commission, in cooperation with the European Parliament, are at present drafting a *Charter for the Aged.* This will examine the possibilities of a minimum Euro-pension (with inflation-proofing), concessions on telephone and transport bills, and a free alarm link for the over-75s.

On *working conditions,* the European Foundation for the Improvement of Living and Working Conditions, in Dublin, has for many years been studying the problems of shift-work, temporary and part-time employment, the impact of new technologies, and preparation for retirement. Its detailed reports can be consulted at Commission Offices.

In addition, the Community has:

For detailed information see coloured pages A14

(a) created permanent bodies to review safety and health in mining, steel and nuclear industry, and financially assisted existing work in these fields;

(b) launched a programme on safety, hygiene and health protection at work, particularly aimed at reducing the risk to workers of exposure to chemical, physical and biological agents.

There have also been rules to limit the dangers of microwaves and lasers in industry, to introduce common safety signs, understandable in any country, and to help with health education.

The *poverty action programme,* which ran from 1975 until 1980, provided some £12 million for pilot studies to help communities in particularly run-down regions of the Community to help themselves, by improving the environment, social involvement and physical amenities, thus making their area more attractive for potential investors and employers. The projects supported in the UK included day centres for poorer families in London and Liverpool, a legal assistance service in Wolverhampton, 'local resource centres' in London, Govan and South Wales, and community and social development programmes in Edinburgh and Belfast.

For detailed information see coloured pages A14

THE TROUBLED INDUSTRIES

Manufacturing industry in the European Community has been deeply affected by technical changes in patterns of ownership and technology over the last 15 years. The long-term problem sectors of steel, textiles and shipbuilding have been particularly ravaged.

STEEL

The beginnings of the steel crisis in Europe (and indeed worldwide) coincided, of course, with the recession dating from late 1973. For the first few years it was accepted wisdom that cut-price competition lay at the heart of the problem.

But by the 1970s it was clear that the facts did not altogether support this. The drop in demand for Community steel was not merely a temporary response to oil price rises, but a reflection of gross over-capacity. Technically out of date, scattered and over-protective, the European industry had lost its competitive edge. Nor would modernising be enough in itself to restore the industry to health: capacity had to be cut and jobs had to go.

And they did. Between 1974 and 1983 the number of steel workers in the Community fell from 800,000 to 480,000 – and many of the latter were on part-time work. Britain accepted less than her share of these job losses in the first five years, more than her share subsequently.

Not even the most vociferous anti-Marketeers have, I think, suggested seriously that there is a connection between Community membership and the decline of our steel industry. Those in the industry itself argue that outside the Common Market, steel in Britain would have fared worse, perhaps very much worse. It can equally be argued that had the Community not found a joint approach to the steel problem, with Britain playing a full and honourable part, it might have split asunder.

The European Coal and Steel Community (ECSC) was formed before the EEC, and gives the Commission more than its usual meagre share in the Community's decision-making. In 1977 the 'Davignon Plan', named after the responsible Commissioner, was launched. It came none too soon. Between 1974 and 1977, capacity utilisation in the industry had dropped from 87% to 64%, and steel consumption, both within the Community and in the world at large, had dropped. Yet companies were still expanding, and politicians in most Community countries were still, with an increasing quaver of the voice, promising 'no job losses'.

The Davignon plan (and Community steel policy as a whole) has at its heart a cartel of a unique kind. Instead of forcing the weakest to

For detailed information see coloured pages A14

the wall (which is what cartels are usually about) its object is to spread inescapable misery as fairly and equally as possible. To achieve this required the re-writing of the rules of the ECSC Treaty, which in principle forbade rescue operations by national Governments when their steel industries were in trouble. In 1977, *all* steel industries were in trouble of an exceptional kind. Huge losses were part of life in the industry, nationalised or private. There was no way of finding private capital for the modernisation and restructuring essential to the industry. It was plain that whatever the Commission, the Parliament or the Council had to say on the matter, State aids were going to be pumped in, on a massive scale.

The Commission therefore took the bull by the horns. In 1977 and 1978 it introduced systems to monitor steel imports and prevent dumping by third nations. Internally, it got agreement on price guidelines and selling conditions to prevent unfair or discriminatory practices. After unsuccessful attempts to persuade Community countries to limit production voluntarily, the Council agreed that a state of 'manifest crisis' existed in the steel industry; this enabled the Commission to enforce restrictions on production, on a quarterly quota basis.

The Commission is also charged with ensuring that crisis measures, which allow specific and temporary State aids to the steel industries of the Community, do not breach the rules of fair competition. As a result:

(a) steel companies notify the Commission of planned investment, which must be compatible with the overall objective of financial viability and fair competition;
(b) there are agreed rules for State aids.

The Davignon Plan, by helping the Community's steel producers to restructure during these difficult years, has reduced capacity from 170 million tonnes to 140 million tonnes – no mean achievement. The Commission is pledged to abolish State aids to the industry (they were in theory to have ended by 31 December 1985) and to lift production quotas on certain steel products. Both member States and EUROFER are at time of writing fighting to maintain them, at least in part. They have, however, told the Commission that they are prepared to cut 11.9 million tonnes of production capacity between July 1987 and the end of 1990.

The most common misconception about the Commission's powers relates to its power to intervene in the steel industry. Even those actually employed in the industry believe that 'Brussels' has the power to close down, say, Ravenscraig or Llanwern. It has, of course, no such authority – nor would it dream of wishing to acquire it. It is the task of DG IV (and in various ways DGs II, III, V, XVIII and others) to ensure that national quotas are kept to and State aids honestly administered, and to help the industry by restructuring aid,

For detailed information see coloured pages A14

employment schemes and regional measures. But how steel capacity is reduced, whether jobs in the industry are maintained or lost, whether mills are kept in operation, reduced in output or closed, are entirely questions for governments. The history of crisis in the EC's steel sector as described above is shown below.

1974 Drop of 20 per cent in output; 35–40 per cent in prices in the EC. Steel capacity use falls from 85–65 per cent.
1976 Simonet Plan for the EC steel sector
1977 Davignon Plan for the EC steel sector
1978 The EC industrial Ministers agree on the need for production quotas for steel
1980 The EC introduces mandatory quotas for steel
1988 End of the quota system for steel
1989 Still 30 million tonnes of over-capacity in the EC steel sector. A reduction of over 20 million tonnes is necessary though with the prospect of the loss of 100,000 steel jobs in France, West Germany, Belgium and Italy. However, the upturn in the world economy since 1986 has meant temporary respite for the EC steel sector with many steel companies reporting their best years since 1974. Currently therefore, the question of steel closures has been put aside as steel capacity use has risen to 80 per cent in the EC.

The Community, through the ECSC and the EIB, has contributed massively to the modernisation of the steel industry, to job creation for those who are forced to leave the industry, and for training and retraining. (See Part VII.)

★ ★ ★ ★

Relations between the Community and the United States have been difficult in the field of steel. Early in 1982 US steel producers accused their counterparts in Community countries (and particularly the British Steel Corporation) of heavy subsidies and dumping. Had the accusations been pursued through the full American procedure, British steel might have been almost excluded from the US market. In the event, agreement was reached at a Community level on cutting back on exports to America by all steel producers – including those in West Germany, who had not been subject to American complaints. Disputes rumble on, but to date have been settled equably and honourably. Export restraint agreements, negotiated between the US and the Community as a whole, have held well.

TEXTILES AND CLOTHING

One of the main problems in the textile and clothing sector has been competition from low-wage producers in the Far East and elsewhere. At the Community level the essential task over most of the 70s and 80s has been to help the Community's mills and clothes

For detailed information see coloured pages A14

manufacturers, (particularly at the bottom end of the price field) to adjust and regain their competitive edge before they collapsed under pressure from cheap imports. At stake were the jobs of one industrial workers in 10 in the Community.

The Commission negotiated, with considerable difficulty, the Multifibre Arrangement with the developing countries and a number of other agreements with low-cost producers in the Far East, Africa, Latin America and elsewhere. All involved voluntary restrictions on exports to the Community. Nonetheless, imports have increased steadily since 1973. One sixth of the Community's textile factories closed, and jobs in the textile and clothing industries dropped at an average rate of over 100,000 jobs a year. In the UK the number of workers in the trade has almost halved since 1971.

Such powers as the Community's institutions possess have on the whole worked well in the extremely difficult circumstances of the past decade. State aid has been kept in check, every attempt has been made to spread the misery as evenly as possible, and a great deal has been done to create the infrastructure and training needed in the hardest-hit regions. The managers of Britain's textile and clothing industries believe, on balance, that Community membership has been beneficial.

Recently there has been special Community help for textile regions, designed to create new jobs, particularly in small and medium-sized enterprises, outside the industry. Areas eligible include Northern Ireland, parts of Tayside, West Yorkshire, Lancashire and Greater Manchester.

★ ★ ★ ★

The textile industry gives a clear-cut illustration of the problems of a Community committed to low tariffs and generous import quotas for the products of the developing world, but at the same time faced with the possible destruction of one of its major and long-standing industries. Getting the balance right is certain to prove increasingly difficult as the recession continues, particularly since the entry of Spain and Portugal, both of whom produce more textile fibres than they consume. Their volume of trade will be closely monitored over the next few years, as will the rapidly increasing imports from Turkey – a candidate for Community membership.

As regards imports from third countries, a series of negotiations distinguished by hard talking and positive scrutability on the part of countries in the Far East, went on throughout 1986. Of 26 draft bilateral textile agreements between the EC and low-cost suppliers, 21 were concluded, with countries ranging from South Korea and Hong Kong (the subject of the toughest bargaining) to Mexico, and Romania to Bangladesh. In future a particularly fierce eye is to be turned upon the (illegal) practice of relabelling imports in one Community country and then exporting them to another.

For detailed information see coloured pages A14

The upper end of the Community textile market continues to fare better. New technology as applied to textiles under the BRITE programme (see next chapter) has specific funds devoted to the manufacture of fabric from 'supple' materials, and for automation and computer-design in the clothing industry. £16 million was made available in the period up to 1988 to support research in these fields.

SHIPBUILDING

A few grim facts. Prices offered by Asian shipyards (Japan, Korea, Taiwan and more recently China) are roughly half those of ships built in Western Europe, and delivery times much shorter. Since the mid-seventies, production of new ships in the Community has fallen by over half, and employment in parallel: 100,000 jobs have gone since 1975. In spite of huge subsidies to the industry, offered by every European government as well as in the East, the Community's share of the shipbuilding market is currently running at between 10 and 18 per cent, depending on whether you assess it on order books or actual sales figures.

Throughout the world, there is around 150 million tonnes of shipping capacity surplus to demand. Putting it another way, if the entire shipbuilding industry of the whole world had done no work for five years, we would still have more ships than the world can use. And the trend is likely to continue. Today's industries are not bulky. Twenty years ago a computer would have filled a large cargo hold. Today a more powerful one would fit into the ship cat's basket. Forecasts for new demand for ships have been scaled down year by year. By 1990, the Commission estimates, the Community's shipyards must axe another 35 per cent of capacity and 50,000 more jobs must go.

We tend to view the problems of the shipbuilding industry as being particularly savage in Britain – an understandable reaction, particularly for those who live in Clydeside or the North-East. In fact, the most brutal cuts have probably come in Sweden – not, of course, a member of the Community. Ten years ago second only to Japan in the number of ships built, and employing 35,000 workers, it is now quitting merchant shipbuilding altogether. Finland, which has what is virtually a barter agreement with the Soviet Union – ships for oil – has faced a crisis, as have the yards of the US, France, Denmark and Holland.

It is fashionable to blame the appalling problems of the shipbuilding industry on cut-price and cut-throat competition from the Far East. Independent voices have been more canny. Japan, during the late 1970s, showed considerable restraint in its shipbuilding policies. The European response (not only in the Community) was to increase government subsidies and to become more protective, not less. During late 1980, figures were published showing that the Japanese industry, despite having to compete

For detailed information see coloured pages A14

against the heavily subsidied industries of Europe and America, was establishing a world reputation for producing good ships, cheaply and on time. And they were competing fairly: wage costs in the industry were not far below those in Britain*. Within one week of the publication of these figures, the Boilermaker's Society in the UK unanimously approved a 40 per cent wage demand, despite the fact that productivity had actually dropped over the previous three years.

In troubled times, it was not surprising that the shipbuilding nations of the Community all found it necessary to offer State aids to the industry. Many of these were technically in breach of the Community's rules on fair competition. They have varied from nation to nation; and include direct aid for construction, tax refunds, preferential credit terms, and governmental guarantees for the order price irrespective of the final cost. In developing and maintaining its position, the West German shipbuilding industry has had considerable support from both Federal and State governments. Government assistance reflects a desire to help the shipping industry as well as the shipbuilding industry directly.

The Commission has tried, with varying degrees of success, to restrain the level of these subsidies and (as with steel and textiles) to spread the inevitable suffering in terms of unemployment as fairly as possible. Since 1978, in theory at least, direct aid to shipbuilders by national governments can only be given for reducing capacity or modernising yards. But much is outwith the Community's power to intervene. For example if you order a ship from a British yard you are asked to pay 70 per cent of the purchase price over eight years at around 7 per cent interest. (These are the OECD approved terms.) But Denmark will offer you 80 per cent of the price over 14 years at 8 per cent; Japan, from 65 to 90 per cent over 10 years at between 2 and 4 per cent; and Belgium 80 per cent over 50 years at 1 per cent interest.

Shipbuilding in all Community countries is an intensely political issue, and an emotional one. The Commission, at best, can only hope to exercise some control over the internal free-for-all (subsidies playing leap-frog) and work for a united front against the challenge from third countries.

But in its current thinking on shipbuilding, the Commission virtually abandons hope that the Community industry as a whole will return to competitiveness. For the first time, it acknowledges the possibility of total collapse and disintegration, and makes its recommendations in the light of this. All hopes of ending State aids (as member states were theoretically bound to do) are abandoned. In future, the Commission suggests emphasis must be placed on building specialised vessels, particularly those incorporating

* By 1984 they had overtaken those in Britain. Japanese shipbuilders are very far from being 'cheap labour'.

For detailed information see coloured pages A14

advanced technology. There should be a clear distinction between production aid and restructuring aid.

The Council, in its first examination of these new Commission guidelines, gave a general welcome to the principles, and added two riders:

(a) a ceiling should be fixed for production aid, which must be totally 'transparent';
(b) aid for restructuring should be directly linked to a reduction in capacity.

There is as yet no shipbuilding fund, as in the case of coal and steel. Shipbuilding areas which have suffered major job losses are, however, given special priority in respect of aid from the Regional Development Fund and the Social Fund (q.v.), and in the allocation of the UK's 'budget refund' money.

For detailed information see coloured pages A14

SMALL AND MEDIUM-SIZED ENTERPRISES

A task force exists to look specifically at the problems and potential of SMEs, and has already managed to get an action programme through the Commission and through the Council, which approved the main lines of policy and strategy and earmarked start-up money. The December 1986 Summit endorsed this; the precise words in the Communiqué are perhaps worth quoting in full:

> The Council welcomed the setting up of the Commission Task Force on Small and Medium-sized Enterprises to coordinate action to improve the environment for business. The Council also endorsed the principles of the Commission's proposals on help for small business, and in particular steps to:
> — improve the administrative environment and reduce the fiscal burdens for small firms;
> — ensure that existing schemes operate effectively for small firms;
> — help the setting up of new small firms;
> — improve the access of small firms to new technology;
> — enable member States to learn from each other's experience.

They also endorsed a new loan agreement worth about £1000 million to be made available to SMEs to help them invest in new technology.

This neatly worded compromise reconciles the opposing views with regard to SMEs of the various Community States – some of which see the problem as being one of making things physically and administratively easier for the small businessman without, on the whole, offering him money, others of which feel that State financial support and direct intervention of various kinds is essential. The guidelines provide for both.

It has been remarked earlier that if every SME in the Community were to take on just one or two new employees, the unemployment crisis in the Community would reach manageable proportions overnight. Evidence from America (and indeed parts of the United Kingdom) demonstrates that this is by no means imposssible if sufficient local effort is put into it. Equally, many small companies produce goods and services which are extremely competitive in the world market-place, provided the macro-economies are in reasonable shape. It is (or should be) easier for the small man to adapt, re-jig or re-style his product more quickly and flexibly than a large manufacturer.

Why, then, are small entrepreneurs in Europe so reluctant to expand, diversify, export and form partnerships? The answers are probably:

For detailed information see coloured pages A14/15

(a) unwillingness to leap into the dark;
(b) lack of knowledge of where money can be obtained, and the flinty eye of the local bank manager;
(c) lack of information more generally – preferably obtainable from a single point;
(d) red tape at home;
(e) red tape at frontiers;
(f) the whole hassle of VAT/translation/lack of trust in partners/ drawing up business plans/expensive lawyers/marketing/trying to teach old Bill to use a computer.

At the risk of oversimplifying, these problems can be divided into three groups: *information,* covering (a), (b) and (c); the reduction of red tape by the creation of a true *internal market* covering (d) and (e); and Community and national help – financial, administrative and technical – to tackle portmanteau problem (f). The Task Force's remit will cover all three, (since, of course, they interlock), but will first concentrate on *informing* SMEs.

The European Commission has made it clear that its task is not one of conferring privileges on small businesses, but of enabling them to overcome restrictions, discrimination and frustration, which are largely the penalties of their very smallness. The Commission's policy is not one of direct subsidy to businesses, but providing new and better services for them. While welcoming projects carried out at member State level (many of which have been helped by European money), the Commission has made it clear that it sees a particular value in action taken at Community level.

INFORMATION

Since 1987 Community information centres for SMEs have been established. Although these work closely with Commission offices in London, Cardiff, Belfast, Edinburgh and elsewhere in the Community, it was hoped to avoid creating a single new Eurocrat. The plan was to invite existing organisations, such as Chambers of Commerce and research institutes, which already give advice to small businesses on a regular basis, to designate one or two employees as Community information officers. They have been trained by the Commission and provided with access to Community data-bases. The idea is that by entering a single door or ringing one telephone number a small businessman should be able to obtain all the information he needs on the potential risks and rewards of taking that 'leap into the dark'. The new centres are able to offer him detailed information on all help (financial or otherwise) available from the Community and how it dovetails with assistance from government, local authorities, enterprise trusts, banks and the like.

The newly-trained officials have had to walk with extreme care the tightrope over the quagmire of political and other rivalries which

For detailed information see coloured pages A14/15

exist in the field. The Centres began slowly but are now well-used and successful.

In Brussels itself, a Business Cooperation Centre has existed for more than 10 years. Its objective is to encourage cooperation between firms in different member States, and it has now been merged in the Task Force. A Business Cooperation Network has been established, linking business advice agencies throughout the Community by computer. This network (which will be made available to the new information Centres) will allow small firms to identify potential partners in other Community States quickly, ensure that invitations to tender for public or private contracts are made available quickly and easily, act as a guide to funds available in other Community countries and shed light upon facts, figures and administrative information which the small businessman needs if he is contemplating exporting or partnership agreements.

RED TAPE

The White Paper on the Internal Market (the Cockfield Plan), with its timetabled progiamme for abolishing barriers to trade between Community states, pays special attention to the problems of SME's.

An attack has already been made on the problems (financial and otherwise) for small businessmen which can be caused by Community legislation. The Task Force, in cooperation with national governments, has looked at all proposed legislation, both to ensure that it does not apply to SMEs when that is unnecessary, and to ease the burden in terms of cost and working time when it is. Where legislation already exists, the Task Force will turn to the more difficult task of 'deregulation' in favour of SMEs, where this is possible and potentially beneficial. A proposal to simplify VAT procedures for small companies has already been approved, and there are proposals to simplify such things as company accounts, company law, and other areas of taxation.

There are plans to allow SMEs to compete more easily (and on fairer terms) for contracts for public procurement, and for helping them to climb over the 'paper mountain' of forms at frontiers, until such time as they are abolished.

ADVICE AND HELP

Your bank manager may be making (by his standards) cheerful noises about an overdraft for expansion or diversification, but he'll need a detailed business plan, complex financial statements and estimates, a marketing plan, and heaven knows what else. Who is going to prepare them, and what is it all going to cost?

You may have a bright new idea, and you may even be sure that no one else has thought of it first. But how do you patent or license it,

For detailed information see coloured pages A14/15

what about its design and development, and how do you go about selling in a new market?

Your bank manager and government departments should, of course, be able to guide you on most of this. But the bank manager you've known and trusted all your life may not be all that enthusiastic on innovation, and government departments tend to send you leaflets which are difficult to understand.

A surprising amount of help is already at hand, cheaply or even free. The problem is knowing how to get it. Partly, this is a task which the new regional Centres are geared to tackle. But a great deal of Community money and effort has already gone into such schemes as Business Improvement Services and Better Technical Services, organised by the UK government with the help of the European Regional Development Fund. These aim to deal with all the problems outlined above – and more. Regional development agencies, local authorities and other bodies sometimes operate similar schemes. The blue pages list sources of useful information.

FINANCE

The Task Force is also concerned with developing and coordinating Community grants and loans to which SMEs can have access. This might be done through the New Community Instrument (sometimes known as NIC, or the Ortoli Facility, £500 million richer since December 1986) in the form of cheap loans operated by the European Investment Bank; through the formation of mutual guarantee companies to facilitate access to credit; by the support of a new company for financial engineering (EUROCONFIN, established in the summer of 1986 to act as a clearing house for potential financial backers of SMEs); through the various funds available for innovation and the new technologies (listed in the following section); and by access to venture capital as well as the better known Community funds already available (see Part VII).

OTHER TASKS

Also included in the Action Programme for SMEs (printed in full in *ComDoc* (86) 45, with a useful summary available from any Commission office) are a range of other measures, including:

(a) steps to develop a favourable environment for SMEs, running in parallel with the implementation of the White Paper on the Internal Market, and including the production of explanatory papers in simple language when changes are made in legislation; links between organisations representing small firms; and the establishment in 1989 of a European Economic Interest Group to further cooperation between them;

For detailed information see coloured pages A14/15

(b) projects to make it easier for small firms to start up and develop, which will look not only at financial and other incentives, but at training of personnel and managers to allow them to adapt to changing circumstances;

(c) advice on exporting, including pilot training schemes, access to trade fairs abroad, permanent 'show-cases' for the products of SMEs in the US and Japan, and help with subcontracting across frontiers;

(d) the sponsorship of conferences, inter-regional cooperation, and better links with large corporations.

Special help for SMEs in the field of the new technologies is dealt with in the next section.

* * * *

Cardinal to the success or failure of all this new activity calculated to encourage the small businessman to think a bit bigger will be the publicity it generates.

Where business and technical services and employment creation schemes for SMEs have demonstrably succeeded (in Strathclyde Region, to take perhaps the best known example) there has been a real story for television and radio commentators and industrial correspondents to get their teeth into: newsy speeches by Ministers and leaders of local authorities; colourful success stories featuring local firms; telephone lines for enquirers, manned round the clock; poster and advertising campaigns; well written, clear pamphlets made available in every outlet possible; the cooperation of banks, development agencies, enterprise trusts, Commission offices and the lawyers, accountants, technological experts and others involved. After the initial launch, care was taken to keep up the momentum: numbers of enquiries, jobs created, partnerships established, first export contracts, briefing seminars and conferences, and all the rest.

Only too often it is the very first hurdle which intimidates the man or woman with a good idea from getting going in the race. It is not enough to establish ways of helping them over that hurdle; they must be reminded, dramatically and often, of how easy it can be to get such help, and how others have profited from it.

See European Commission (1988) 'The European Community and Cooperation Among Small and Medium Sized Businesses'. *European File*, Brussels.

For detailed information see coloured pages A14/15

THE NEW TECHNOLOGIES

The cliché 'Sunrise Industries' leaps readily to the typewriter. But the sun rose some time ago.

In 1973 Messrs Heath, Brandt and Pompidou signed a joint statement, warning that unless the countries of the Community quickly formed a team they would lose sight of their competitors in the new technologies (notably America, with a commanding lead, but being remorselessly tracked by Japan).

These words were largely ignored by the Council of Ministers, national governments and most firms for a decade. Between 1973 and 1985, the US created several times as many jobs in the new industries as the Community, and Japan twice as many. (Meanwhile the sun was also rising in Korea, Taiwan and Hong Kong.)

In research and development the story has been no more cheerful for Europe. American expenditure has far outstripped that of the whole of the Community; Japan spends about as much as Germany and the UK added together. And much of the money being spent in the Community is no longer pioneering anything: it is devoted merely to catching up. In the micro-electronic fields, for example, Europe was until very recently between two and four years behind the US in research, and was importing 80 per cent of its integrated circuits or producing them under licence. In telecommunications, the US has 39 per cent of world sales, Japan 12 per cent; no Community country has more than 6 per cent.

It was never going to be easy to persuade the companies and nations of the Community to mount a joint defence to the admirable trade onslaught of America. But it took too long for national governments to recognise that pious words, followed by the total resumption of cut-throat competition at the internal level, were not going to work. In a series of detailed policy papers prepared over many years the Commission amassed evidence to show that only the Community as a whole could offer scientists, innovators and industrialists the large-scale mobilisation of manpower, money and marketing to challenge the Americans and match the growth of the new industries in the East. The problem is that, until recently, little has actually been done about those papers. As a result many of Europe's best scientists now work in America.

As early as 1974, at the request of the Council, the Commission produced two draft programmes. The first was a plan to mobilise skills, research and technology at the Community level. The second was for the joint development of 'informatics' – the omnibus word covering such things as the electronic processing of information, office automation and telecommunications. They called for

For detailed information see coloured pages A15

collaborative research, feasibility studies, and coordination of procurement policies. These were regularly dusted off, considered in the Council with much thoughtful nodding of heads, and dumped once again in the pending tray. National and company rivalries reduced collaboration to a polite formality.

The turn of the tide probably came in 1979, with the creation of Round Table discussions for the heads of electronics industries in the Community. The fact that these tycoons were at least willing to talk to each other frankly and in confidence was the first sign of a changing mood – and a changing market. Informatics in terms of world trade was already worth over 200 billion dollars a year, and was growing at between 8 and 10 per cent per annum. The Community's share of high technology exports, as a percentage of total exports, had been static at just under 25 per cent since 1963; America's share had risen from 29 per cent to 34 per cent, and Japan's from 16 per cent to 35 per cent.

And the tempo was accelerating; it helped to concentrate the minds of those round the table enormously, if a little late. Eight out of ten personal computers sold in Europe were being made in the US. Of every 10 video recorders, nine were being made in Japan. In the new industries as a whole, a positive balance of payments for the Community vis-a-vis the world as a whole had been turned into a 10 billion dollar deficit.

In the early 1980s came the establishment of the first real Community strategy for the modern industries and the first hard results. The European Space Agency and Airbus Industries began to get into their stride. In 1980, Euronet Diane was inaugurated. DIANE (Direct Information Access Network for Europe) now marshals 300 data bases and information banks spread throughout the Community, containing over 60 million facts and references covering most of human knowledge. Linked through national post and telecommunications agencies, it is rapidly extending from the Community nations into other systems in Europe, and via satellite links to the United States and the Third World. DIANE is now supplemented by two other electronic information systems – INSIS (Community Inter-Institutional Information System) and CADDIA (Cooperation in Automation of Data and Documentation for Exports, Imports and Agriculture). Any organisation or individual seeking information can get easy and relatively cheap access to these databanks, which, with DIANE itself, are now merged in international communications networks, thus doubling the data base.

ESPRIT

1982 saw the launch of the pilot stage of ESPRIT – the European Strategic Programme for Research and Development in Information Technology. This experimental programme, costing £25 million,

For detailed information see coloured pages A15/16

linked 12 of the largest Community companies involved in information technology, plus over 600 other businesses, universities and research bodies, in collaborative research on some 200 projects. The principal aim was to develop the necessary skills and infrastructure for chip manufacture through the development of new tools such as electron beam machines, plasma etching and computer-aided design. It was a decided success, not only in the research results themselves, but in the change of attitudes it engendered.

The pilot stage over, a larger-scale ESPRIT programme was launched in 1984, the Council of Ministers voting £350 million to help to pay for it over five years, with the industry itself matching this contribution. The programme was drawn up after detailed consultation with companies, Governments, and research bodies. It took into account the report, submitted in 1982, of the team working on Forecasting and Assessment in Science and Technology (FAST). This 10-strong body of experts, established in 1978, was charged with examining the contribution which new technologies could make to the economic recovery of Western Europe, and the creation of jobs.

The aim of ESPRIT is to raise the levels of European technology to that of America and Japan by the 1990s, and to persuade Community nations to pool research and development – or at least to work towards common goals, and compete in developing and sponsoring the brightest ideas. It will concentrate on both immediate and long-term strategy, with particular respect to growth and changes in the market.

During ESPRIT's first year of full-scale operation 441 projects were submitted. Of these, 173 (involving 448 organisations, including companies, universities and other research bodies) were given the go-ahead. An average of five transnational partners are involved in each, and SMEs did particularly well, participating in over half of the projects.

The current scheme, with a budget of around £1 billion and a Community input of some £500 million, places the accent upon such research areas as advanced micro-electronics, office automation, software technology, computer integrated manufacturing and advanced information processing, though priorities may change in the light of circumstances, and tenders are invited annually. The success of ESPRIT should have benefits not only for European industry, but for employment and for the consumer. The Council has called for increased concentration upon schemes which are 'saleable' to industry, and preference for proposals from SMEs.

Everything has gone according to plan as far as ESPRIT is concerned. ESPRIT has enabled the European dimension to be introduced into the management of firms. Trans-European cooperation has produced tangible beneficial effects to Community

For detailed information see coloured pages A15/16

industry: high performance software designed to speed up industrial automation, components for chips in the telecommunications sector, and common technical standards. ESPRIT 2, the second phase of the Community programme is under way and bears a strong resemblance to ESPRIT 1.

BRITE

This programme (the acronym stands for Basic Research in Industrial Technologies for Europe) was launched in 1985. Its aim is to provide help for advanced technology in traditional industries – aeronautics, motor vehicles, chemicals, textiles, engineering and the rest – and thus 'to provide an incentive to the creation of a significant and advanced technological base on which Community industry can draw to maintain its international competitiveness'. Community funds (initially some £80 million over four years) will go to 'precompetitive' research and development involving cooperation between participants in two or more member states. This must involve innovative research of high technical quality, and preference will be given to major projects (normally £650,000 or more) which it is hoped will lead to technological breakthroughs in industrial productivity, product reliability, and originality of design or quality. The Community contribution will normally be 50 per cent of the total cost. To date, several hundred organisations are involved.

There are two separate programmes:
(a) covering new materials and new production technologies;
(b) covering pilot and demonstration projects specifically concerned with flexible materials.

These areas were chosen after consultation with industrial experts throughout the Community; this consultation will continue and priorities may change.

Projects likely to be considered for Community funding under programme (a) are those involving precompetitive R & D into:
(1) Reliability, wear and deterioration of new materials;
(2) Laser technology and powder metallurgy;
(3) Joining techniques;
(4) New testing methods, including non-destructive, on-line and computer-aided testing;
(5) CAD/CAM and mathematical modelling;
(6) Polymers, composites and similar materials;
(7) Membrane science and technology;
(8) Catalysis and particle technology.

Programme (b) will cover the automated handling, joining and assembly of flexible materials, and new ways of introducing them into manufactured goods.

Participation in the BRITE programmes is open to all companies, research institutes, universities, etc., within the Community. At least one partner in a project must be an industrial firm. Apart from

For detailed information see coloured pages A15/16

funding these programmes, BRITE will try to help existing pre-competitive R & D in these fields by organising meetings and seminars and allocating project officers to keep in touch with work in progress.

Of the first successful awards under BRITE, the partners involved comprised 60 per cent industrial firms (including 24 per cent SMEs) 21 per cent research institutes, and 19 per cent universities. They included automatic sewing systems for the textile industry, reliability testing methods for marine and off-shore structures, reducing friction in internal combustion engines, and developing sealing compounds for use in the aeronautics industry at high temperatures.

A detailed information package for potential applicants for BRITE is available from the Commission in Brussels (Directorate-General for Science, Research and Development, Joint Research Centre).

BRITE has been generally well received. It has been given considerable support by industry and by the research world. As a result the European Commission is proposing to increase the budget by some 60 million ECU so as to encourage further participation by SMEs. A new programme BRITE 2 has now been launched by the EC.

BIOTECHNOLOGY

Microbes have long worked for us in a cheerful, costless and non-energy-consuming way – beer, wine and yoghourt being among their better-known products. Today we are well and truly into the era of genetic engineering, hybrids and cloning, which for many of us seem less appetising.

However, the 'bio-society' is here, and there is no opting out of it. It already wields immense influence in agriculture, food-processing, energy, chemicals and pharmaceuticals, human health and behaviour; and the economic stakes are enormous. Almost half of manufactured goods are biological in origin. By the end of the century, it has been estimated, the world market for biotechnology may top 100 billion dollars. The Community is behind America – indeed, US expenditure in research work on biotechnology is already twice of that of the Community, even more in the case of industrial usage. The brain drain from Europe to other areas of the world has been greater than in any other field in recent years.

Against this background the Commission proposed a three-part action programme extending over five years, with an initial budget of about £120 million and the backing of 16 leading chemical groups in Europe. It would concentrate on three sectors:

    (a) the laying of a sound foundation for Community-wide research and training in biotechnology, and the co-ordination of information;

    (b) specific research and training projects in areas such as disease prevention and agriculture;

For detailed information see coloured pages A15/16

(c) the establishment of a code of practice, with particular reference to safety and health for worker and consumer alike.

In 1985 the Council agreed a modest first stage programme based upon these plans but with a budget one third of the suggested size.

More than 1300 research projects have been submitted under this programme. Of the research projects selected the following are particularly noteworthy: the study of protein architecture, the application of biotechnology to industrial micro-organisms, *in vitro* methods of analysing the pharmacological and toxicological properties of molecules and determination of the risks associated with genetic manipulation. One part of the programme also focuses on the scientific training of researchers, in particular the award of post-doctoral fellowships to encourage mobility among scientists.

In parallel with this, work must be done to coordinate national policies. Wide differences exist between national legislation as regards the dissemination of research results and cooperation between firms. There is also a patent problem: can you copyright a micro-organism? Lastly, there is considerable hope that biotechnology will serve the Third World well in the fields of agriculture and disease control. But the often rushed experiments of the past must not be repeated.

'It is now quite clear' says a recent issue of the magazine *Technology in Europe,* somewhat menacingly, 'that the fate of the CAP is largely dependent on the future of biotechnologies. Their use should enable the major problems of European agriculture to be resolved by encouraging new uses of products of the soil and increasing the productivity of foodstuffs for which there are markets, while at the same time preserving the environment and improving the quality of the goods offered to consumers.'

The paper goes on to add that the immediate need is for pilot projects involving trials with new crops and harvesting systems, biotechnological ways of increasing the value of animal and plant products, inventories of the potential of Europe's soil according to climatic zone, etc. The Commission is to ask for some £200–300 million for these projects, to be matched by like sums from member States concerned. (Farming, as they say, is all about optimism.)

TELECOMMUNICATIONS AND INFORMATION TECHNOLOGY

Although the telecommunications industry accounts directly for only 1 per cent of GDP, it is directly involved in the jobs of almost two workers in every three in Western Europe. Enormous changes are afoot. The use of optical fibres has vastly increased transmission capacity. Micro-electronics has dramatically reduced the size of installations and slashed maintenance costs. With us already, and soon likely to be commonplace, are the tele-transmission of written

For detailed information see coloured pages A15/16

texts at unbelievable speed, the scanning of data-bases, computers which 'talk' to each other, radio telephones, video conferences, and (at a friendlier level) a whole range of aids for people living alone.

Something like 90 per cent of telecommunication hardware in the world is out of date; the market is potentially enormous. During 1983 the Commission brought together a group of senior officials responsible for telecommunications in member states. They drew up an action programme with these aims:

(a) to create and stimulate a Community-wide market for terminals and network components (nine different types of switching systems at present coexist unharmoniously);

(b) to bring standards closer together, institute regular study and planning at 12-nation level, and encourage and improve cross-frontier services;

(c) to improve training and R & D;

(d) to extend and strengthen telecommunications in the poorer and more remote regions, with the help of Community funds.

This last objective has already seen considerable progress. Money from the Regional Development Fund, the EIB and (in Britain) budget refunds has gone massively into improving telecommunications in the peripheral areas of the Community. A framework for consultation, analysis, forecasting and planning has been established; it includes participation by representatives of national telecommunications administrations, industry, and finance Ministries. In 1984 the Council agreed plans for harmonisation of standards and products, and for marginally freer access to public contracts for new installations.

RACE

For most of us, 'telecommunications' means speaking on the telephone, although devices such as telecopiers and auto-banks make us aware that there is a bit more to it. And we are told by those who should know that business will in future increasingly depend upon rapid access not only to the voice and the written word, but to graphics and video.

A single network for Europe is perfectly possible, and necessary: if Community countries continue as in the past to try to maintain separate networks with different standards we will be priced out of the market.

To help pre-empt this, the programme entitled RACE (Research into Advanced Communications in Europe) was tabled by the Commission in March 1985, and adopted by the Council with commendable speed (although with a budget reduced by two-thirds). Its object is to draw up plans for a pan-European telecommunications network, and to establish it between 1995 and the turn of the century. The RACE programme covers the following fields: high-speed integrated circuits, integrated optoelectronics,

For detailed information see coloured pages A15/16

broadband switching, passive optical components, high-speed processing components, dedicated communications software, flat panel display technology.

The first, or 'Definition' phase got under way in early 1986. Awards were made to 31 projects, worth some £28 million, harnessing the combined expertise of telecommunications administrations, manufacturers, broadcasters and university researchers. The Definition phase ran until early 1987, and was in two parts: the first involving drawing up a model for integrated broadband communications (IBC), the second looking at technical options. UK companies won a larger share of work on these projects than any other member state – 52 out of 192 participants are British.

An important step forward was taken in November 1986, when Ministers agreed in the Industry Council to set joint Community standards for an Integrated Services Digital Network (ISDN). The aim is that by 1988 better and wider services will be made available in our homes and offices through the ordinary telephone line. These will include simultaneous voice, text, graphic and data transmission, and should eventually revolutionise our shopping habits, banking, meter readings and leisure. Sending a business letter by telecopier, which at present takes something like a minute, should (for starters) come down to about four seconds. Advantages for hospitals, the police, anti-terrorist organisations and international traders should be spectacular.

In Phase I of RACE (running from 1987 to 1991) it is hoped to develop the technological base for the single European network, carry out trials and tests, and work for common standards and specifications. In Phase II (1991–95) it is hoped to get the network into a state of preparedness for implementation before the end of the century.

The stakes are high: the estimate is that total Community investment in telecommunications equipment will amount to £100 billion (in today's money) during RACE's time-scale.

RACE is complementary to ESPRIT, and the programmes will be integrated.

INSIS

Taking its own warnings to heart, the Community in 1982 established a Community Interinstitutional Information System (INSIS). This is currently spending some £5 million a year in seeking to improve the workings of the Institutions themselves, thus both saving time and money and offering a pilot study for broader work at a European level. It covers:

- electronic text transmission and temporary storage;
- the development of teleconferences, rather than the expensive transport of bodies and documents;
- links between data bases;

For detailed information see coloured pages A15/16

- services for computer illiterates.

A similar scheme, known as CADDIA (Computerisation of data, from market organisations and trade) aims to give quicker and more ready access to information on the Common Market, the Community's commercial policies, and the CAP. The succinctly titled CD (Coordinated Development of Computerised Administrative Procedures) plans to do likewise for trade, both internal and external, and EUROTRA (Machine Translation) is working towards slashing the costs of the acres of translation which must be done every day in the Community as documents are translated into the working languages – 72 pairings in all.

INFORMATION TECHNOLOGY GENERALLY

Sometimes known in Community jargon as 'informatics', the phrase 'information technology' covers not only the various programmes already listed, but a number of other Commission-funded programmes concerned with the more effective and integrated use of computing, telecommunications and audiovisual technologies. Most of these are recent. They cover such ground as:

- information for industry (product and pricing news, world market developments, trade regulations, property rights and the like);
- specialised scientific, technical and commercial information on biotechnology;
- electronic publishing;
- computerised information on government assistance available throughout the Community;
- concerted action in the field of artificial intelligence and pattern recognition;
- easier access to 'grey' literature – unpublished documents in the fields of research, technology and the social and economic sciences. (Two programmes currently operate: the European Association for Grey Literature Exploitation – EAGLE; and SIGLE, the System for Information on Grey Literature in Europe.)
- the establishment of databanks concerned with materials used in engineering;
- new techniques for open learning (DELTA, the Development of European Learning through Technological Advance);
- the establishment of recognised standards and testing services for the information technology sector;
- exploring the potential of technology in the fields of medical research, industrial productivity and road safety (a recent report suggests that £16 billion a year and thousands of lives could be saved just by applying I & T technology to avoid motor vehicle collisions).

For detailed information see coloured pages A15/16

This is an incomplete list, and there are additions to it virtually every month. See the blue section for a list of sources of information, and on keeping up to date.

EUREKA

This French initiative, launched in 1985, was at first greeted somewhat coolly in the UK – partly, no doubt, because it was mistakenly portrayed in the press as 'France's answer to Star Wars'. There has, however, been a striking volte-face since government money (virtually ruled out at first) is now available from the £300 million Support for Innovation budget, together with funds from the Commission.

EUREKA is a framework for promoting collaborative projects in a wide range of fields of advanced technology. It involves 19 countries (the Community plus EFTA and Turkey) and the Commission. Its aims are to improve European competitiveness in world markets in the civil application of new technologies, including information technology, robotics, advanced manufacturing, marine technology, environmental protection, telecommunications, materials, biotechnology, lasers and transport technologies.

Through EUREKA (which has its own office in Brussels) governments and the Commission can provide information and contacts for those making partners across frontiers; identify and in some cases help to overcome barriers to collaboration; and offer financial support for projects which qualify. It is central to the scheme that businessmen and industrialists will take a leading role in identifying, helping to pay for, and carrying out such projects.

Collaboration between participants in more than one country is essential, and before projects are given aid they must identify a clear potential market for an end product.

Of the first projects announced during 1986, the average cost was high – around £25 million. British companies are involved in about half of them. They included, in rough order of success rate, information technology, communications, medical equipment, transport, new materials, advanced manufacturing, and marine, environmental and biotechnological research. Firms are eligible for support of up to 50 per cent of their share of applied research costs, and up to 25 per cent of their share of development costs. By the end of 1986 109 projects had been selected, costing about £4000 million in government and industrial investment.

It is for companies or research institutes to identify topics on which they wish to collaborate and to seek prospective partners. Although EUREKA can assist in this, it has been made plain that it is for companies themselves to take the initiative.

The EC's support for EUREKA is part of its attempt to achieve an integrated market by 1992 and takes the form either of participation in EUREKA projects or encouraging the promotion of technological and industrial cooperation in Europe.

For detailed information see coloured pages A15/16

In Britain, advice is available from the EUREKA Projects Office, Room 210, DTI, Ashdown House, 123 Victoria Street, London SW1E 6RB.

STIMULATION ACTION

Competing in the invention, development and application of new technologies involves not only hardware and software, but brains, and the rewards (financial and in terms of challenge and facilities) offered to their owners. The brain drain from Europe to America has been in its way as serious as the chauvinistic refusal to cooperate in research and development which characterised Western Europe in the 1970s.

In the Community Stimulation Action Plan, now in its second stage, the aim is to create a 'Researchers' Europe' by breaking down the national, disciplinary and institutional barriers which still hamstring Europe's scientific potential. The Community has funds for laboratory twinnings, research grants enabling researchers to work in laboratories in other countries for up to three years, and direct help for multinational research teams and companies. The work done must be of the most advanced standard, but can be in any of the exact and natural sciences.

In the experimental stage of the programme (1983–84) 86 projects were financed with a total budget of £5 million. They involved 218 laboratories and over 1000 researchers from all Community states. The programme achieved some notable successes, enabled researchers to gain experience on large-scale installations sometimes not available in their own countries, and shows signs of establishing multinational partnerships which will endure. 'By concentrating the Community's widely scattered resources,' says the report on the first phase, 'and bringing researchers from different nationalities and disciplines into contact with one another, the level of European research has risen spectacularly.' The Community Stimulation Action Plan has now been put on a multiannual basis. A detailed guide for applicants is available from Directorate A, DG XII, in the Commission in Brussels.

Priority areas include mathematics and computer science, advanced optics, chemistry, biocommunication, earth sciences, oceanography and scientific instrumentation.

EDUCATION AND COMETT

Another aspect of the brain drain concerns proper training and job opportunity. There has sometimes been in Community countries, a lack of rapport between schools and institutions of higher learning and employers in the new industries. Too often the brightest scientifically minded pupils have been unable to get much in the

For detailed information see coloured pages A15/16

way of help or guidance on the subjects they might profitably study and the uses to which their talents could be put. Too often the best science graduates have knocked on the doors of American companies and have been whisked across the Atlantic for training, often never to return.

During Industry Year (1986) the Commission promoted many studies and conferences on links between school and industry. The same year saw the first stage of the action programme of the Community in Education and Training for Technology (COMETT). This has three objectives: to promote a European, as opposed to a purely national, approach to training in the new technologies; to organise joint training programmes to combat specific skill shortages resulting from rapid technological change; and to stimulate the exchange of experience between Community countries in the field of university – industry cooperation in training.

Specifically, it will provide funds for students wishing to work in hi-tech industries in a Community country other than their own. Ten thousand students should gain fellowships to spend six months training on the job in industry, and there will be facilities for exchanges of employees in industry and university staff in the same field, both for teaching and research. About £45 million was spent between 1986 and 1989.

The first phase of COMETT concentrates on creating a European network of university/industry partnerships, exchange and joint training schemes, and establishing an EC data base. Grants to multilateral projects meet 50 per cent of the cost, up to a ceiling of about £250,000.

The Commission also offers *sectoral grants* to promote training and mobility of young European scientists. This offers a chance for training and research work in another member state. The grants are modest – £780 per year, with a maximum of three years – but cover both students and post-graduates and most fields of research in the new industries. Information: DG XII, Division A–2 in the Commission in Brussels. Applications may be submitted at any time.

On the matter of education for existing workers in industries affected by technological change, much useful work has been done by the European Foundation for the Improvement of Living and Working Conditions, in Dublin. A booklet entitled 'The Role of the Parties Concerned in the Introduction of New Technology' is available (price £3) from the Foundation at Loughlinstown, Shankill, Co. Dublin.

'SPRINT' – INNOVATION AND TECHNOLOGY TRANSFER

A 'Plan for the Transnational Development of the Supporting Infrastructure for Innovation and Technology Transfer' was adopted

For detailed information see coloured pages A15/16

in 1983 and work began on it at the beginning of 1984. Retitled SPRINT (Strategic Programme for Innovation and Technology Transfer), it completed its experimental period in December 1986. A new and more ambitious SPRINT programme followed.

The philosophy behind the plan is to ensure that inventions are put quickly and effectively into practical (and commercial) use. There is a decided emphasis in favour of SMEs, and although Community funds are available it is implicit in the plan that it can only be successful if national governments, local authorities, venture capital and transnational advisory services and research organisations are involved.

The best summary of the plan is contained in issue No. 43 of the Newsletter on New Technologies and Innovation Policy (see page A15), as updated by subsequent issue 54, and in a European File (18/86). SPRINT'S priorities include:

(a) the development of 'human networks' for accelerating the flow of information on innovation and technology transfer, and developing trust;

(b) stimulation of cross-border exchanges in these fields by collating technical information and supporting specialised information media;

(c) improving national and regional innovation policy through exchanges of experience and help with co-ordination.

Much of the money available has so far been spent in promoting conferences and study visits, and in the direct encouragement of bodies already working in the area of innovation and technology transfer. The Commission in implementing the plan has the help of the Consultative Committee on Innovation and Technology Transfer (CIT), the Standing Technological Conference of European Local Authorities (STCELA) and the European Association for the Transfer of Technologies, Innovation and Industrial Information (TII), together with the European Venture Capital Association (ECVA) of which more below. Working groups have been established in such fields as industrial design, protection of industries property and innovation in traditional industries (textiles, footwear etc) A Community Directory of assistance available in all member States for research innovation and technology transfer has been published. (Kogan Page, £32.00.)

In the light of the advice of these bodies the Commission issues periodic calls for proposals for various forms of transnational cooperation. These are published in the Official Journal and in the Newsletter mentioned above. Further information: DG XIII in Luxembourg, who publish a useful paper: 'Industrial Innovation: a guide to Community action, services and funding'.

For detailed information see coloured pages A15/16

VENTURE CAPITAL

The European Venture Capital Association (EVCA) was founded in 1983. It is a non-profitmaking organisation with headquarters in Brussels, and its remit is to manage and invest venture capital in Community countries to finance innovation (particularly on the part of SMEs), and to establish standards of business ethics and professional competence.

During its first, three-year stage, it involved around 50 founding members with total investment portfolios of about £1 billion. Though in its early years risk-investors showed a pronounced preference for established companies, later estimates showed a growth of 41 per cent in venture capital available in the Community, with Britain the largest provider. A report on the scheme for that year is available from the Commission (DG XIII).

In 1986 the Commission put forward proposals for establishing an insurance scheme for risk investments in the new technologies, to be backed by Community funds. Provisionally entitled Eurotech Capital, it would be operated by some 15 private sector financial institutions spread across the Community, with the Commission acting as broker.

EUROPEAN BUSINESS AND INNOVATION CENTRE NETWORK (EBN)

The EBN was established in 1985 with £250,000 initial funding from the Commission. With a start-up membership of 14 organisations in seven Community countries it has grown rapidly. Its function is to stimulate entrepreneurship and improve the chances of success of new businesses, particularly small ones working in the new technologies, and to help enterprise trusts, science parks, innovation consultancies and other agencies. It acts as a clearing house for information and advice, and has established a range of Business and Innovations Centres. A note on the work of the EBN is available from PO Box 25, B–1040 Brussels 26, or from 'Business in the Community' at 227A City Road, London ECIV 1LX.

REGIONAL AID: 'STAR' AND 'VALOREN'

It is recognised that the least-favoured regions of the Community find it least easy to profit from new advances in telecommunications and energy, yet need them most. Two new Commission programmes, costing some £76 million over five years and agreed by the Council in late 1986, are aimed at helping to remedy this.

STAR will make it possible for some of the most disadvantaged regions to acquire the latest telecommunications equipment; VALOREN to help them fully develop their energy potential, including such local resources as peat, wind and hydroelectricity. Again, preference will be given to work by SMEs. Italy and Spain

For detailed information see coloured pages A15/16

seem most likely to benefit from these programmes; in the UK, only Northern Ireland is likely to qualify.

★ ★ ★ ★

Community aid for ENERGY, the ENVIRONMENT and technology in THE DEVELOPING WORLD are dealt with under their respective sections in this part of the book. See also the note in Part VII and the entries in the blue pages.

THE 'FRAMEWORK PROGRAMME' AND THE FUTURE

The Summit meetings of 1985 at Milan and Luxembourg got a bad press, but in fact achieved one of the most significant agreements in the history of the Community: a pledge to establish a European Technological Community, involving far more extensive collaboration in high technology research and marketing between countries than has hitherto been attempted or even contemplated.

The Commission had for some years been drawing up a Framework Programme for such collaboration. ESPRIT, BRITE and the other programmes listed in previous pages formed a central part of it. But the Programme itself is considerably more ambitious, being intended to coordinate all the Community's research and technological developments.

The draft programme has been considered several times in Council, reported on by the Parliament and the Economic and Social Committee, and thus amended and reshaped so often that it must have kept the Commission's word-processors and their operators in full-time employment for many months. The problems are not unfamiliar. The Commission recommends spending in the order of between £5 and £6 billion over the five-year period, more than twice annual spending in the recent past. The European Parliament considers this too little. The Council of Ministers (and in particular Germany, France and the United Kingdom) consider it far too much. At time of writing the likeliest compromise is a form of short-term funding with options for renewal.

As is often the case, the best summary of Commission initial thinking is probably contained in the current Programme presented by President Delors in 1986. In view of the importance of the subject, it is worth quoting from this in some detail.

It foresees that action to promote technological cooperation must be:

> (i) flexible, in that it attempts to combine direct action with shared-cost action (on the lines of ESPRIT), concerted action (on the lines of COST) and participation in variable-geometry projects;

For detailed information see coloured pages A11, A15/16

(ii) effective, in that it builds on rather than replaces national programmes, increasing coordination between them and thus enhancing their value (Community R & D budgets represent no more than 2 per cent of total public R & D expenditure in the member States). Community action should play a more significant role in the areas covered than it has in the past (on the lines of the ESPRIT programme, which mobilises 25 per cent of all pre-competition research in information technology); it should multiply synergic effects and make it possible to keep European research at the forefront of the world scene (eg through the fusion programme);

(iii) diversified, in that financial instruments geared to the different phases of technological cooperation between Community firms could facilitate the implementation of programmes; this is why the Commission will be taking initiatives with regard to financial instruments.

As to the approach adopted, the Commission will see to it that its technological cooperation and development effort proceed hand in hand with its trade, internal market and competition policies, with a view in particular to improving the dissemination of innovation (financial instruments, and access by small businesses to innovation). The Commission will endeavour to ensure that firms can enjoy the benefits of common standards based on international norms. This standardisation policy should promote the liberalisation of public procurement contracts, particularly in the telecommunications field, make for compatibility between new equipment and services, and lead to the development of multi-vendor systems open to competition.

The new Framework Programme will place all these elements (flexibility, effectiveness, diversification and consistency) in perspective to give shape to the European Technology Community and take advantage of the opportunities opened up by the agreement reached in Luxembourg. If Europe is to have a durable technological base, innovative technological development must take place in a genuinely competitive environment so that European industry can expand and maintain comparative advantage on world markets.

Most recent proposals from the Commission provide for 60 per cent of planned expenditure to go to projects which will improve competitiveness in European industry. There is a decided implication that aid for research without hard commercial implications (and financial backing from the private sector) is unlikely to win support, particularly if proposals are submitted by large industrial concerns or universities. There is also emphasis on more selective criteria for assistance, regular monitoring of the Programme throughout its lifetime, and a general increase in private funding. The relationship between the Framework Programme and

For detailed information see coloured pages A11, A15/16

Eureka has yet to be defined, except that the Research Council of 9 December 1986 suggested that Community research would tend to be 'fundamental and pre-competitive' whereas EUREKA projects would be nearer the market-place.

★ ★ ★ ★

One problem in erecting such a Framework is that you must do so on shifting ground. The speed with which new developments and new priorities arise in the field of the new technologies is staggering. As the section in this book has had to be completely re-written and extended by approximately 200 per cent in less than a year, so the Commission's various guidelines for the Framework Programme tend to be out of date before they are seriously considered by the Council of Ministers. Thus, for example, new topics (the use of space, marine technology, transport engineering, campaigns against cancer and AIDS) which were barely mentioned in the Commission submission to the Council of one year, had priority and detailed proposals for action the next. The list of acronyms grows every month: among those not hitherto mentioned are DRIVE (Dedicated road safety systems and intelligent vehicles in Europe), BICEPS (Bio-informatics collaborative European programme and strategy), CODEST (Committee for the European Development of Science and Technology), COST (European Cooperation in the field of Scientific and Technical Cooperation), ESA (European Space Agency), EUTELSTAT (European Telecommunications Satellite Organisation), EUMETSTAT (European Meteorological Satellite Systems), APOLLO (Article Procurement with Local On-line Ordering), CERN (European Laboratory for Particle Physics), and RE (Researchers' Europe, the tag which is used to describe new Commission plans to extend the Stimulation Plan to include Spain and Portugal and the new association agreements with non-member states, and to look at the social implications of the new industries).

To keep abreast of all this, *European Information Service* and *British Business* are as usual indispensable. The best overall summary known to the writer is contained in Appendix II to the Economic and Social Committee report on New Technologies. This can be consulted at any Commission office: the reference number is CES 732/85. To update this, subscribe to the Newsletter on new technologies and innovation policy, available from DGXIII-A of the Commission in Luxembourg.

APPLYING FOR HELP

A distinction should be made between 'old' and 'new' money. Funds for development and training in the new industries in certain fields has for some time been available from the Farm Fund, the Social Fund and the ECSC; this is touched upon in Part VII.

For detailed information see coloured pages A15/16, A22

'New' money for R & D (apart from the special case of the Community's own research establishments at Ispra, Culham and elsewhere, not covered here) is normally awarded by contract, subject to open tendering. (Occasionally the tendering procedure is preceded by 'calls for expression of interest', which enables the Commission to draw up a list of potentially suitable organisations when a programme has been given general approval but not formally funded.) Calls for proposals are published in the Official Journal, usually once or twice a year, will be summarised in *British Business,* and are available through the service Tenders Electronic Daily (TED). Those who have responded to a call for an expression of interest will be notified at the same time.

As a rule the Community's financial contribution will not exceed half the total cost of the project, and may be as low as 25 per cent. But 100 per cent funding is possible when the Commission has an exclusive interest in the project concerned. If research is later commercially exploited, part of the Community grant may be repayable; this is made clear in detail on application forms enclosed with tender notices.

As a rule of thumb, before submitting an application for Community R & D funding, you should be able to show that your proposal:

(a) has a transnational character, involving collaboration between organisations in two or more member states;

(b) conforms with the general aims of Community R & D demonstration programmes, namely to obtain basic data, stimulate useful invention, and pool brains and effort;

(c) has a good chance of eventual commercial exploitation, or 'Communautaire' value;

(d) is neither open-ended nor 'blue-skies' research, and will result in publishable results.

Two sectors are most directly involved: research and educational institutes (in universities, polytechnics, colleges and government-funded agencies) on the one hand, and industrial companies (particularly SMEs) on the other. It is becoming more and more necessary to demonstrate established links between both sectors. Research should either complement (but not duplicate) work being done at a national level, or make possible very large-scale projects which individual member States cannot finance or staff themselves.

Tender forms (available from Community offices in the UK as well as direct from Brussels) give detailed – sometimes over detailed! – instructions on the information which the Commission requires. They do not always, however, give an indication of the time-scales involved. These are not short.

Assessing proposals, evaluating them in confidence, with details of applicants stripped out, selection, consultation, contract negotiation and final signature adds up to a complex process.

For detailed information see coloured pages A15/16, A22

Unsurprisingly, decisions on applications are rarely made in under eight months, and sometimes take up to a year or more.

Clearly, applications for funding which arrive before the deadline published in the tender announcement warm the cockles of the hearts of those in DGs XII and XIII who will have to deal with them. But don't slap your application in too hurriedly. In the new technologies, priorities change rapidly. There is, for example, a dramatic difference between the Framework Programme for 1984–87 and the Programme for 1987–91. The earlier budget awarded almost as much to energy research as everything else combined. The latter relegates energy to a quarter of the total, puts it in second place to funds for information technologies, and introduces a major new fund line covering telecommunications and transport under the general heading 'The Life Blood of the Large Market'. The sum recommended for applying new technologies to industry remains roughly the same, but no longer includes biotechnology, which has a separate entry, and there are new budget lines for marine resources and the 'Europe for Research Workers' scheme.

Keep up to date, therefore, by reading *European Information Service* and *Better Business.* Before actually typing up and despatching your application, check with someone in the appropriate Directorate-General in Brussels in case there have been developments since the tender was issued of which you should be aware.

TELEVISION

Visitors to Brussels are often surprised to discover that on the TV set in their hotel there are 16 buttons, all revealing something different when pressed. On a typical evening one can summon up news or feature programmes from France, Germany, Belgium, Holland and Britain. There will be Italian films, Danish cartoons, a choice of soccer, motor-racing or skating, and quite often a play performed in English with French sub-titles, or vice-versa. (Plus, of course, incomprehensible soap operas, quizzes and panel games.)

This is a modest glimpse of things to come. In the 1990s viewers in most European countries will be able to watch perhaps five satellite TV channels, 30 national stations transmitted by cable, and a host of other programmes broadcast by neighbouring nations.

Both the European Parliament and the Commission have given much thought to the implications of this. Between 1982 and 1984 two Parliament resolutions and two Commission reports were published. They are wide-ranging, and make an interesting (and occasionally terrifying) read.

The economic opportunities of the television explosion are already enormous. The television satellite and ground equipment industry, booming even today, will probably be measured in tens of billions of pounds a year by the year 2000. The advertising potential

For detailed information see coloured pages A15

of a market of several hundred million (with television sets which will translate for you at the flick of a switch) hardly bears thinking about, particularly if you are a newspaper proprietor. Programme makers, now producing between 1000 and 5000 hours a year in the four largest Community states, will have to meet a demand several times as great. The question is whether they will meet it properly, or whether we will be submerged in a deluge of drivel. At present Europe cannot even agree on a single television or video system. Advertising laws vary radically. So do those allowing or banning programmes containing pornography, violence, or racist views. Libel laws are fiercely penal in some countries, almost non-existent in others. Copyright rules are an international shambles.

The time to consider these matters at a European level is, of course, now, not in five, ten or twenty years when America and Japan have stepped gladly in to fill every gap left by the failure of Community television industries to work together.

The Commission Green Paper on a common approach to broadcasting underlines the right of free transmission across frontiers, the right of writers and performers not to have their work 'stolen', and the right of children to be protected from programmes which may be harmful. Commission and Parliament reports also offer some positive suggestions:

(a) existing measures to protect consumers from misleading advertising should be extended to television across frontiers;

(b) where libel laws differ, there should be a comparable right of reply by people who have been unfairly attacked, no matter where they live;

(c) there should be financial aid (perhaps on the Canadian model) for good programme making;

(d) there should be an 'anti-dumping' policy, to deter the spread of the lowest common denominator;

(e) bodies like the European Broadcasting Union should be encouraged and helped to diversify, perhaps by offering pan-European programmes broadcast by European satellite;

(f) there should be special programmes for young people at the European level, devoted to news, feature material, and political and cultural coverage related specifically to the Community itself.

After many months of consultation and preliminary discussion in the Council, the Commission produced a draft Directive (COM86/146), widely leaked in advance in early 1986.

The proposals were treated by the media as though they were applicable to the situation in 1986, whereas, they are in fact directed at the dreadful future. Modest suggestions on control of advertising and the percentage of home-grown documentary, feature and entertainment programmes were portrayed as bureaucratic meddling

For detailed information see coloured pages A15

in the affairs of the BBC and ITN programme schedules of today, rather than an attempt to come to terms with the deluge of satellite and cable broadcasting 10 years hence.

The draft Directive recommends, in essence, a Common Market for broadcasting and broadcasters by breaking down barriers to cross-frontier radio and television. It suggests minimum acceptable standards for all member states – while in no way inhibiting the right of individual countries to have stiffer laws. Strict controls on advertising are recommended, particularly in the distinction between the advertisement and the programme content, and on matters such as decency, racial, religious or sexual discrimination, religious or political offensiveness, and the advertising of tobacco products (the paper suggests total prohibition) and alcohol (no glamorising).

There are provisions for the protection of young viewers against exploitative advertising and pornography, gratuitous violence or incitement to race hatred in programme content, and measures for protecting copyright.

The most controversial clauses in the draft concern advertising time and the European content of programme schedules.

On advertising time, the draft proposes a 15 per cent limit. Countries would have the right to set a lower figure for domestic channels, but would not be allowed to ban commercial broadcasts from other Community states. This has been widely opposed in Britain, as has the plan for a total ban on tobacco advertising.

The proposals on European content have simply been misunderstood. The draft Directive says that member States shall ensure that internal broadcasters reserve at least 30 per cent of their programming time (not consisting of news, sporting events and game shows, advertising or teletext services) for the broadcast of programmes made in the Community, either in individual countries or jointly. This means precisely what it says: that in, say, Britain, TV air time should include at least 30 per cent of material made in Europe – *including Britain*. The percentage should increase gradually to 60 per cent. (At present we use over 80 per cent.)

To put it another way: member states must agree not to use more than 70 per cent of their air time to broadcast programmes from America and Japan some of which already make 'Dallas' look like Shakespeare.

The Council has not so far considered the draft Directive in detail. The attitude of the British Government is a little difficult to assess, since the same speech, made on 2 July 1986 by Giles Shaw, Home Office Minister for broadcasting, was headed 'UK backs proposals for developing trans-frontier broadcasting' in the DTI magazine *British Business,* and 'Minister attacks EEC plans for TV law' in the *Financial Times.* The respective reports began: 'The UK fully supports the aims of the European Commission and the Council of

For detailed information see coloured pages A15

Europe in the developing of transfrontier broadcasting' (*British Business*) and 'The Government is against the creation of a legislative framework by the European Economic Community for the regulation of cross-frontier television' (*FT*) You pays your money. . . .

A House of Lords Select Committee report on the Green Paper itself was unusually negative for that body. It rejected fixing limits on advertising time, said that bans on advertising tobacco would be unacceptable in member States, and believed a statutory 'right of reply' would be unlikely to be widely accepted.

In June 1986, the Council of Trade Ministers agreed on common standards for direct broadcasting by satellite and its onward transmission by cable – the 'MAC packet'. This brought little joy to the Japanese, who are reputedly backing a much more sophisticated system.

★ ★ ★ ★

1988 was European Cinema and Television Year. Its objectives were, at time of writing, laid out best in COMDOC. They were:

(a) to promote awareness of the importance of a strong and competitive European audiovisual industry;

(b) to promote, by means of such an industry, a European identity, a better balance between the large and small cultural areas of the Community, and greater mobility for programme makers;

(c) better cooperation in Europe on financing, producing and distributing cinema and TV programmes, and a closer partnership between the two media.

The Council of Europe collaborated with the Community and there were national steering committees with responsibility for coordination and fundraising; direct funding by the Community was modest.

For detailed information see coloured pages A15

WORKERS' PARTICIPATION AND COMPANY LAW

Ivor Richard, until 1985 Commissioner for Social Policy, spoke during his last weeks in office to the CBI on 'Industrial Democracy' which is the Community's tag-phrase for enlightened participation in industry between the employed and their employers. He had, he said, a relationship with the Confederation based upon trust and understanding: 'You don't trust me, and I don't understand you!' The quip got a roar of laughter, but encapsulates a real problem.

There are those in the Community, on the right as well as the left of politics, who are bewildered by the UK's attitudes to the relationship between the two sides of industry. Conversely, there are those in Britain, in all Parties, who do not consider it a proper part of the Community's policy-making to attempt to draw up common codes for workers' participation in industry.

It might be sensible, therefore, to begin by outlining *why* the Commission feels that the Community should be involved in what it admits is 'the undeniably controversial and difficult issue of the role of employees in relation to the decision-making structures of companies'. (The reasons, and the quotation above, are taken largely from the Green Paper entitled 'Employee Participation and Company Structure', published by the Commission in 1975.)

The Commission addresses itself to two separate but interlinked problems. The first is the need for a 'common market for companies'. Widely differing laws in various Community countries inhibit companies, and do not enable them to take advantage of the huge 'home market' on offer. Only the more aggressive multinationals, many of them controlled elsewhere, have the strength to cope – and they use that strength, too often, in a cavalier fashion which works against the Community's policy for reducing disparities between regions.

The second problem, in the words of the Green Paper, is the increasing recognition 'that those who will be substantially affected by decisions made by social and political institutions must be involved in the making of those decisions. In particular, employees are increasingly seen to have interests in the functioning of enterprises which can be as substantial as those of shareholders, and sometimes more so'.

Two aspects (the economic and the social, or the practical and the philosophical, if you like) of a deeper problem which is less openly discussed. Many in the Commission and the Parliament go a great deal further. As they see it, the 'social partnership' – the relationship

For detailed information see coloured pages A16

between employers and workers – is in danger of breaking down in certain countries.

In most industrial nations (the argument runs) both sides of industry, however fiercely they may bargain on pay, working hours, or conditions, feel that they are essentially on the same side. There is a strong tradition of consultation between employers and the employed; workers feel they have a real part to play in the decision-making process of the companies for which they work, and that includes such central matters as hiring, firing, diversification and long-term strategy. Where such consultation does not exist, disputes are neither pre-empted nor settled by negotiation; they result in strikes and confrontation. Putting it bluntly (though they rarely do in public), many people in the Community believe that, for example, Italy, Greece and the UK have failed for 40 years to get relations between the component parts of industry right, and as a result have not been able to play their full and appropriate part in an industrial strategy for the Community as a whole. Until company laws are brought closer together, and some form of workers' participation exists Community-wide in industry, the problem (runs the argument) is insoluble.

* * * *

Before tackling these hottest of potatoes, we might look at what has already been agreed at Community level in terms of workers' rights, since (in view of the contentiousness of the whole subject) they add up to a fairly cheerful story. There are three Directives.

The first concerns *collective redundancies.* In force since 1977, this brings national legislation into line, and aims, *inter alia,* to prevent the 'export' of unemployment from one area to another. Any employer planning to make major redundancies must send a detailed statement in writing to the representatives of the workers concerned, and agree to immediate discussions with them to try to reach agreement on ways of avoiding or limiting the redundancies and ameliorating their consequences. He must also inform the relevant public authority, which can delay the redundancies for a month or more to try to help.

The second concerns the *rights of workers* who suddenly find themselves working for a new employer as a result of a takeover bid, closure or merger. Here the new employer must accept, automatically, the rights and obligations of the previous regime as regards contracts and collective agreements until the deal expires (or for at least a year). Trade unions must be given full access to employers, offered reasons for the transfer and its likely consequences, and informed of any changes or proposals which might affect their future. Continuing consultation must be established. A third Directive, in force since 1983, guarantees the payment of *back wages* and other outstanding claims from

For detailed information see coloured pages A16

employees when a firm is insolvent, bankrupt, or ceases payments. This is achieved by setting up guarantee companies, which are not liable to seizure during bankruptcy.

Modest achievements, but real ones. We now look at the Commission proposals which encounter the most extreme resistance in the United Kingdom.

'VREDELING'

The 'Vredeling proposals', named after the Dutch Commissioner who initiated them, were introduced in 1980. Properly termed the *Draft Directive on Procedures for Informing and Consulting Employees,* they have had a chequered career. Shortly after they were published they were attacked in detail by the European Parliament, and have been amended and watered down many times since. (For details of the basic document and subsequent discussion papers and changes, see Part IX.)

The current proposals are along these lines:

All firms with more than 1000 employees should be required to keep their workers fully in the picture about the company for which they work, its tactics and its prospects, by making available to them all company information not deemed to be secret for commercial reasons. At least once a year, workers' representatives should be given a detailed account of the structure of the company, its employment and investment hopes. Should the management of a subsidiary company in a larger concern fail to give this information, workers would have the right to approach head office directly (but in writing, not in person, as was once proposed).

In addition, workers' representatives in subsidiaries of a major company should be entitled to prior information on the reasons for, and potential impact of, any closure, move, reduction or significant alteration in output or activities; new agreements with other firms; major changes in organisation, working methods, or manufacturing techniques; the introduction of new technology; and proposals which might affect health or safety. Before a company can take a final decision the workers should be given 30 days to give their opinion.

The draft proposal includes safeguards for the protection of secret and confidential information. There are special rules for undertakings concerned with religion, charity, politics, culture and information, and right of appeal to a tribunal or equivalent body.

The Vredeling proposals, even in their modified form, have proved very unpopular with many employers in the Community, and in the UK in particular. The CBI has expressed its members' concern that information useful to their competitors might be leaked, that management could be undermined, and that the information operation would be too costly and time-consuming for some companies to bear. The European Trade Union Confederation and most British trade unions have, however, welcomed the

For detailed information see coloured pages A16

proposals (although they suggest amendments).

The Council last formally discussed the Vredeling proposals in June 1986. They gave the Commission a pat on the back, told them to keep up the good work, and promised to discuss the proposals again in 1989. The results are still awaited.

WORKERS' PARTICIPATION

The Commission's proposals on Workers' participation are formally termed the *Fifth draft Directive on Public Companies.* They are more a palimpsest than a draft, having been scribbled over so many times it is sometimes difficult to discern their original purposes. The best guide to the Commission's original thinking is the Green Paper referred to above. In brief the declared objectives are to:

(a) reconcile different national legal systems to allow the formation of genuinely European companies;
(b) establish workers' rights at a European level, in order to promote good industrial relations;
(c) define the responsibilities of both sides of industry (and of shareholders) in such a way as to improve business decision-making and encourage investment.

The Fifth draft Directive was introduced in 1972 and hotly debated in that year both by the Economic and Social Committee and the Parliament. After years of consultation, discussion and amendment, it was republished in 1983. In its latest form it is intended to apply only to companies with 1000 workers or more in Community member States. It suggests that all such companies should have some form of supervisory body, or that executive managers should be in the minority on a board containing supervisory members. There are four suggested methods of worker participation, and each member State could decide which it wished to choose:

(a) equal rights of workers and shareholders to nominate between one third and one half of the supervisory board members, with the final say for share-holders in the case of a tied vote;
(b) equal rights with shareholders to object to nominees on a coopted supervisory board, with the final decision left to an independent tribunal or equivalent body;
(c) the creation of a separate body composed solely of workers' representatives, with rights of consultation and information identical to that of the supervisory board, but no right of veto;
(d) any other system agreed by collective bargaining, corresponding to the principles of one of the previous models.

In all cases, the choice of employees' representatives would

For detailed information see coloured pages A16

accord with the right of all workers to vote, freedom of expression, proportional representation and a secret ballot.

★ ★ ★ ★

The Commission's proposals for workers' participation are, in the words of *The Times*, 'hardly likely to shake multinational structures to their foundations'. Nor is it a simple case of the Fifth draft Directive being opposed by big business and supported by trade unions. Indeed, the Commission Green Paper of 1975 was resisted fiercely by both sides of industry, the 'bosses' seeing it as an attempt to interfere with the proper role of management, the 'workers' as an attempt to infiltrate tame 'bosses' pets' into senior positions in trade unions.

Over the years attitudes have polarised. The CBI is against the draft Directive in principle. The TUC is broadly for it, although it has expressed reservations about the right of non-union members to play a part in a company board, whatever its kind.

The Council last discussed the draft in December 1983, when Britain was largely alone in protesting against the principle of legislation. Company law experts are at present studying the draft in detail; yet more amendments can be expected. In the meantime, the Commission is studying ways in which workers affected by the introduction of new technologies can be brought into discussion and decision-making, and how workers can more easily acquire a financial stake in their own company.

★ ★ ★ ★

There has been, in this writer's experience, a reluctance on the part of some managers and personnel officers in large British companies even to think about the Community's proposals on information and workers' participation, in the belief that they have been virtually written off. This may prove to be misguided. Commitment within the Commission is real, and is far from a mere expression of party political ideology. Both the 'Vredeling' proposals and the Fifth draft Directive have at least technically been given the blessing of the Council of Ministers. I do not think they will go away; too many people in the Commission and the Parliament believe in them.

COMPANY LAW IN GENERAL

A great many proposals aimed at smoothing the path for a Common Market for Companies have been adopted or are in the pipeline; many more are in the drafting stage. They cover (the list is incomplete):

(1) The Sixth Directive (adopted 1982, now theoretically incorporated in national legislation) on the assets and liabilities of public limited companies which are wound up;

For detailed information see coloured pages A16

(2) The Seventh Directive (adopted 1983) on consolidated financial statements;
(3) The Eighth Directive (adopted March 1984) on professional qualifications of auditors;
(4) The Ninth Directive (in early draft) concerned with protecting minority interests, employees and creditors in a dependent company;
(5) The Tenth Directive (published in draft) on mergers of companies of different member states;
(6) The Eleventh Directive (published in draft during 1986) on disclosure requirements of branches;
(7) A proposed Regulation for a European Company Statute. First published in draft in 1970 and amended after much consultation in 1975, this seeks to establish law for European companies which would be directly applicable in all member States. It is being interminably examined in working groups, and any agreement seems a very long way off.

There are also a multitude of proposals and draft Directives in the fields of banking, capital markets, transferable securities, stock exchanges, insurance, taxation, social policy, and commercial and private law. An excellent summary of these various proposals (and of Directives already agreed) is available from Price Waterhouse EC Services, Rue Ravenstein 60, Bte 7, 1000 Brussels. It is entitled EC Bulletin Number 74, 'Harmonization Status Report on Company Law and Business Related Subjects'.

THE 'SOCIAL PARTNERS'

The Community tries to maintain, through all its institutions, regular and balanced contact with what it calls the 'social partners' – both sides of industry. In the case of employers, initiatives have scarcely been necessary; all the major employers' bodies have long established links with Brussels and Strasbourg. In the case of Trades Unions, contacts have greatly expanded and improved in recent years.

The European Trade Union Confederation (ETUC), with headquarters in Brussels, is wider in membership than the Community alone (representing unions in 19 countries) but takes a particular interest in proposed EC legislation and has extensive contacts with the Economic and Social Committee and the Parliament. Through its research unit (the European Trade Union Institute) it provides useful material for trade unionists, researchers and educators. There are also a range of industry committees.

The Community has established, in Dublin, a European Foundation for the improvement of living and working conditions, and in West Berlin a European Centre for the Development of Vocational Training (CEDEFOP).

Two particularly useful documents for trade unionists are a

booklet, *European Community Institutions and Publications,* available from the Trade Union Division of DG X in the Commission, and the periodical *Social Europe.*

For detailed information see coloured pages A16

CONTRACTS AND TENDERS

Every day, many millions of pounds are up for grabs in new contracts for public works and the supply of goods and services to public bodies in the Community. Public supply contracts are of vital importance to most big businesses in the Western world, and of increasing interest to SMEs. Since many of these contracts are not awarded by national governments but by regional and local authorities, the amount at stake is difficult to assess. But a Commission estimate published in June 1986 put the total at about 9 per cent of the gross domestic product of the Community. Even discounting defence expenditure, what we are talking about is something in the region of £90 billion a year.

All firms established in the Community have, in theory, the right to compete on equal terms for all public contracts (with a few strictly defined exceptions). But some have proved more equal than others; and national governments and local authorities have found ways of bending the rules, or delaying their application. The Commission published in June 1986 a programme of action to correct this.

PUBLIC CONTRACTS

The Official Journal publishes invitations to tender for public contracts in its daily 'S' supplement. These must include:

(a) all works contracts of over about £600,000 to be awarded by governments or local authorities throughout the Community;

(b) all supply contracts of more than about £120,000 to be awarded by local authorities, certain public bodies, governments for their rental and leasing requirements, and defence ministries for non-military products such as textiles and shoes.

These contracts are open to any firm in the Community without discrimination on grounds of nationality. Two kinds of tender are permitted: open (where direct tenders are invited) and restricted (where contractors must apply to be considered for invitation to tender). In practice about half the tenders are open; only the United Kingdom almost always employs the restricted system. The advertisements to tender must be published within nine days of becoming public, and not less than 36 days must be allowed for the receipt of tenders in the case of open invitations; under the restricted procedure the latter period may be shortened.

Of supply contract notices recently published, the highest proportion were for footwear and clothing, food products, and metal structures. Between 5 and 10 per cent of contracts were for electrical

For detailed information see coloured pages A16

engineering products, petroleum products, office and data-processing equipment, and paper. There were many contracts in respect of textiles, motor vehicles, plastic products and chemicals, but the range is very wide: on a typical day they included envelopes, computer equipment, omnibuses, caster sugar and heating oil.

Since 1980, the Official Journal has also published all contracts (except rental and leasing agreements) to be awarded by central or federal authorities worth more than about £100,000. These are open to tender by any firm in the EC.

There are exceptions. It is not obligatory to publicise contracts to be placed by public transport authorities, or those concerning transmission or transport for water or energy, or tele-communications. In certain cases contracts may be awarded by direct negotiation or by private treaty without publication of a contract notice, but there are strict rules to prevent the abuse of this provision.

All well and good. But the existing rules have not worked as well as they should – occasionally because of national obstructionism, often because time-scales for tendering have been too short, or it has been difficult for interested firms to get the information they needed, when they needed it. The Commission, after much consultation during 1984 and 1985, submitted in June 1986 proposals for establishing a genuine internal market in public purchasing. This incorporates a carrot and a stick: the carrot being the promotion of an information campaign to make national obligations and opportunities for suppliers better known, the stick being the threat that Community loans and grants to governments and local authorities will be conditional on compliance with Directives already agreed.

The paper recommends fuller and quicker information for firms; simpler, agreed technical standards; and above all more time. It suggests that the Directives should be extended to cover transport, water, energy and telecommunications. Tougher action (through the European Court, if necessary) should be taken if governments or local authorities continue to break the rules, or reserve too many contracts for special treatment.

The Commission note was given a general welcome by the Council in June 1986 as a useful contribution to cutting costs for public bodies, increasing the competitive strength of the industries concerned, and completing the internal market.

★ ★ ★ ★

The Community has the duty to ensure that firms anywhere in the Community should be able to discover details about contracts in good time, tender for them without discrimination, and be judged fairly by the awarding body. There, in theory, its responsibility ends. Winning the contract will depend upon the traditional virtues –

For detailed information see coloured pages A16

good market research, sensible tendering in the appropriate language and currency, and all the rest.

In practice, however, the European Community can be of help, in particular to small businessmen, as can government departments and a number of other agencies.

The small businessman, in particular, may only be able to break into the public contracting market if he can find a partner in the country in which the contract is being offered. Here the Business Cooperation Centre in Brussels can be helpful. Its address is 6 rond-point Robert Schuman (2/9), Brussels 1040, and the telephone number Brussels 235 39 49.

Leaflets on tendering and on doing business in the EC are available from the National Westminster Bank Group, Office of EC Affairs, 41 Lothbury, London EC2P 2BP. There is also a free booklet on Public Supply Contracts in the European Community, available from any Commission Office.

A study of the problems of subcontracting across frontiers is at present being undertaken by the Law Department of the University of Essex. The aim is to prepare a guide to subcontracting throughout the Community, with special attention to opportunities for SMEs. An article on this project was published in the Law Society *Gazette* of 12 March 1986, and summarised in *British Business* on 11 April.

THE DEVELOPING WORLD

The nations of the Community have their own aid programmes. Community aid does not attempt to compete with this, but to complement it. It offers a variety of forms of aid, but here we are concerned specifically with the European Development Fund (EDF). This exists principally to help over 80 of the world's least developed nations in Africa, the Caribbean and the Pacific under the Lomé Convention. The EDF, with a budget in the order of £4300 million over the current five-year period, offers direct grants and loans at particularly low rates of interest. The nations concerned put to the Commission outline programmes for spending the grants or loans they are given, and specific projects within this framework. These are agreed by the Commission, and calls for tender are put out. Only the ACP countries themselves and the 12 Community nations may tender, preference being given to local firms. Bids to tender can be submitted jointly by a Community firm and a local firm.

The amount of business at stake is substantial, and risk-free, since the Community itself pays contractors. To date Britain has too often failed to get its fair share of contracts although we are often (particularly in Commonwealth ACP countries) well placed to win them.

Four major sectors share most of Community aid:

(1) Rural development (the majority of EDF funding);

For detailed information see coloured pages A16

(2) Industrialisation;
(3) Economic infrastructure;
(4) Social development.

Loan money (made available by the European Investment Bank at extremely favourable rates of interest) is much concerned in mining, tourism, industry, agro-industry and energy projects. Recently a particularly high priority has been accorded to small and medium-sized companies in the ACP countries.

HOW TO TENDER

An excellent leaflet entitled 'Opportunities for Contracts under EEC Aid Programmes' is available from the UK Permanent Representative's Office in Brussels. The British Overseas Trade Board can give an indication of the outline programmes submitted by individual countries, together with detailed description of individual projects and tender documents. The magazine *British Business* has regular articles on opportunities available. Helpful documents can also be obtained from any Commission office.

Works and supply contracts are awarded by open tender, notices of which are published by the BOTB, and in the Official Journal 'S' series. But there is no substitute for direct contact with the Commission (the Development Directorate, DG VII), the European Investment Bank and the UK Permanent Representative's Office in Brussels. It is also worth considering writing to the British Embassy in the countries concerned, and/or to the Community's delegates to third countries, a full list of which, including telephone and telex numbers, is given in the Commission Directory.

CONSULTANCIES

EDF money is often used to finance detailed and expert studies. Consultants who wish to apply for such contract work *must* register with the Commission before they can be considered. (See the UKREP note mentioned above.) No advance publicity is given for consultancy opportunities, and there is therefore no substitute for regular contact by telephone or letter if not in person. The Commission prepares a short list of possible consultants and sends it to the ACP government concerned, which does the actual choosing.

* * * *

In the past, British companies have often complained (with some justice) that it is far more difficult for them to tender for contracts, either in the Community or under the EDF, because their competitors clustered round Brussels get a head start. The latter can smell contracts in the wind earlier than is possible from Birmingham

For detailed information see coloured pages A16

or Glasgow; they get the details days before they are available in published form.

Since the arrival of TED (Tenders Electronic Daily) things have become easier. All contracts to be published in the Official Journal are now available hours or days ahead on the Euronet Community network. This is a selective service – the system can be programmed automatically to display only those tenders which might interest the user. The annual access fee is £36, and on-line transmission costs 10 pence a minute. Shared subscriptions make the service very cheap indeed.

An 'Action Pack' on TED, giving full details and much information on tendering, is available from the Office for Official Publications, PO Box 1003, Luxembourg (Luxembourg 49 00 81), or from Commission offices.

For detailed information see coloured pages A16

TRANSPORT

Most of us tend to think of transport as applying to people – putting bottoms on seats of planes, buses and trains. And that is certainly an important part of a vital industry. But for every ten stone traveller in Europe, many tons of inanimate exports are on the move. A Common Market cannot work properly if people in one area are unable to buy the products of another. It should, in theory, be as easy to buy a bottle of Guinness in Milan as it is to buy an Italian refrigerator in Dublin. But sometimes the present transport system cannot cope.

Transport is an important industry in its own right, employing 6 per cent of the labour force directly and 15 per cent if one adds road-building, railway construction, and the manufacture of planes, ships and motor vehicles. It is a vital contributor to tourism – a bigger industry still. It uses a quarter of all the oil consumed in the Community, and represents more of the Community's GNP than agriculture. Most aspects of the Common Market depend upon it.

This importance was specifically recognised in the Treaty of Rome, Article 3 of which requires that member states should adopt 'a common policy in the sphere of transport'. Much, as we shall see, has been done at the Community level. But we are still far from having a Common Transport Policy.

Indeed, during 1985 the Council of Ministers was found guilty, by the European Court, of failing in its duty to create one. At the end of that year it agreed to the creation of a free transport market by 1992, and instructed the Commission and COREPER to explore the prospects of:

(a) simplifying and gradually eliminating controls and formalities at borders, which at present cost the Community around £500 million a year;
(b) creating a Transport Infrastructure Programme which would offer the advantages of easy travel for goods and people throughout the Community, including its peripheral areas;
(c) the organisation of a transport market by road, rail, air and sea;
(d) better safety measures in all aspects of transport, and particularly on the roads.

The first of these proposals is incorporated in the White Paper on completing the internal market. A single administrative document is now available for transport vehicles which cross frontiers, which speeds up matters and saves money. In addition, two important decisions were taken by the Transport Council in June 1986. The first concerns road haulage

For detailed information see coloured pages A16/17

quotas, which restrict the operations of companies trading in other member states. These are to be immediately increased, and quota restrictions abolished by 1992. The Commission is currently drawing up fhe proposals required of them, together with a study on vehicle taxation, excise duty on fuel, and road tolls, all of which can distort competition.

The second Council decision concerned vehicle axleweight. From 1992 a minimum drive axle weight of 11.5 tonnes will be permitted for five-axle or six-axle vehicles. The UK and Ireland have been granted a temporary derogation from this and will be retaining their own limits (10.5 tonnes for drive-axle weight, 38 tonnes for total laden weight) to give them time to put in hand any necessary work on strengthening roads and bridges.

The Commission published its draft Transport Infrastructure Programme in June 1986. This is aimed at increasing the social and economic cohesion of the Community by improving transport links generally, and in particular those involving road/sea and road/rail links, high speed rail routes between major urban centres, and special help for peripheral areas. Although the emphasis is on dovetailing national transport programmes, the draft recommends large-scale Community aid for such programmes – ranging from the massive (the Chunnel) to the small and specific (eliminating bottlenecks in traffic flow). Funds available should be increased by about 60 per cent by 1990, the possibilities of mobilising private capital should be explored, and EIB loans should be made available with budgetary guarantee from the ERDF.

On air transport, the Commission, which has long attempted to do something about the high cost of flights within the Community as compared with similar flights within, for example, the US, submitted proposals to the Council on 30 June 1986. These recommended keeping the existing system of bilateral agreements between airlines and between member states, but with more flexibility and a better deal for the consumer. Airlines would be able to decide their own tariffs (provided they covered operating costs on the route in question) and would not be obliged to enter into capacity-sharing arrangements. Only if the market share of an airline fell below 25 per cent on internal routes would the national government concerned be able to intervene. (There were, however, extensive exemptions from the normal rules of competition, largely in favour of better service to air travellers.) The paper suggested a trial test for the new rules over four years.

The Council failed to reach agreement on these proposals. The Commission then threatened to institute court action against ten national airlines (including British Airways and British Caledonian) for being in breach of the rules of the Treaty of Rome in regard to abuse of a dominant position. The stalemate continues.

The campaign for cheaper fares within the Community has been

For detailed information see coloured pages A16/17

most actively pursued by the European Parliament (and in particular by Lord Bethell).

On shipping, proposals submitted during 1985 and approved in principle by the Council recommend joint action against international protectionism, coupled with greater freedom to provide shipping services within the Community itself: carriers authorised for international inland navigation would be allowed to carry out operations in another member state. There would be provision for imposing duties on third countries found guilty of unfair trading practice. A House of Lords report on the proposals approved of them in general, and suggested speeding up the timetable for their implementation.

Road Safety Year (1986) had as its aims first, to focus attention on road safety, by campaigns and exhibitions, and in the long term to speed up legislative proposals for car testing, braking, tougher standards for licence examinations, and more frequent and thorough inspection of vehicles used for transporting dangerous goods. The many campaigns mounted throughout the Community have concentrated on alcohol and driving, use of safety belts, speed, child safety, and the problems of motor cyclists. The impact of all this activity on road accident casualty statistics has however been negligible. A possible explanation for this disappointing outcome may be found in the theory of risk compensation as outlined by Dr John Adams, a reader in geography at University College London (copies of his book on 'Risk and Freedom' may be obtained directly from him). A study of possible uses for new technology in road safety was inaugurated in conjunction with the DRIVE project.

Over 50 new rules on safety devices for motor vehicles have now been agreed at the Community level.

★ ★ ★ ★

Over the past 10 years, international traffic has increased twice as fast as national traffic within the Community, and this growth shows no sign of slowing down. When Britain joined, 6½ million tonnes of goods were transported from one Community country to another by road, rail or water. The figure seems likely to rise by the end of the century to over 11 million tonnes. The number of people travelling internationally will probably double over the same period.

The shape of transport is also changing. Over a decade or more, investment has tended to favour roads and air transport, at the expense of rail and water – which are often more economic in terms of energy consumption. But the situation shows signs of reversal: more money is being put back into the railways (and inland waterways in Continental Europe).

Very large amounts of Community money have gone to the UK and Ireland for roads, railways, bridges, ferries, airports and harbours, both in the form of grants from the Regional Development Fund and

For detailed information see coloured pages A16/17

loans from the European Investment Bank. This has made a real contribution to the infrastructure of the British Isles, and has saved ratepayers considerable sums in interest charges. The Commission has drawn up a list of other principal transport bottlenecks within the Community, and hopes to award them special priority in the allocation of Community funds, particularly when they affect more than one Community country. A new Community financial instrument, designed exclusively for the transport sector, has been proposed by the Commission, but so far has failed to win the hearts or minds of the Council of Ministers.

On the fair trade aspects of transport policy, the Community has several agreements already under its belt. International road and rail goods tariffs have been brought into line, as have the qualifications required of those wishing to enter the road haulage trade. The tachograph, introduced in Britain with such alarums and excursions a few years ago, is now acknowledged as a valuable tool for road haulage practice, and has already saved an unmeasurable number of lives, as well as several drivers from prosecution. There are a range of mutual agreements on safety standards for goods vehicles. Agreement should also soon be reached on new safety rules for bus transport (covering the design of coaches as well as their operation).

★ ★ ★ ★

Apart from its impact on trade, transport is of obvious importance to those who wish to visit another Community country, or to work there. Advances in the field of travel and tourism (and the stumbling blocks which remain) are touched upon in the section entitled 'Travelling and Working in Europe'.

For detailed information see coloured pages A16/17

ENERGY

When some mad villain attacks a tanker in the Gulf, the result can have more immediate effect upon the Pound, and thus the British economy, than months of careful planning by the Government or work by the Treasury and the City.

This sombre and disillusioning fact is a reminder of the importance of energy to the United Kingdom, but also the Community as a whole. Particularly since the successive oil price fluctuations of the 70s and 80s, the Community has been forced to come to terms with the implications of a future when energy supplies are no longer cheap, plentiful or guaranteed.

The Community is the world's largest oil importer. Despite North Sea oil production, it still relies on Saudi Arabia, Libya and Nigeria for a third of its supplies. And although imports of oil dropped by almost 50 per cent between 1973 and 1983, the import bill increased five times. Faced with these circumstances, energy policy has begun to develop in the Community – albeit slowly and late. Under targets established in 1980, member states have pledged to reduce power consumption. (At present economic growth is almost exactly paralleled by growth in energy use; by 1990 we are committed to reduce the latter by 30 per cent.) Dependence on oil is to be gradually diminished; the aim is that solid fuels and nuclear power should account for 70 or 75 per cent of electricity generation; gas consumption (at present serving 18 per cent of our needs) should be increased; and new sources of energy (solar, geothermal, hydro-electric, wind power, biomass) explored and developed jointly. Above all, energy-saving schemes are to be encouraged and assisted.

Emphasis is also placed on security of supplies. There is now regular consultation on maintaining gas supplies, if necessary across frontiers. All Community States have a legal requirement to maintain oil stocks equivalent to 90 days' supply, and fuel stocks at power stations equivalent to 30 days' supply. Rather less public arrangements have been agreed on immediate measures to be taken if the oil market is disrupted in the short term, and to monitor its stability in the long term.

At an international level the Community as a whole has signed agreements with the principal nuclear exporting countries (the US, Australia and Canada) on stability and safety of supplies; similar agreements are being explored with external producers of gas and coal. Conscious of the energy needs of the Third World, the Community's loans and grants to help energy developments in the non-oil producing countries have increased greatly, and are now running at over 700 million dollars a year.

For detailed information see coloured pages A17

The Community finances a massive programme of research into safety in the nuclear industry, and the disposal of radioactive waste – the latter, admittedly, with a marked lack of success to date. It has given major loans to nuclear power stations, including several in the UK. The JET (Joint European Torus) project, at Culham in Oxfordshire, is helping to explore the possibility of 'clean' power produced by the fusion of deuterium and tritium. The costs are great (about £220 million to date) but the stakes are higher still: one gramme of deuterium, which is easily extracted from sea water, may one day produce more energy than 2000 gallons of petrol.

In future, however, the hope is that far more progress will be made on new sources of energy, and the crucial question of conservation. At present about a third of the Community's total energy consumption is swallowed up in heating, ventilation, lighting and hot water supplies in our homes and offices. We could cut this consumption by between 30 and 65 per cent.

Another 25 per cent of total energy consumption (44 per cent of oil consumption) goes on transport. Changing social habits could save perhaps half of this. (One person driving to a place of work in a large car will seem, a few suggestions hence, to have been criminal irresponsibility.) In industry, which uses 35 per cent of total energy consumption, further huge savings are possible.

Of the Community's budget for energy, the largest part goes into such fields as the JET project, nuclear safety, and the work of the Joint Research Centre. Europe is making spectacular progress as far as the harnessing of controlled thermonuclear fusion is concerned. Some 3600 people – a third of whom are researchers – are involved in the Community fusion programme in the member countries, Sweden and Switzerland. The ultimate objective of the Community fusion programme is the construction of a demonstration reactor. The EC has set aside 690 million ECU for the programme over the period 1985–89.

Grants in the non-nuclear energy field have, however, grown rapidly in recent years, applications far outstripping the sums voted by the Council. The purpose of the awards is to help improve the management of energy resources and reduce energy dependence, and also to promote industrial and agricultural competitiveness, improve living and working conditions in energy industries, and strengthen development aid. The aim of the current programme is both to investigate potential resources and to improve existing technologies, thus developing new techniques, processes and products, and carrying out pilot projects with a view to demonstration and eventually commercial exploitation. It involves both industry and universities as well as public and private research centres.

Grants can be offered in nine fields, grouped under two main headings:

For detailed information see coloured pages A17

1. *Development of renewable sources of energy.* This covers solar energy, biomass, wind and geothermal energy.
2. *Rational use of energy.* This covers conservation, use of solid fuels, new synthetic fuels and fuel cells, better use of hydrocarbons, and the analysis and modelling of energy systems.

Unfortunately, there is not enough in the Community's coffers to support projects under all these headings each year; they also vary considerably as to size and duration. During 1986, for example, grants were only available for solar radiation and photovoltaics, improving biomass energy by use of Ethanol plants, wind energy in medium-size installations, and liquid fuels. Tenders for contract grants are advertised periodically, and published in the Official Journal. The tender announcement gives full details of the terms under which grants can be given; further advice is available from the Department of Energy, Thames House South, Millbank, SW1P 4QJ or from DG XII E in Brussels, telephone 010–322–235–5832.

The Community can finance up to 49 per cent of the cost of successful projects. If the project leads to successful commercial exploitation, up to half the Community grant may be repayable. The contractor will remain the owner of patentable inventions and know-how acquired during the course of the project, but must agree to the dissemination within the Community of the results of the project, and exploit his success in accordance with the rules of fair competition.

During 1985, Community support for R & D in non-nuclear energy was given to 550 projects out of 1451 applications. Sixty per cent of projects were from SMEs. Of earlier projects, about half those supported have so far become profitable.

During the period from 1985 to 1988, £120 million was available in Community funding for non-nuclear energy R & D including help for the hydrocarbons sector. An excellent booklet, 'EEC Support for Research and Development in Non-Nuclear Energy, Notes for Applicants' is available from the Department of Energy at the address above. A most welcome recent development is that applications in English alone are now accepted.

* * * *

When considering applying for energy demonstration funds it is important to know what work is already going on in other Community countries, some of which may be more advanced than in Britain. The Community's annual Reports, and specialised occasional bulletins available at Commission offices, can provide useful information about the type of project most likely to be supported.

* * * *

The dramatic fall in oil prices during 1985/86 means that many of the

For detailed information see coloured pages A17

new and renewable sources of energy suddenly found it difficult or impossible to compete. Determined not to lose the momentum established, the Commission produced a draft resolution aimed at reminding member States of their commitments. It is also in process of revising its Plan for Coal (leaked with explosive results during 1985) and its wider draft resolution on energy objectives for 1995 (COM 85/245).

For detailed information see coloured pages A17

THE ENVIRONMENT

If abolishing frontiers is one of the aims of Community policy, it has to be admitted that pollution got there first. The polluter long ago jumped across the borderlines, creating more problems for his neighbours than for himself. The debris which litters the banks of the Rhine in Holland has all too often been put there by citizens of quite another country. Gases and chemicals discharged into the air may fall to the earth in the form of acid rain hundreds of miles from the source of emission.

But if Europe's environment is a transnational problem, it is also highly appropriate for cooperation at the Community level. Curbing pollution and protecting the environment generally saves resources, works for the improvement of the quality of life, gives admirable opportunities for cooperation in research and practical work, is capable of harnessing the energy and enthusiasm of young people, and also looks to the future in a very particular way.

The Community's resources are limited and have been concentrated so far on two broad fields of activity:

(a) preventing pollution
(b) managing land and resources more effectively in an environmental sense.

The principle that 'the polluter pays' is becoming increasingly accepted in industrialised nations, and was adopted at the Community level in 1975. Since 1979, Community money has been available for *pilot projects on new technologies* which can prevent or reduce pollution, or otherwise help to protect the environment. The Community has also financed many conferences, seminars and detailed reports, drawing on the experience of those in the field throughout the Community, and those non-governmental organisations represented in the European Environment Bureau.

The *safety of nuclear installations* and the storage of *radioactive waste* have been the subject of a series of programmes with extensive Community resources, covering the study of the ecological impact of traditional power stations, the remote detection of pollution, and agricultural and chemical ecology. There have been major studies on the *climate,* weather forecasting, recycling of *waste, pollution-free technology,* and information on man and his quality of life.

There are rules on curbing *atmospheric pollution* by reducing the emission of lead and other substances by motor vehicles, and limiting the discharge of sulphur dioxide and other particles into the air. Many of the rules have been agreed and implemented.

The impact of *chemicals* on the environment is also dealt with in

For detailed information see coloured pages A17

part by legislation covering biodegradability standards for detergents and containers, the classification, packaging and labelling of pesticides, solvents and paints, the use of dangerous substances in industry, and the evaluation, testing and control of new chemical substances before they are marketed. There are agreed rules for *worker protection against lead and asbestos* in industry. The Community nations have agreed to exchange information on stockpiling of dangerous substances, and on the prevention of industrial accidents.

Noise is a pollutant, and maximum levels have been established in the case of new motor-vehicles, aircraft, grass-cutting machines and tractors, and machines in factories and workshops.

On *water,* a number of Directives already agreed deal with the quality of bathing water, drinking water, and fresh water used for fish farming. There are rules on the discharge of dangerous substances into rivers, lakes and the sea, and on steps to be taken at a Community level when oil is spilt onto the sea. Water is, of course, an indispensable raw material of industry, and Community policy ranges more widely than the immediate problem of pollution. (A free leaflet entitled 'The European Community and Water' covers the subject briefly.)

The word *'waste'* is becoming something of a misnomer insofar as urban and industrial by-products are concerned. Much waste can be prevented; much can be recycled. Five million tonnes of solid waste is generated in the Community every day. It pollutes land and rivers – often at great expense, containing as it does large quantities of costly, imported raw materials. Waste can be extremely dangerous in the process of transport, particularly between countries, and there is a Directive which should prevent a repetition of the controversy which surrounded the transport of barrels of dioxin from Seveso in 1983.

The wider employment of *waste recycling* would not only improve Europe's environment but would save vast sums of money. It has been estimated that we throw away, every year, about £7000 million in reclaimable materials. Community funds are available for research into the treatment and recycling of paper, and municipal and industrial waste.

The Commission is responsible for coordinating the approach of member states to the conservation of fauna and flora. The Community now bans products made from baby seals, whales and other cetaceans. It protects 74 species of birds, and limits the hunting and sale of others. It exchanges information with countries throughout the world as well as between member countries themselves, and undertakes joint research with other European nations.

In its various aid and cooperation agreements with the Third World, the Community contributes to water management, the struggle agains the encroaching deserts of Africa, the preservation of tropical forests, and the establishment of forms of agricultural and energy supply consistent with the environmental needs of the nations concerned.

In March 1985 agreement was also reached on reducing *pollution from car exhausts.* Stricter controls will be introduced over a six-year period beginning in 1988 with new cars in the bigger, thirstier ranges. Manufacturers will be able to choose between the three-way catalytic converter pioneered in Germany and the 'lean-burn' engine used elsewhere and preferred by British manufacturers. By 1993 all new cars sold inside the Community will run on lead-free petrol.

The last two or three years have seen far greater awareness of the problems of the environment. A number of factors have played a part in this: the 'acid rain' campaign, the well reported activities of Greenpeace and the success of the Green parties, an extremely active and well informed committee in the European Parliament, and most recently the Chernobyl disaster and its aftermath. The Commission took advantage of this climate of opinion to produce a document, New Directions in Environment Policy (COM 86/76) which starts from the premise that a proper environmental policy is not only essential to preserve the quality of life for generations to come, but an economic imperative. 'Environmental protection is not an option,' says the document. 'Strict environmental protection can be regarded as merely a properly conceived economic policy.'

The Council of Environmental Ministers has reached agreement on a whole range of measures, including transfrontier shipment of dangerous waste, curbing pollution of the sea by land-based sources, dumping of certain dangerous substances, rules on the use of sewage sludge in farming, protection of animals used in experiments and scientific research, new rules for safety at work and many more. There is to be a full-scale investigation of the Chernobyl disaster and its implications for nuclear safety and health protection, radiation levels in food, crisis procedure in the event of accidents and the problems of radioactive waste. The Commission is at present preparing detailed proposals for the Council.

There has also been some progress on the difficult problems of acid rain (limitation of emissions from large combustion plants), the sulphur content of gas oil and the disposal of waste oils at sea. A scheme for offering grant aid to farmers who undertake to farm in such a way as to preserve or restore the environment, agreed by the Council in 1985, has been given a somewhat lukewarm welcome in Britain. A list of environmentally sensitive agricultural areas put forward by the Countryside Commission and the Nature Conservancy Council as cases for possible assistance is reported to have been drastically pruned by MAFF.

1987 was designated 'European Year of the Environment'. Since then the European Commission has redoubled its efforts to enhance

For detailed information see coloured pages A17

public awareness in Europe of the importance of protecting the environment and to promote the application of the principles set out in the fourth action programme (introduced in 1986). This programme encouraged the integration of environmental policy into all other policies, whether national or Community. Priority activities and objectives are protecting the ozone layer, protection of the aquatic environment, air pollution, noise abatement, conservation of the natural heritage, controls on chemicals and industrial hazards.

IMPACT STUDIES

After long discussion the Council approved, in March 1985, the Directive on Environmental Impact Assessment. This has have far-reaching implications for governments, industries and local authorities throughout the Community.

Under the Directive member states must, before beginning work on certain major projects, make an assessment of their impact on:

human beings, fauna and flora;
soil, water, air, climatic factors and the landscape;
the interrelationship between these factors;
material assets and cultural heritage.

This will apply to crude-oil refineries; power stations; installations designed for storage or disposal of radioactive waste; cast-iron, steel, asbestos and chemical installations; major roadways and airports; large ports; and waste-disposal installations for the burning, treatment or storage of toxic and dangerous wastes. (There are derogations possible in certain cases.)

Moreover, member states must submit for evaluation other projects in which they consider there may be a major environmental impact, including projects in agriculture, mining, energy and metal-working.

The public must be informed of the proposed project, and its assessment in environmental terms (and given an opportunity to express an opinion) before the project is initiated. The Directive came into force at the beginning of 1989.

For detailed information see coloured pages A17

MONEY

Aid is discussed in Part VII. In this section we look at what is known in other Community capitals as 'the British problem'; the budget more generally; taxation; and the European Monetary System (EMS).

My file of newspaper cuttings on the single subject of the UK contribution to the Community budget is four feet thick. Since the problem has now, in theory, been solved, three feet nine inches of it have been bundled up and despatched, with a curse and a blessing, to the basement. It would be a comfort to feel that the far larger volume of newspaper cuttings in German, French, and the other Community languages will be as readily jettisoned and forgotten. They will not.

For several years the work of the Council and its 'summits' was brought to a virtual halt by failure to agree on the proper British contribution to the budget in net terms. Britain's demands for refunds, year by year, were soundly based. But the manner of their presentation, in the press and television of British itself, has left a legacy of illwill among our neighbours and partners which may take a long time to live down.

The UK's net contribution to the Community has never approached that of West Germany. We have had huge refunds. Yet it has been commonplace for TV commentators and editorial writers in the popular press of Britain to describe us as 'the paymasters of the Community', and public opinion polls indicate that we still believe we are.

What was actually at stake, over these years of rancorous argument, was whether Community membership should cost us a penny, tuppence or thruppence a head per day. For this we get a seat at the board of directors' table when every Community decision, internal or international, is made – with the entire cost of our agricultural support system thrown in as a bonus.

Britain has yet to take full advantage of the enlarged market, while her subscription to the 'club' has increased. Community ministers are realists, and understand the problems which faced British governments.

The press correspondents and the public of other Community countries are less sophisticated. They find it difficult to forget the oil which comes out of the North Sea every year as a free gift, which we did not possess when we signed the Treaty of Accession, and which pays for our entire contribution to the Community budget several times over. They are not convinced that we can really be poorer now

For detailed information see coloured pages A17/18

than we were then, and that it is the fault of the Common Market.

* * * *

At all events, a long-term solution to the 'British problem' has at last been agreed. As a result of the Fontainebleau Summit of June 1984, there will in future be safeguards to ensure that Britain does not pay more into the Community budget than she can afford. It is a complex agreement, but goes like this: Britain's VAT contribution to the budget will be viewed as a rough index of her prosperity. Our gross contribution will be considered as our VAT contribution plus the same percentage of the Community's receipts from customs duties and agricultural levies. For example, if in a given year Britain's VAT contribution proves to be 20 per cent of the Community's total take, then Britain's gross contribution to the budget will be considered as 20 per cent of the Community revenue as a whole. From this total, Community aid to the UK will be deducted. This will be deemed to be Britain's net contribution, two-thirds of which will then be returned to Britain in the form of a rebate. (A detailed note on this difficult subject is available from any Commission office.)

THE BUDGET

The Community budget represents less than 1 per cent of the Gross National Product of the member States; the argument about its size is less contentious than how it is spent.

Currently, agriculture and fisheries account for between two-thirds and three-quarters of total spending. This is a considerable drop from the 80.6 per cent recorded in 1973, but still far too high. Subsidising stocks of food for which there are few buyers leaves far too little to tackle the problems of today – unemployment, aid for the Third World, the challenge of the new technologies, the environment, disaster relief, regional and social policy, and so on.

The success of the Common Agricultural Policy is real. It has improved efficiency and prevented shortages of food. But the CAP long ago ran slap up against the limits of the market. Europe is awash with dairy products and, at times, grain and beef. While many areas of the world are starving, this is a disgrace and an affront to mankind. Reform remains essential.

A beginning, at least, has been made. The Community's current policy for restricting CAP expenditure limits guaranteed prices, increases the producer's share of the cost of disposing of surpluses, and imposes penalties for over-production in the dairy sector, which is largely responsible for the CAP's huge storage costs. Nonetheless, CAP expenditure has already meant one increase in the VAT contribution to the budget, and will assuredly mean another unless reforms are implemented.

Determining the size and shape of the budget is a complex process.

For detailed information see coloured pages A17/18

It begins with a draft prepared by the Commission. This takes into account expenditure already committed or expected, probable income, and the guidelines and priorities laid down by the Council of Ministers and the Parliament. Like every domestic or national budget, it must make a series of calculated bets on such matters as food prices, the values of currencies, changes in earning power, and what is happening in the world at large. Once agreed by the Commission it is put to the Council of Ministers for debate, lengthy discussion, and invariably amendment. Once the Council has adopted the revised draft (which it can do by a qualified majority) it goes on to the European Parliament, and an increasingly rough passage.

Parliament has the right to reject the whole budget – a power exercised several times because it disagreed both with its overall size and the priorities awarded by the Council. It can also alter the budget marginally up or down, probably by about 10 per cent either way. (In this, at least, the European Parliament is unique in the world.) Parliament has used its budgetary powers as a political lever; in some senses its most positive achievement has been to establish machinery for the resolution of budgetary conflict between the Commission and the Council. Parliament is also a valuable ally of the Court of Auditors in keeping an eye on how the money is actually spent, and whether the Commission has monitored this properly.

Much of the money which the Community administers falls outside the budget. The European Development Fund (see p. 116), the European Investment Bank and the European Coal and Steel Community borrow on the world markets and lend on their own initiative and standing.

Nor does the budget by any means reflect total expenditure on Community policies. Pump-priming is a most important element of Community spending. Relatively modest expenditure by the Community has led to expansion in trade, greater competitiveness and productivity, and economics of scale which have dwarfed the size of the initial investment. The Community budget has strengthened the voice of Europe in healthy disproportion to its size.

1986 saw a new and serious budget crisis. The draft budget, agreed in late 1985, was a delicate compromise, negotiated after months of intense and detailed argument. For the first time it established financial guidelines for CAP spending, insisting that it should grow more slowly than the Community's own resources while stocks were reduced. The VAT ceiling was increased from 1 per cent to 1.4 per cent and provision was made for the accession of Spain and Portugal – all for an increase of 3.2 per cent over the previous year, less than the cost of inflation.

The Parliament threw this out in December 1985, and indeed the President of the Parliament signed a budget adding some £400 million, with the recommendation that much more should be spent

For detailed information see coloured pages A17/18

on regional and social policies, and in fields other than agricultural ones. The Council of Ministers challenged Parliament's right to do this, and the matter was put to the European Court, which in June 1986 declared the budget signed by the Parliament as being unlawful.

Hurried redrafts were made. But by this time the fall in the dollar had brought about an inescapable rise in agricultural spending. This, coupled with massive reductions in Britain's payments into the budget on the terms agreed in Fontainebleu, meant that the eventual budget was far higher than the version which the Parliament had eventually signed. It was not until July that the 1986 budget was agreed, by which time a great deal of money had been committed or spent, and it was clear that future budgets would cause similar problems.

Commission thinking, to quote the current Programme, is that 'budgeting on a year-to-year basis has proved inadequate for the sound management of Community policies'. It is recommended that budgets should be adopted on a multi-annual basis (perhaps covering four years), with annual reviews in the light of Community developments. According to the Programme, 'since there must be extreme budgetary rigour, clear, sometimes difficult political choices will have to be made' – which is putting it mildly.

In its report on the financing of the Community budget in February 1987, the Commission published a five-year financial perspective 1988–92. These forecasts – made at constant prices – may be summed up as follows: the growth in FEOGA guarantee expenditure, the doubling of other funds (regional, social, etc, known collectively as structural funds though not to be confused with the 'structural' or guidance section of the agricultural budget), the promotion of research and other essential Community policies, the introduction of new policies and measures for the correction of budgetary imbalances. The structure of the budget would be substantially changed leaving agricultural guarantee expenditure accounting for slightly over 50 per cent. The 1988 budget and the future financing of the Community's activities were the main items on the agenda of the European Council meeting in Copenhagen on 4 and 5 December. Sadly, not enough common ground was found for decisions to be adopted. However, under the terms of the Single European Act a new 'own resources' system for Community financing has been proposed.

TAXES

With the Common Market a quarter of a century old we are still stopped by customs men at national frontiers. The smuggler yet plies his unlawful but profitable trade.

The problem, of course, is the difference between taxes and excise duties in different Community countries. There is, as yet, nothing

For detailed information see coloured pages A17/18

remotely resembling free trade in wine, whisky or tobacco. As the White Paper on the internal market dolefully puts it: 'There is no way of removing frontier controls for goods subject to excise duties whilst the present significant differentials in coverage and rates exist'.

There is another problem. The Common Market is founded on the free movement not only of people and goods, but of services and capital from one Community country to another, on fair terms. Different company taxation can lead to terms which are very far from fair. Bringing closer together the tax burdens suffered by companies in various countries is necessary, both to avoid the perpetuation and extension of the 'golden triangle' of investment location, and to try to make production costs and return on investment as far as possible equal, irrespective of in which area of the Community a company chooses to operate.

Tax harmonisation should help to solve many of these problems, and make travel and business between Community nations less complicated. But it is easier said than done.

At the level of taxation on personal income there are wide differences between countries. There is also, to put it mildly, a very considerable distinction between what citizens of certain countries *should* pay and what they actually *do* pay! VAT ranges from 8.2 per cent of total tax receipts in Britain to 21 per cent in France. Excise duty is responsible for 21 per cent of the national tax in Ireland but only 4.7 per cent in Holland. There are great differences in taxes on companies, too. Corporation tax accounts for 3 per cent of total tax revenue in Italy but 13 per cent in Luxembourg.

Attempting to reconcile these widely disparate approaches has so far been a lengthy and largely unproductive business. Partly this has been for the obvious reason that sovereignty in tax matters, which is basic to the democratic process, is properly regarded as a fundamental prerogative of national parliaments. Partly it has been because tax adjustments (sometimes frequent and dramatic) have proved an indispensable national weapon during the recent rolling economic crisis in industrialised Europe. But tax harmonisation remains a necessary step in gradual moves towards economic and monetary union.

Five priorities have been established in the field of taxation:

(a) a uniform basis for VAT assessment;
(b) bringing excise duties closer together;
(c) harmonising taxation where it directly influences capital movements inside the Community;
(d) further equalising taxation on companies and firms;
(e) extending duty-free concessions to private travellers who cross frontiers within the Community.

In some of these areas there has been a degree of success. VAT is

For detailed information see coloured pages A17/18

now assessed on a uniform basis. There are agreed rules for reimbursing VAT to non-residents, and plans for harmonising arrangements for VAT collection on works of art, antiques and secondhand goods. Spot checks will soon replace formal controls at frontiers between member states, and a single document is being introduced for shippers and transporters. Tax-free allowances and small gifts have gradually been increased in value for private travellers between member States. Two Directives provide for cooperation and mutual assistance between member States in trapping tax evaders and preventing fraud. Taxes on capital formation are now uniform throughout the Community.

But little progress has been made on a proposal for a common system for company taxation, the approximation of systems for taxation of dividends at source, or on the elimination of some forms of double taxation.

Probably least progress has been made on excise duties. This is scarcely surprising, since such duties are a very important part of Government income in all Community countries, but vary spectacularly. Proposals for harmonising the structure and basis of taxation on excise duties on tobacco and alcohol, the big earners for governments, have met with little success in the Council. At the time of writing, five countries are the subject of actions in the European Court of Justice on such matters as discriminating against whisky and cognac.

★ ★ ★ ★

More generally, there is a raft of proposals, draft Directives, and amendments to existing legislation, covering not only taxation and excise duties but banking, insurance, security transactions, capital documents, stock exchanges and company law. To attempt to summarise them here is unnecessary since the White Paper on the Internal Market tackles the task. Within its overall remit of abolishing barriers to trade, the Paper lays out Commission thinking on all these fields, and a timetable by which the necessary legislation should be agreed.

THE EUROPEAN MONETARY SYSTEM

The idea of money which you can spend anywhere in Western Europe is a straightforward and attractive one, which the non-economically minded can understand. It is also demonstrably coming nearer.

The purpose of the European Monetary System is, however, considerably wider in purpose than this. It aims to create a zone of monetary stability in the Community, provide a framework for collective discipline in economic policy, and contribute to a convergence of economic performance in the Community,

For detailed information see coloured pages A17/18

particularly in respect of inflation and the balance of payments.

The economies of the Community nations are highly interdependent: half of all EC trade is internal. During the 1970s, the very future of the trade and agricultural policies of the Community was threatened by wild swings in currency values.

The EMS, established in 1979, has as its objective the creation of a zone of monetary stability, economic convergence, and the control or reduction of inflation. It has worked, on the whole, very well. All Community countries except Greece and Portugal are members; all except these three and Britain participate in the system's exchange rate mechanism. The European Currency Unit (ECU) is used by the Community institutions and widely in the public sector for borrowing and lending. It is composed of a 'basket' of currencies backed by major banks, and its value is calculated daily: it is currently worth about 65 pence.

A central rate in ECU is fixed for each currency in the system, which can be varied by mutual agreement. Such central rates are used to establish a grid of bilateral exchange rates, expressed and published daily in national currencies. These rates, like the old snake, move in a 'tunnel' – a margin of fluctuation of at most 2.25 per cent up or down. (There is special dispensation for Italy and Spain which announced its attention to become a full member in Spring 1989.) If currencies show signs of exceeding these limits, central banks must intervene.

The EMS contains a new element, in the shape of a 'warning bell', which gives advance warning when a country is nearing the roof or the floor of the 'tunnel'. This enables gradual rather than dramatic action to keep currencies in line.

After slightly difficult beginnings, the EMS has established its value to the full members beyond doubt. It has survived the second oil shock, the extraordinary ascendancy and subsequent decline of the dollar, and the worst of the recession.

Particularly during 1984/1986, exchange rate movements within the Community have been roughly similar against the dollar in all countries except the UK. By comparison with the swings in the Yen and the Pound, the EMS has provided a zone of relative tranquility.

In 1980 the average rate of inflation in the Community was 11.5 per cent. It is currently running at 5.4 per cent. As the Commissioner in charge has put it: 'In times of crisis the existence of the EMS and the importance attached to it have prompted the adoption of difficult, brave decisions which kept the Community in one piece.'

Since 1985 the ECU has been an official reserve asset. Non-EC central banks now hold official ECU in their reserves – a particular advantage for countries such as Austria and Switzerland, which have extensive trade links with the Community but are not members. Even the Soviet Union now trades in ECUs. The declared ambition of the Commission is to establish the unit as a world reserve currency on a par with the dollar and the yen.

★ ★ ★ ★

For detailed information see coloured pages A18

There is great disappointment in other Community countries that the UK has not allowed the Pound to enter the System. The reasons for this unhappiness are psychological as well as practical: the absence of the Pound is seen as another example of Britain's unreadiness to enter wholeheartedly into the Community enterprise. The British Government has several times declared that the time was not ripe for the Pound to enter the System. Since the Pound has, since the EMS was set up, fluctuated wildly from over two dollars to just over one dollar, it is hard to see how the time can not have been very ripe indeed at some point of the pendulum. There is almost complete unanimity in business circles and financial institutions in the UK: the Pound should join, and soon.

At its meeting in Hanover on 27 and 28 June 1988 the European Council recalled that, 'in adopting the Single European Act, the Member States of the Community confirmed the objective of progressive realisation of economic and monetary union'. The President of the Commission, Jacques Delors, was empowered to set up a committee whose task would be to study (and eventually propose) concrete stages leading towards this union. In early 1989, the committee reported (see Committee for the Study of Economic and Monetary Union 'Report on economic and monetary union in the EC' available from the European Commission).

For detailed information see coloured pages A18

CONSUMERS

There has been a consumer choice explosion in the Community, particularly in the last decade. Shops now offer fifteen cheeses where they used to offer five; confectionary made in half a dozen Community countries sits side by side on counters from Sicily to Copenhagen. Electrical goods, kitchen equipment, clothing, tobacco, fruit and vegetables, glass – there is a profusion of options.

This poses problems. How can consumers be protected against faults in products from other countries? How can they get redress if things do go wrong? How can they be sure that what they eat is wholesome? How can they be certain that safety glass is equally safe, no matter which car they choose to buy?

Such questions are not new. Indeed, there have been thousands of laws in separate nations covering consumer protection since goods began to be exported. The trouble is that laws differ, and are applied with differing degrees of severity. Many are fair and sensible; others are designed purely to keep out inconveniently attractive or low-priced products, thereby protecting local industry.

What we want as consumers is basically simple: more for our money, a range of choice, a guarantee that what we order is what we actually get, and redress if goods are faulty. But consumer protection is very far from simple, even in a single country. That the law is difficult to enforce is clear from the growth of consumers' societies and their magazines; the problem is exacerbated when people are buying products manufactured hundreds of miles away, in countries with different laws.

Consumer protection in the Community context means not only supranational legislation, but the creation of conditions in which consumers can participate in the decisions which concern them as buyers and users, and in which consumer organisations can exert influence on manufacture, distribution, selling practice, and guarantees not only at home, but in the Common Market as a whole.

There has been a Community consumer policy since 1972, and it already has a decent track record. Several dozen major rules have been agreed which bring national legislation into line on consumer health and safety without impeding the free movement of goods.

On *foodstuffs*, there are Directives governing labelling (shelf-life, contents, additives, etc), safe packaging, truthful advertising, permissible levels for colouring matter and preservatives, and the composition of certain products – honey, fruit juices, etc – to ensure that they do not mislead purchasers. There are also provisions for monitoring the effects of certain foods on health, particularly fruit and vegetables which may contain pesticide residues. There are

For detailed information see coloured pages A18

rules on trade in fresh meat and its quality, and on frozen foods.

Cosmetics are subject to rules on labelling and packaging; agreement has been reached on the mutual banning of some 350 substances which might have an adverse effect on health, and the monitoring of others.

Several Directives govern the marketing and presentation of *pharmaceuticals* and of *toxic substances.* In the case of *motor-cars and trucks* there are agreed rules on resistance to shock, control of pollution, safety glass, exhaust gas emissions, rear-view mirrors, etc.

On *prices,* there have been a great many examples of Community action to prevent cartels or dual pricing policies, particularly in the case of medicines and alcohol.

Directives have been adopted on *energy consumption* (electrical appliances will eventually be labelled indicating the cost per hour of operating them), and the *unit price* of foodstuffs (is 440ml at 69p cheaper than X fluid ounces at 84p with 20 per cent added?) will be made simpler and clearer. There are also plans for particularly explicit labelling of frozen foods.

Those hooked by the more unscrupulous methods of *door-step selling* will now have a 'cooling-down' period of seven days, time to think it over after having been persuaded to sign a contract of £35 or more. (This will *not* affect door-step deliveries of food and drink.) On *hire purchase* and other consumer credit transactions, contracts must indicate the true rate of interest in clear and simple terms.

An agreement on *toys* will forbid the use of toxic paints, dangerously sharp fasteners in woolly animals, etc. More detailed proposals are in the pipeline for the prevention of *domestic accidents,* (which cost more in a year than the entire Community budget) particularly poisoning, fire and electrocution, caused by faulty appliances and other goods. Studies are at present being carried out on the *fire risk* presented by some clothing, furnishing and fittings, and the safety problems of *cleaning fluids* and other potentially dangerous substances used in the home. *Lead-free petrol* was made available in garages in the UK well before the date specified in the Community agreement. A directive on the use of *asbestos* in consumer products has been provisionally agreed by the Council. Discussion is well advanced on an agreement on discouraging trade in *counterfeit goods.*

The two most important agreements of recent years concern *manufacturers' liability* and *misleading advertising.* They have also had the roughest reception.

The Directive on Product Liability was finally agreed in July 1985, although member states were given three years to implement it. Anyone who suffers injury or damage to property as a result of a defect in something he or anyone else has bought can now take legal action against the producer of the article, *whether or not he has been negligent.* The Directive sets no limit to liability (though members

For detailed information see coloured pages A18

states can set one, provided it is high enough to give the consumer real protection).

Clearly the Directive is excellent news for insurance companies and consumers, less so for manufacturers, some of whom have uttered dreadful warnings of price rises – scorned by the consumer associations, who have long argued for an even tougher set of rules. Companies will be able to plead two special defences: 'state of the art' – meaning that scientific or technical knowledge was not sufficiently well developed at the time the product was circulated to detect the defect; and the 'development risks defence' – if the manufacturer can prove that the defect developed after the product was put into circulation. It is up to national governments to decide whether these defences are permissible: the UK has announced that they probably will be, to the fury of the Consumers' Association.

The Directive to curb misleading advertising has been around in various forms since 1975. When first published in full draft it covered unfair as well as misleading advertising; the first adjective was later dropped, since it became apparent that member states were unable to agree on what 'unfair' meant. Even in its watered down form it was greeted with howls of rage in the British press, prompted by some of the more successful companies and their advertising agents, but also for the sound reason that the original wording of the Directive might have meant standards in Britain actually dropping, and that the powers of the self-regulating Advertising Standards Authority might be undermined. These objections were overcome in a later draft, and the Directive was finally agreed in June 1984. During 1985 the DTI circulated a consultation document on ways in which it might best be implemented as from the end of 1986.

The purpose of the Directive is to protect both consumers and businessmen from 'any advertising which in any way, including its presentation, deceives or is likely to deceive the persons to whom it is addressed or whom it reaches'. (Political advertising is exempt!)

In many respects Britain already has standards more rigorous than those demanded by the Directive, and will of course keep them. But the new laws will give more power to the Director General of Fair Trading, on whose recommendation the courts will consider the possible prohibition of advertising which may be misleading in terms of the Directive. The real controversy has concerned the possibility that the Director General of Fair Trading should in future be empowered to act in respect of *broadcast* advertising, which is at present regulated solely by the Independent Broadcasting Authority and the proposed new Cable Authority.

Much argument lies ahead on this particular front. However it is resolved, the need to have controls on fraudulent claims in advertising is certain to become more important and more urgent as 'armchair shopping' via television develops exponentially.

Three other important initiatives are promised. The Commission

For detailed information see coloured pages A18

is charged with working for the improvement of:

(1) *commercial services linked to products.* Proper repairing, supply of parts and guarantee conditions are all vital components of the purchase price when one is buying a car, a television set or a washing machine. But the quality of service and the reliability of estimates varies enormously from company to company and country to country;

(2) commercial services *not linked to a product:* organised trips, package holidays, insurance, consumer credit, etc, where again standards differ greatly and where there are sometimes no authorities to whom to appeal if things go wrong;

(3) the *relationship between consumers and public administrations* particularly in the field of transport, and the possibility of some form of trans-border 'ombudsman' to settle disputes.

The accent in future will be on better consumer *information.* This will cover true prices, the real value of guarantees and warranties, comparative tests, simpler and better labelling, help with cooperation and visits between consumers organisations in various countries, and the development of consumer education in both secondary and primary schools, particularly with regard to nutrition.

In early 1986 the Commission published detailed proposals for 'A New Impetus for Consumer Protection Policy'. This was welcomed by the Council in June, and the Commission is currently drawing up proposals for formal submission. A House of Lords Report (17 June 1986) backed the paper in general and made some useful suggestions.

★ ★ ★ ★

A Consumers' Consultative Committee exists to make the voice of the consumer heard in Brussels and Strasbourg. It is composed of representatives of the principal European consumer organisations, and gives them a chance to coordinate their actions and speak to the Commission and the Parliament more directly. The Committee publishes detailed opinions and is consulted when draft papers on any subject are being prepared if they have implications for the consumer. British consumer organisations have been particularly active and effective on the Community front. They have excellent links with the institutions and their counterparts on the Continent, sponsor many conferences and seminars on consumer topics, and produce a variety of booklets and 'state of play' papers.

For detailed information see coloured pages A18

YOUTH AND EDUCATION

Fifty eight million citizens of the European Community are in full-time education. They will shape its future, and have traditionally been among its most enthusiastic supporters. But how long may this last?

None remembers a war in Europe. Few are now reminded of the Community's achievements by their parents, who take them for granted. Three-quarters of young Europeans complain, in public opinion polls, that they do not have enough information about the Community and its policies. Nor have they, as their parents had, much obvious reason to believe that it is good for them: young people account for 20 per cent of the potential workforce, but 40 per cent of the unemployed.

Tackling this, by job creation and training (see the section on Employment, and also Part VII), and establishing better links between school and work, must clearly be the first priority. Seventy five per cent of the Social Fund is now devoted to the under 25s, and since 1983 member states are pledged to grant a 'social guarantee' to youngsters who leave school without qualifications, whereby all will have the opportunity of a minimum of six months' training.

But there are longer-term issues at stake. If the Community is to mean anything to its peoples, if we are to pool our energies, enthusiasms and ideas and learn to become better neighbours, the process is best begun at school.

There are few references to education in the Treaties, and it took ministers of education 20 years before they could agree on proposals for joint action and money to support them. The sums available are still nugatory, but a start has been made, and the present outlook is more encouraging.

Commission objectives, apart from the first task of smoothing the transition from school to working life, are:

(a) More exchanges of information, students and teachers;
(b) Equality of opportunity in education;
(c) Foreign language teaching;
(d) Education in European current affairs;
(e) The wider use of new technologies in schools.

On *exchanges,* the Community has (surely rightly) concentrated on encouraging 'twinned' initiatives rather than paying bills. There are, however, three new schemes called COMETT, ERASMUS and YES. They have the same aim in different fields: to help forge a new generation of young Europeans who are

For detailed information see coloured pages A18/19

more flexible than their elders, know and understand each other better, are reactive to change, and conscious of their future role as good citizens not only of their own country but of the Community as a whole.

COMETT (Community in Education and Training for Technology) was agreed at the end of 1985 and is currently running. The plan is to help more than 10,000 computer science and electronics students gain a six-month place in industry in another Community country. There will also be places for 350 academic staff and 350 business graduates. The budget is for £56 million for the initial stage, and national governments as well as the Community will contribute. The programme will also look at new and better ways of teaching, including distance learning systems and new technological methods, in coordination with the DELTA scheme (see below). The ultimate aim is to establish a European network of university/ industry training partnerships, with joint schemes and projects in the new technologies and a Community-wide data base. Enquiries: by letter to Dr A Kirchberger, DGV in the Commission in Brussels, or from COMETT Technical Assistance Unit, 71 Avenue de Cortenberg, B1040 Brussels.

ERASMUS has a somewhat forced translation (European Community Action Scheme for the Mobility of University Students) but a better *raison d'être*: the fact that there was considerably more traffic between the students of Europe when Erasmus was teaching in the late fifteenth and sixteenth centuries than there is today. Unlike COMETT, it is concerned not only with the new technologies but with all disciplines 'from medicine to the arts, from economics to history'. The scheme is also considerably more ambitious in its financial recommendations.

The objective is to ensure that by 1992 at least one European student in 10 will be able to undertake at least 3 months of their degree studies in another member state. Cooperation in the fields of research or continuing education are not eligible for ERASMUS financial support. In 1987, 5500 student grants or scholarships were available, double that number in 1988, and five times as many in 1989. There will also be funding available for the holding of intensive 'teach-ins' for gifted students. Other plans include preparatory visits by university staff, the setting up of a European University Network, and pilot schemes to make academic recognition of degrees acquired abroad less difficult. The Commission wants about £110 million in funds for the scheme, and will go on asking for it (with the support of the Parliament).

The most recent programme, Youth for Europe (Youth Exchange Scheme) is part of the 'People's Europe' concept (see Part VI). This is aimed at a younger age-group – the 16s to 25s – and should enable 80,000 of them to make a visit of at least a week to another member state of a fairly nitty-gritty kind, enabling trainees to be placed in

For detailed information see coloured pages A18/19

work situations where they can see at first hand the problems and opportunities which they share as Europeans. It will build on the excellent groundwork established by such bodies as the Central Bureau for Educational Visits and Exchanges and the Young Workers Exchange programmes, but will aim at a wider mix in terms of social, economic and cultural background.

Funding will be very far from lavish – probably an average of £200 per exchange for travel and pocket money – and cooperation at local and national level by youth organisations, quangos, local and national government, and industry will be an essential part of the scheme.

In its proposal, agreed in early 1986, the Commission asked for about £20 million, 80 per cent of which went to the exchange visits and the rest to support and planning measures, including study visits for youth workers, preparatory visits, and information campaigns. The scheme has been given a general welcome by the Council and the Parliament and the current rate of funding is £10 million over three years.

All three schemes should build on background already established. The Community has sponsored many seminars on the exchange of information on teaching, developed wide contacts with national education services at various levels, and in particular established EURYDICE (the *Education Information Network in the European Community*). Created in 1980, this has completed the experimental period of its operations. Educational organisations in member states provided data about their systems and methods, which are then made available to policy-makers in education and later to a wider public. A list of documents prepared by the Central Unit of EURYDICE is available from 17 rue Archimède, Bte 17, 1040 Brussels.

Two types of grant are available for helping in the exchange of information and experience. The first (for administrators and researchers) is for *short study visits;* the second (involving universities and other institutions of higher education) helps with *joint study programmes.*

In the case of short study visits, grants normally cover the whole cost of a week's visit to another member state to study general or technical education in action. They are primarily intended for those involved in teaching secondary pupils; officials of education departments are not usually eligible.

Joint study programmes attracted 193 awards during 1985, many to the UK. (A typical grant went to institutions in Belgium, France and Britain to exchange practical ideas in better training for nurses.)

Some twenty grants are made every year for research into *European integration.* These are intended for young university lecturers at the start of their career; the maximum award is £2,500.

For detailed information see coloured pages A18/19

A useful contribution to exchanges of all kinds has been the publication of the *Community Handbook for Students,* designed to plug the information gap which inhibits students in higher education from pursuing courses in Community countries other than their own. It gives detailed information on conditions of admission to higher education in other states, procedures for applying, and details of fees, grants (where available) and social conditions. The National Equivalence Information Centre in the British Council (10 Spring Gardens, SW1A 2BN) can advise on how foreign qualifications are likely to be viewed in Britain, and it is hoped that similar bodies will be established in all member states.

A Commission report on *equality of education and training for girls* in the 10–18 year-old range, written as long ago as 1978, recommended a co-operative action programme of research, teacher training, and special pilot projects. A modest sum to launch this initial programme has been requested. There are also schemes designed to help with the more effective education of migrant workers, the handicapped, and the illiterate.

A scheme established in 1986 offers small grants to help set up and develop youth initiatives – projects created and managed by young people, for young people. These can involve areas such as community work, information and advice for young people, use of the media and new technologies, and help for disadvantaged youngsters. Applicants (between 16 and 25) must raise half the cost of the project themselves; the accent is on teaching new knowledge and skills and readiness to share experience acquired. A leaflet and application form, 'Young People's Projects' is available from any Commission office.

Wider *teaching of foreign languages* is seen not only as being essential to the better operation of the Common Market, but to the wider aims of the Community – the right to live and work anywhere, better political and economic understanding and cooperation. A draft programme drawn up by the Commission suggested that:

(a) all Community citizens should be offered every chance to learn at least one other Community language;
(b) language teachers should have part of their training in the appropriate country, and regular 'refresher' courses;
(c) new language teaching methods should be developed, particularly for adults and less gifted children;
(d) exchanges between language teachers should take place Community-wide;
(e) there should be more pupil exchanges, and a pilot network of schools teaching in several languages.

The programme was welcomed by the Parliament and the Economic and Social Committee, and has been the subject of many pious words by Education Ministers in Council. In 1989 the European

For detailed information see coloured pages A18/19

Commission outlined the new LINGUA programme to encourage the teaching and learning of at least two EC languages throughout the Community.

During 1986 the Commission called for interested bodies to put up ideas for developing European learning through technological advance. This DELTA programme should last for five years, and will cover the developing of learning systems at a European level, testing and development of open learning, and the establishment of a future work programme for Community action. The first objective is defined as 'overcoming distance and access constraints, based largely on existing infrastructures, systems, equipment and technology', moving on in later years to use of artificial intelligence, two-way video communication, and such other marvels of science as may emerge.

The first call for expressions of interest is closed; there will be more in years to come. An outline of DELTA is in Official Journal No. C 60/3 of 15 March 1986.

On the more general question of education about Europe, there has long been a feeling that far too much attention in the classroom has been paid to teaching about past battles, and far too little to the problems, achievements and failures of the past 40 years. Until recently the problem of out-of-date textbooks was exacerbated by almost total opposition among local authorities in Britain to allow what was seen as 'propaganda' material into the classroom. Hearteningly (and perhaps because material about the Community has in fact become less propagandist) this attitude has changed dramatically. Requests for simple, illustrated material and maps now pour into Commission information offices. There are also available two specific aids for teachers: a set of slides and an accompanying teachers' handbook entitled 'The European Economic Community – Past, Present and Future', aimed at senior pupils, and a project for primary schools entitled 'Your Europe' by Sarah J. Pope. Both are part-funded by the Commission. The first is available on loan from Commission information offices; the second is available, price £9.95, from Holmes McDougall of 137 Leith Walk, Edinburgh.

A useful guide to those wishing to study or work in Europe has been produced by the European Democratic Group. Chapters include: studying in Europe, holiday work, post-graduate training, exchange schemes, earning your living and opportunities for longer-term work. 'A Student's Guide to Europe' is free from 32 Smith Square, London SW1P 3HH.

For detailed information see coloured pages A18/19

TRAVELLING AND WORKING IN EUROPE

In theory, a British passport is not only a licence to pass without let or hindrance through the 12 countries of the European Community: it also enables you to find work there, anywhere, at any time, with equal rights to those enjoyed by the citizens of the country you happen to be in.

In practice, of course, the streets of Paris, Rome or Hamburg are no more paved with gold than the streets of London. In a Community with an unemployment rate on a par with Britain's (and in some regions higher) finding a job is likely to be more, rather than less difficult than finding one in Britain itself. Nor will professional or trade qualifications necessarily unlock any doors.

Travelling in Europe is simpler than it has ever been, and you are automatically entitled, as a citizen of the Community, to free medical care and social security. But there are exceptions to this rule and major differences in the way you achieve treatment or social benefits.

Go prepared, whether travelling or looking for work.

TRAVELLING

A Community passport is being phased in. In the meantime your own works in all EC countries, and a simple travel document in most. Two other documents are essential: Form E111, required for medical treatment should you fall ill or have an accident, and Leaflets SA30 and SA36 which go into the matter in detail. Both are free from DHSS. Get them before you leave. If you should have the misfortune to suffer illness or an accident which means a period of convalescence, get immediate advice on your rights locally.

If you are driving in the Community you will need an international driving permit – cheap, and available through the motoring organisations, which also offer packs of useful advice on such matters as reflective triangles, differing laws, unfamiliar traffic signals, and penalties for driving offences. (Driving a 'one-eyed' car at night in Belgium can result in drastic action by the police, probably a fat fine on the spot; if you cannot pay it you may find yourself in a police station, pronto.)

Life may become easier for drivers if a Commission draft paper on road safety (backed by the European Parliament) becomes law. It aims, *inter alia,* to make road signs and signals easier to understand, establish higher standards for the testing of vehicles for roadworthiness, limit speeds for buses and vehicles carrying dangerous goods, prescribe tougher penalties in certain countries for drivers under the influence of drugs or alcohol, and encourage

For detailed information see coloured pages A19

measures to help the most accident-prone-groups – the young, the elderly and the handicapped – plus much more.

In early 1986 the Commission published proposals for Community action in the tourism sector, which already accounts for about 7 per cent of consumer spending and at least five million jobs. These recommend easy-to-understand symbols and information concerning hotels used throughout the Community, more staggering of annual holidays, and better consultation between the tourist boards of the various states. A first study of the holiday preferences of 12,000 EC citizens was published in July 1986.

During 1985 a 'Traveller's Charter' was proposed by the Commission. This would include a freeze on holiday prices in the last 30 days before departure, and suggests that holidaymakers should be given compensation as well as refunds when their holidays are cancelled at the last minute. Travel agents in the UK have yet to give their detailed response to these proposals.

WORKING IN EUROPE

As citizens of the Community we have the right to move freely in any Community country and work there. This does not give you the right to choose your job; but it does include treatment on the same basis as nationals of the country of your choice when it comes to wages, working conditions, taxation, social insurance, the right to send for your family and dependents, the right to rent or buy a house, to qualify for vocational training, and to join a trade union.

You are also entitled, provided you have a full British passport, to go to the country of your choice and stay for three months while you look for work. You will be paid unemployment benefit during that period, *provided* you have been available for work in Britain for a month previously, and provided you immediately register with an employment office in the country of your choice. (These rules do not apply at present to Greece, Spain or Portugal.) If you cannot find work after three months you may be asked to leave the country.

These are the broad outlines. Today, with unemployment (particularly among the young) a serious problem in every Community country, it is essential to read the small print.

Start with a call at your Jobcentre. A free leaflet, 'Working Abroad', is available there. They should also be able to give you DHSS leaflet SA 29, entitled 'Your Social Security and Pension Rights in the European Community'.

You should also be able to get, from the Jobcentre, an indication of what sort of vacancies may be available, and where. Generally, skilled posts are more easily acquired than unskilled ones. The most likely openings are for secretaries, accountants, teachers, nurses, and specialists who may find a place in a UK company based in Europe or a multinational.

A second language is essential in many parts of Europe, and

For detailed information see coloured pages A19

increases your chances of employment dramatically everywhere. Put another way, your chance of finding a job, even in Holland or Germany, if all you can offer is English, must nowadays be rated as Lucky Accident Only.

If you can, find work before you pack your bags. The Jobcentre can help with this. If they have nothing immediately available they will use their established links with the employment services in other Community countries. This costs you nothing.

If you get an offer, make sure you are clear about exactly what it means. Surprisingly often there may be a chance of getting at least temporary accommodation thrown in with the job. Make sure about the situation for your family, if you have one. Be certain of whether you must pay your own fare, or if your employer is paying all or part of it, what your rights are in law if you leave the job. If everything is in order, move fast. Phone. Job-hunters (and employers) don't hang about on the Continent.

WHAT TO DO WHEN YOU GET THERE

You will not need a visa or work permit in any Community country except Greece, Spain or Portugal. But you must, when you enter a country to look for work, immediately register with the local police, arrange for a residence permit, and contact an employment office.

Provided you prepare in advance, you should get unemployment benefit as soon as you register for work in a Community country. Apply before you go at your local DHSS office. But not all countries are equally speedy or efficient in paying social benefits, and finding a job may take longer (and cost more in transport and accommodation) than you think. Make sure you have enough money to live on for at least a month.

If you are self-employed or propose to set up a company you must conform to the rules relating to the right of establishment. These vary: a full guide is available from HMSO, entitled 'Freedom of Movement for Persons in the European Community'. If you retain your UK resident status while working elsewhere in the Community you will usually be able to transfer such funds 'as may be needed to establish a home in the new country of employment', and can rent or buy a house anywhere in the Community *on the same terms as any local citizen.* That is the point: housing laws vary widely. Check in advance with the embassy of the country concerned. If you are taking children with you, plan in advance for their education.

PROFESSIONAL QUALIFICATIONS

Freedom to work anywhere in the Community does not imply that you can demand to do the same job there as you do in Britain. The Community is moving towards interchangeability of professional qualifications, but progress has been slow.

For detailed information see coloured pages A19

Pharmacists, nurses, dentists, vets, midwives, architects and hairdressers can, in theory, work anywhere. Employment is relatively easy for road hauliers and lawyers. Some 80 Directives make freedom of movement in jobs and professions easier in agriculture, the power and water industries, banking, finance and insurance, the liberal professions, and many others; but there are snags – read the small print before you go.

EMPLOYMENT WITH THE COMMUNITY'S INSTITUTIONS

Jobs with the Commission, the Council, the Parliament, the Court, and the other Community institutions do not crop up often. Each body recruits separately by open competition; such competitions are invariably advertised, almost always in *The Times* and usually in several other national and provincial dailies. (Technical jobs are advertised in the appropriate trade journals. They will also be mentioned in the Official Journal.)

Virtually all competitions require practical experience and a working knowledge of another Community language in addition to English. If you reply to an advertisement you will be given an application form for a competition; should your qualifications merit it you will be boarded, usually in London. Successful candidates in these competitions are placed on a reserve list against future vacancies; there is no guarantee that being successful in reaching this reserve list will eventually result in a job.

Most entrants into the Community's institutions join at or near the beginning of their career, although in the upper grades specialists are recruited separately. For certain posts a degree (or equivalent experience) is essential; for others, largely in the clerical grades, posts are reserved for those who have not been able to obtain a degree.

For posts in translation and interpretation, at least two languages other than English are required. Interest in the subjects covered by the Community, and a good working knowledge of these languages are considered more important than total fluency in any language other than your native tongue.

THE 'STAGIAIRE' SCHEME

Certain in-service trainee posts are available. They are strictly temporary, and last from three to five months, with no guarantee of future employment. The Commission organises twice a year in-service training periods lasting between three and five months for candidates from universities and from the public and private sectors. The training periods start on 1 March and 1 October each year. The purpose of in-service training with the Commission is: to give trainees a general idea of the objectives and problems of

For detailed information see coloured pages A19

European integration; to provide them with practical knowledge of the working of the Commission departments; to enable them to further and put into practice the knowledge they have acquired during their studies or professional careers. There are about 200 places a year, and competition is stiff. Candidates must apply about six months ahead of their intended starting date. If they are shortlisted, they are chosen in the light of opportunities in the Commission.

Payment is strictly breadline, but there is a camaraderie and flexibility in the stagiaire scheme which makes the finding of accommodation relatively easy. A good working knowledge of a second language (two others in the case of those applying for linguist work) is again essential.

Information: any Commission office, or direct from DG IX, Training Division, The Commission of the European Communities, 200 rue de la Loi, Brussels 1049.

PART VI

POLICIES IN PROCESS OF CHANGE

Painting the Forth Bridge poses a well-known dilemma. Once you have finished, you must start all over again, which gives you a job for life. On the other hand, your work is going to look pretty scruffy and out of date for a lot of the time.

Thus with this sort of book. Certain Community policies (agriculture, for example, or the ideas for a new kind of Community) are changing day by day. Try to offer more than guidelines, and you will never make it to the printers. This is even more the case now as we run up to 1992.

This is a particular pity in the case of the international role of the Community, arguably the most important of all. As a force in the world, the Community is often more fully recognised in Tokyo, Belgrade or Washington than in London or Paris. The Commission Directorate-General which deals with External Relations (DGI) is by far the largest. Apart from having some 50 senior officials in Brussels, it has Delegations (often, in effect, EC embassies) in 80 nations outside the Community, and is in daily touch with the 100-plus ambassadors from third countries based in Brussels.

The impact of the Community at international level, in politics as in trade, is worthy of a book of its own; but how would you write it? Even during the weeks which I spent at the typewriter on this superficial pocketbook, so much happened on the world stage in which the Community was involved that any attempt to encapsulate it would have been hopeless.

The concerned reader, then, must not miss his *Financial Times*, *Independent* and European Information Service. All that can be offered here are a few markers. The weekly press releases from the European Commission are also an invaluable source of reference.

POLITICAL COOPERATION

The concept of political cooperation is implicit in every clause of the Community Treaties, but is rarely mentioned. Nor, until very recently, has it been spoken about publicly by politicians. No mystery in that. Political cooperation is the most direct form of

For detailed information see coloured page A19

pooling sovereignty – a practice sensibly adopted by governments in most parts of the world, but admitted nowhere. The President or Prime Minister who attends a 'summit' conference or a state funeral understandably wishes to convey the impression that it was he or she who came back with the goodies having given nothing away. So, too, the Minister who attends a Council meeting in Brussels.

However, we now find the Community negotiating more and more at the international level, not with 12 different voices but with one. This is true not only of the long-established meeting-places of the world – GATT, the United Nations – but at a day-by-day level. The impact of 12 ambassadors in Washington or Moscow saying the same thing with different accents is worth a great deal more than the sum of its parts. It could not be achieved without the cooperation, at the top levels, of the governments of the Community.

At the other end of the scale, terrorists, sky-jackers, drug dealers and other internationally active rogues fear, above all things, transborder cooperation. Enmity and lack of political trust between nations provide them with the tools of their wretched trade, and the refuge they need when they are rumbled.

Sitting between two super-powers, the Community cannot itself become one, if only because of the diversity which gives it its spirit and value. The EC has however been described as a 'civilian power'. But it does have diplomatic ties, in its own right, with more than 100 nations. The Commission takes part in Western economic summits, alongside the US, Japan, and four of its own member states. It signs, on behalf of 12 nations, agreements worldwide on matters which go far beyond those of a customs union. The Community has taken joint public stances on such events as the crises in Afghanistan and Poland, the continuing problems of Africa, Central America and the Middle East, and the invasions of Cambodia and the Falklands.

It is not too often that we may credit Britain, and her entry into the Community, with a dynamic and positive contribution. Too frequently in the past (with Denmark and more recently Greece) we have seemed to be driving with the handbrake on, ready at any moment to slam into reverse.

But it is fair to assert that political cooperation in the Community has changed out of all recognition since 1973, and for the better – not least in the Community's relationship with the rest of the world. For this, Britain can properly claim some of the credit.

Since the late 1970s, senior foreign office officials of Community countries (known as Political Directors) have met monthly or more often to prepare for Council meetings. This Political Committee has expert help, good and fast communications at its disposal, and a shadow team of administrators. Until now, it has had no standing in terms of the Treaties, but quietly got on with the job of political cooperation.

For detailed information see coloured page A19

However, at the end of 1985 the Council put matters on a formal basis. A new Secretariat of European Political Cooperation was established under the Council Presidency, continuing the work of the Political Committee but extending its remit, particularly as regards advising the Presidency in political contacts, both within the Community and in third countries. One important role is its responsibility for ensuring that the discussions and outcome of political cooperation meetings are made available in agreed texts in all Community languages. (The old Political Committee worked only in French and English; this made for speed, but meant that what had actually been said and agreed did not always correspond with what those present *thought* had happened, and the price of quick 'agreement' was occasionally followed by statements by individual governments making it plain that they had agreed to no such animal.)

Of equal importance are the guidelines laid down for relations between the apparatus of political cooperation and the European Parliament. The new Secretariat will, of course, still leave political cooperation essentially in the hands of individual governments; there will be no 'voting', majority or otherwise. The Commission will have an important advisory role, but no direct part to play. The Parliament, however, is now to be involved up to the hilt. The Presidency of the Council must regularly inform the Parliament of topics at issue (in advance, where possible), keep Parliament informed quickly on texts agreed, give the appropriate parliamentary committees informal briefing at least four times a year, and take the views of the Parliament into account in its deliberations. The President will address the European Parliament at the start of his term of office, and again at the end of it. Once a year he will give a written, detailed account of progress in the field of political cooperation, and speak in the debate on it. Above all, contacts should be quicker and more full: 'By joint agreement, special information sessions at ministerial level on specific European political cooperation topics may be organised as required'.

There is to be intensified cooperation between diplomatic missions of member States in third countries, better exchange of political and economic information, and joint planning in the case of a local crisis, including droughts, floods and other disasters.

Heads of Commission delegations abroad are to meet regularly with ambassadors and high commissioners from member states to coordinate views, and to examine 'the possibility of providing help and assistance in third countries to nationals of member states which have no representation there'. (A Commission proposal of April 1986 goes a great deal further than this, hinting at the possibilities of joint Community diplomatic missions in smaller countries.)

This brief summary does not cover all the ground; nor does it do

For detailed information see coloured pages A19/20

more than imply the possible difficulties. (The best summary of the proposals is in Commission Bulletin No. 2 of 1986.) But the advances are real. In the cool eye of history, political cooperation may seem the most important achievement of the Community in its second generation, and the UK's most valuable contribution to it.

EXTERNAL TRADE

The Community is a trade entity, with a common external tariff and a coordinated negotiating stance in much of the world's industry and commerce. More and more the member States are conducting their trade affairs, both with the industrialised nations and with the developing world, on a joint basis.

Although intra-Community trade has steadily increased in importance, external trade still accounts for around a quarter of the GDP of the Community countries as a whole. Committed to the highest possible degree of freedom in international trade, the Community must nonetheless strive to safeguard the future of its own internal economy during increasingly difficult times. Few international trade issues are clear-cut. Relations between the Community and the US, for example on such major matters as steel, textiles and agricultural products, are complex in the extreme; there are no blacks or whites and many different shades of grey.

Reference has been made repeatedly to non-tariff barriers which still exist even in the Common Market. They are as nothing compared with those which exist in Japan against goods made in Europe. (For years Perrier water was kept out of Japan on the grounds that it would have to be boiled for health reasons before it could be sold. A British confectionery company selling sherbert was told that the yellow colouring could damage Japanese eye-sight and would have to be changed. Each Dutch flower bulb had, during 1985, to be tested for 'quarantine' reasons in Japanese fields before it could be marketed. A bottle of Scotch whisky exported to Japan attracted, until recently almost eight times the duty levied on the local product; 66 per cent of Japanese surveyed during 1986 believed that 'Monde Napoleon Brandy' was imported from France. It is made in Japan.)

Black and white? Ah, no. We have seen what happened in France when Japanese videorecorder imports threatened the domestic product. (They were successfully kept out by a one-man non-tariff barrier located in a tiny town – the only one in France through which videorecorders could be imported.) The Japanese people, have, for years, insisted on buying the products of their own industries for old-fashioned patriotic reasons. Japanese exports have succeeded throughout the world, not because of low wage levels (Japanese salaries are, in real terms, now above the Community average) but because of their work ethic and the excellence of their products.

For detailed information see coloured page A20

The same can not, alas, be said for many of the Community's other competitors in the Far East and elsewhere. While playing its full part in GATT, OECD and other international bodies concerned with trade, the Community has its own trade policy instruments, operated by the Commission. These concern protection against dumping and subsidised exports from third countries; monitoring the common rules for imports into the Community (particularly from the state-trading countries and from China); and a set of common rules for exports to third countries. The New Commercial Policy Instrument, agreed in September 1984 by the Council, arms the Commission with means of acting quickly in the case of complaints of industrial injury arising from dumping, illegal subsidies at home, or unfair pricing or restrictive policies on Community exports to third countries.

A useful background report (B11/86) available from Commission offices and entitled 'The European Community and Japan' gives a detailed account of the deep rooted problem of the Community's trade deficit with Japan and the Commission's recommendations for tackling it, including increased dialogue and cooperation, opening up the Japanese market, and economic liberalisation under the GATT rules. In an attempt to acquaint Community businessmen with Japanese industry and management, a series of language courses followed by work experience are funded by the Commission. So far some 150 young executives have taken part; about 40 places are offered each year. Details: any branch of Peat, Marwick, Mitchell & Co.

US/EC relations, particularly during GATT negotiations and over steel and agriculture, make spectacular headlines in the press. 'For a full week,' wrote Fred Bridgland, the Brussels correspondent of *The Scotsman,* in August 1986, 'Europe has not been at war with the United States.' The reason, he added, was that there was no one around in Brussels to quarrel with, and the Press ('who can always recognise a good trade war when it dreams one up') were on holiday too, with the exception of Mr Bridgland.

In fact, for all the sound and fury of the newspaper headlines, relations between the Community and the US have again and again been resolved in a spirit of genuine openness and compromise. As George Bush noted in a press conference in Brussels, the Community 'is a healthy family with which the US wants to do business for a long time'. He pointed out that we share bilateral trade of over 100 billion dollars, being each other's biggest trade partners by an enormous margin. He went on: 'It is a real accomplishment that no trade war has broken out between the European Community and the US. We kept our cool and managed to avoid the catastrophe of a trade war which did so much harm in the 1930s. This "negative positive result" has been due to the ability to talk problems over in the

For detailed information see coloured page A20

consultative procedure erected between the Commission and the US.'

He noted that every leading cabinet official in the US dealing with economic matters was in Brussels on that day; others who spoke at the conference were Mr Block, Secretary of Agriculture, Mr Baldridge, Secretary of Commerce, and Mr Regan, Secretary of the US Treasury. It must be some time since such a gathering graced any capital – and it gives a dramatic illustration of the importance America attaches to its trade relations with the Community. On the other side of the world, China, Russia and the Comecon countries are now steadily involving themselves with the Community, more intensively and at higher level; during 1986 the Soviet Union for the first time officially recognised the existence of the Community.

Detailed consideration of these matters, and the Community's importance in terms of world trade, must remain outside the scope of this book, though references to it occur throughout. Apart from reference material listed in the blue pages, three publications are worth mentioning. *Japan – The First Step* is a directory of facilities and services for European Companies considering entry into the Japanese market. A series of articles on the European Community and GATT, including an excellent summary of the Community's external relations and commercial policy, is contained in the November 1986 issue of the Commission's *Staff Courier*. Both can be consulted at any Commission office. Lastly, the magazine *Europe*, published by the Commission's Information Office in Washington, is available for consultation in any Commission office, or can be bought direct ($19.50 per year for 10 issues, plus postage) from 2100 M Street NW, Suite 707, Washington DC 20037. It contains a mass of material on US/EC relations written from the point of view of authors on either side of the Atlantic.

The 'bible' on external trade agreements is entitled 'Agreements and Other Bilateral Commitments linking the Communities and Non-Member Countries', published annually by DG I in the Commission, and available in all Commission offices and EDCs.

THE DEVELOPING WORLD

Short of world war, the greatest problem which mankind faces is surely the potential conflict between north and south, rich and poor. Halting the arms race, fighting through the recession, getting our environment right – all these will avail us nothing if we fail the Third World. It is a moral issue, but also potentially a mortal one: if the gulf between rich and poor continues to widen, global conflict must be inevitable.

Little though the Community does to help the developing world, it does more than anyone else. Indeed, in terms of both public aid

For detailed information see coloured page A20

and trade, more than the United States, the Soviet Union and Japan combined. This having smugly been said, a few facts:

- In Western Europe and America we are about $5000 a year richer in real terms than we were 20 years ago. For more than 2 billion people in the Third World, real earnings have increased by less than $70 a year. In parts of Africa, people have actually become poorer.
- About 750 million people in the world exist in a state of abject poverty.
- The worst casualities of the Western industrial recession are the poor countries, not the rich.
- Agriculture in many Third World countries is becoming less, rather than more efficient.
- The imminent AIDS catastrophe in America and Europe may be as nothing compared with that in Africa. Europe has one doctor for every 500 persons; much of Africa has one for every 25,000.

* * * *

The Community depends on the Third World for 90 per cent of its raw materials and more than half of its energy. The Third World takes more than a third of our exports. Even naked self-interest makes it essential for us to do better by the poor peoples of the world.

The framework exists. The Community takes part in the North-South dialogue and increasingly speaks on behalf of its member States at international meetings. It was the first major body to implement the recommendations of the UN Conference on Trade and Development, and it has responsibility for representing its member states in GATT.

In its scheme of generalized preferences the Community helps the export income of over 120 countries and some 20 dependent territories. This enables them to export the vast majority of their manufactured and semi-manufactured goods to the Community with reduced or zero customs duties. The scheme is non-discriminatory, and corresponding exemptions from duty are not asked for in return.

The Community has its own emergency aid funds which, although pitifully inadequate in relation to the size of the problem, have no strings attached and can often surmount political difficulties in a way bilateral aid can not. It is one of the priority targets of the present Commission to persuade national governments both to meet their individual promises in terms of Third World aid, and to increase the Community's emergency funds.

In the Lomé Convention, and its various agreements with the Southern Mediterranean and in the Middle East, Asia and Latin America, the Community has established aid and cooperation of a

For detailed information see coloured page A20

new kind. Lomé, in particular, establishes a contract between utterly different areas of the world which excludes economic or ideological manipulation or discrimination. Linking well over 80 countries of Africa, the Caribbean and the Pacific (the ACP countries), the Convention, launched in 1975 and renewed in 1979 and 1985 and currently under renegotiation, allows 99.5 per cent of the exports from those countries to enter the Community free of all duties, while asking nothing similar in return. It offers large-scale aid in the form of both capital grants and cheap loans, stabilises those countries' export earnings in difficult years, and gives much expert technical help.

But the importance of Lomé in its inception and during subsequent renewals lies perhaps elsewhere. The ACP nations themselves got together, thrashed out a common stance (despite problems often radically different one from the other) and negotiated with the Community as one. That was, and is, a remarkable thing in the world of today. However, there are many who believe that the EC's relationship with the Lomé group is neo-colonial in nature. This view is based upon the trade balance between the two trading groups, the bias in the relationship towards primary as opposed to processed products, and the small amount of EC monies awarded to the Lomé group under the stabilisation of export earnings programme (STABEX). Moreover, as regards the Community's external relations with the Mediterranean countries, there have been major problems since 1986 when Spain and Portugal joined the EC. The Maghreb countries, in particular Tunisia and Morocco, who have traditionally depended on the EC as an export market for their fresh fruit and vegetables, have claimed that Spanish producers have squeezed them out of the market. EC enlargement has indeed upset the delicate balance of EC external relations in the Mediterranean region.

It is not an easy time for Community countries to do better in terms of helping the developing nations. Money is hard to find even for problems at home. Enlargement of the Community has meant more pressure on the limited money available for internal funding. National treasuries, under attack from all sides, find it difficult to refrain from pointing to the fact that aid to the Third World has often been improperly and unwisely used in the past.

The Commission promises, however, to keep member governments in square face with the problem. In its new guidelines it gives as its first priority financial and practical help for self-supporting and long-term development policies, based on better land use and more efficient agriculture, particularly in the very poorest countries of Africa. This, rather than food or economic aid (essential though both are) is the key to rolling back hunger and poverty, and building an economic framework where other aid can be put to most effective use.

For detailed information see coloured page A20

There are plans for an attack on desertification and the destruction of forests, more and faster food aid (with a condition that at least 10 per cent of such food should be bought on local markets), and a contribution to the rehabilitation of broken economies and the gross indebtedness of the developing world.

But all of this costs money. And the treasuries of member states have been lamentably unwilling to find it. In 1981 the industrialised countries made a solemn pledge to double their development aid by the end of 1985, or raise it to a level corresponding to 0.15 per cent of their gross national product. The result, according to an UNCTAD report, has been a disgraceful failure. When the promise was made, Denmark, Holland, Norway and Sweden already exceeded the 0.15 per cent target. They still do. Only Belgium has reached the target since. Most other industrialised countries (including the US, France and Britain) actually give *less* now than they did in 1981, while the number of hungry mouths in the Third World has grown.

Those who wish to keep in touch with the Community's approach to the Third World should be put on the distribution list for an admirable magazine called *The Courier*. It is free, published every two months, and available from the Commission in Brussels (235–6367).

There is much other recommended reading: see Part VIII.

AGRICULTURE

To devote a mere page or two to what up to now has been the Community's most important common policy, and one which continues to consume two-thirds of its annual budget, requires some justification. Four reasons follow.

First, the Common Agricultural Policy is no more static than the sun, the rain or the wind. Anything written about it is apt to become out of date in weeks rather than months. Secondly, it is written about daily in the press, and (in admirable detail) in the journals of the agricultural industry.

Thirdly, while the functioning of the CAP is immensely interesting to farmers, it is pretty hard going for the rest of us.

And lastly, because documentation on the CAP is available at length and in detail. A token tribute to this massive information effort is paid in Part VIII.

* * * *

The Common Agricultural Policy is complex but the problem about it is simple. It costs too much, because it was shaped to deal with a situation very different from that of today. Price levels are still guaranteed at a rate high enough to keep part-time, disadvantaged or inefficient farmers in business. This has made it difficult to avoid

For detailed information see coloured page A20

over-production by efficient, large-scale operators, which in turn has sometimes led to surpluses of food (and poor quality wine) far above the level of sensible buffer stocks. Such surpluses are expensive to store and difficult to dispose of. (They are, nevertheless, considerably less troublesome than shortages.)

The need to reform the CAP has been repeated again and again in a hundred different ways by the Commission and paid enthusiastic lip service by the farm Ministers, Foreign Secretaries and Heads of State of every Community country for many years. They then went on to award their farmers more money. The political difficulties inherent in an attempt to balance the needs of farmers against the demands of consumers have, after all, been with us since farming and politics established themselves as means of employment.

In March of 1984, and after as detailed and tense a series of negotiations as the Community has ever lived through, the Council approved a series of Commission proposals. These defended the principles and impact of the CAP, but demanded the curbing of over-production; suggested ways of protecting the poorest farmers from the economic impact of the essential reforms in order to avoid forcing them off their land and increasing the ranks of the un-employed; and spelled out clearly what had to be achieved within a budget which was showing, in real terms, no growth at all.

The Council solution was, as ever, a compromise satisfying no-one completely, but with which member governments could live. It introduced quotas for milk production (the most serious problem) and strict penalties for breaking them. Production curbs already existed for sugar beet; they were extended to cereals, wine, oilseeds and tomatoes. A time-table was drawn up for dismantling Monetary Compensatory Amounts (the artificial attempt to even out farm incomes between nations caused by currency changes).

These reforms got off to a fair start, but were soon overtaken by events: not, on this occasion, the harvest, but the drop in value of the American dollar. World food prices fell, more Community food was sold into intervention, and the subsidy on exports had to be increased. Dairy farmers (who had obeyed quotas during 1985) were, during 1986, breaking them by over 10 per cent throughout the Community. America, which had to come to terms with the entry of Spain and Portugal into the Community, felt the financial draught equally severely, and 'EEC AND US IN NEW TRADE WAR' became the headline stored in newspaper computers for regular recall throughout 1986. The target date for dismantling Monetary Compensatory Amounts was quietly abandoned.

Worse, it became apparent that the sums earmarked for farm support in the Community budget (two thirds of the total) were not going to be enough. There was certain to be an overrun, a demand for a supplementary budget, and nothing in the kitty to meet it.

For detailed information see coloured page A20/21

In the first half of 1986 dark murmurings were heard in Paris, London, Bonn and elsewhere of the 'renationalisation of the CAP' – a return to a system of national support for farmers, moving the cost largely away from the Community budget.

This notion – which would inevitably have led to a subsidy battle, won by Germany – understandably filled the Commission with dismay. The result was a series of hard-hitting speeches by Vice-President Andriessen, the then Commissioner responsible for agriculture, in which he spelled out some uncomfortable budgetary facts, and gave a new impetus to the guidelines for 'A Future for Community Agriculture' already published in 1985 and supplemented in 1986.

In the green paper thus entitled, the Commission looks ahead over 15 years, emphasising the continuing need for the CAP as a single market, and for Community preference, offering financial security to farmers and avoiding shortages. But certain conditions have to be accepted, however politically unpopular they might be. Surpluses must be disposed of and never again allowed to reach their current dimensions. Early retirement should be offered to 'main-occupation' farmers aged 55 and over and help given to younger farmers to produce new and better products. Land should be taken out of use and farmers compensated for so doing (a proposition relaunched in late 1986 by Mrs Thatcher). Milk quotas should be tightened still further and severe penalties imposed on over-production. There should be a suspension of guaranteed prices for milk powder sold into intervention, and a reduction of buying-in price in respect of beef. These approaches – and many others – are still being debated, with increasing urgency, in view of yet more budget battles to come. By the first half of 1989 it was clear that the Commission's policies for curbing agricultural surpluses were having some impact, though there is still some way to go. The processes and changes occurring in rural areas in the EC are profound, and it is clear that the EC must adopt new concepts and programmes to deal with these. Of particular concern is the protection of rural environments, and the Commission has already introduced a scheme for linking agricultural set-aside with environmental conservation.

★ ★ ★ ★

Browsing through the lengthy list of proposals put forward by the Commission every time a meeting of Farm Ministers is to be held does not make for a convincing read. A tone of near desperation tends to creep in; promises for the flowering of future Community action are made boldly, but one senses a worm in the bud. The last Commission pamphlet seeking to explain the CAP in simple terms

For detailed information see coloured page A20/21

is now five years old; the sheaf of background notes and press releases commenting on developments month by month cannot always hide the frustration encountered when sensible (indeed, vital) ideas for reform are yet again thrown out by the Council of Ministers.

It is difficult to apportion blame for this, and pointless to try here. The CAP is the most intensely political of issues, and the most liable to sudden and dramatic change, for which it is sometimes impossible to prepare within the time-scale of the Community's deliberations.

What is to be done?

There are problems of over-production in the beef and cereals sector; there may soon be a melon mountain and lake of olive oil. But incomparably the most intractable problem concerns milk, and the butter and powder into which it is made. At time of writing some 1.5 million tonnes of butter and one million tonnes of milk powder are sitting in expensive stores with no market in sight. As we shall see in the next section, they are largely useless to the Third World. Much of the butter is now so old that only the Soviet Union is prepared to buy it, at prices far below what it cost to acquire it from our farmers in the first place. The problem is therefore two-fold: how to get rid of the overflowing contents of the cold stores, and how to prevent them refilling again.

There is no shortage of ideas for the disposal of surplus butter, ranging from the difficult to the lunatic. It should be dumped in the sea; burned; buried in coal mines; fed to calves; sold at cut-price to the old and the poor. Imitation milk and milk products should not be allowed to masquerade as the real McCoy; there should be bigger sales drives on the world market; imports from New Zealand should be curbed (a favourite with the French).

Nor is there a lack of suggestions for preventing further over-production. Apart from those listed above, the Commission has suggested the suspension of guaranteed prices for intervention buying of milk-powder, tighter administration of the quota system, and invoking the powers of the European Court for breaches of the rules. It has been suggested that grazing land should be used for forestry, with long-term loans at advantageous rates made available by the Community. A particularly ingenious idea, put forward during 1986 by Dr David Chapman, recommends that intervention buying should be scrapped altogether, and a voluntary system of insurance against fluctuations in price established in its stead. This, he argues, would lead to lower prices for consumers without reducing the incentive for farmers to be efficient. There should be a limit on the amount which could be insured per farm, thus favouring the small farmer.

With diffidence the present writer suggests returning to first

For detailed information see coloured page A20/21

principles. It is both prudent and politically essential to keep small, disadvantaged farmers from going out of business; that was one reason why the CAP was created in the first place. But if this is done by guaranteeing prices for milk and milk products high enough to keep these less efficient farmers on the land, how can it be practicable to prevent overproduction by the exceedingly efficient farmers of Denmark, France, England and elsewhere?

Quotas may be essential. But they are difficult to operate and invigilate. Is it not time to face the difficult reality that open-ended price guarantees should be scrapped, the intervention price gradually lowered, and social support provided for disadvantaged farmers, not by governments (which would lead to a subsidy leapfrog) but by the CAP through FEOGA? This is doubtless a desperately difficult concept to sell to farm Ministers; but it is difficult to see what else can possibly work.

★ ★ ★ ★

So far this brief look at the CAP has concerned its internal problems and inconsistencies. This, alas, reflects coverage of that policy in the media of the Community as a whole. Natural enough; but in the longer term the CAP may be the yardstick against which the Community is judged in global terms, not to its credit.

Certainly it is difficult for the Community to argue with conviction against protectionism in America or Japan when it is seen to be so self-protective of its own food producers. With one voice, the eight nations of rich, over-fed Western Europe declare that they must do more to help the Third World improve its agricultural techniques and come to terms with starvation and drought. This may be sincere, and deeply felt. But with another voice the Community agrees to food deals with Russia at world prices which are (at least in part) kept low by the very workings of the CAP itself.

This is the province of the next part of this chapter. For the moment, it should be noted that any attempt to dismantle the CAP, or for the UK to attempt to pull out of it, would be violently opposed by every sector of the British farming industry and most food distributors. It would, in any case, be politically impossible if the Community were to remain intact. The entry of the UK into the Community has had effects for farmers, distributors and food producers so extensive and complex that it is outside the scope of this short introduction to summarise or quantify them. A selected reading list is given in Part VIII.

FOOD AND PRICES

The Common Agricultural Policy may be a matter of exquisite tedium to the non-farming British citizen; the reverse is true of food

For detailed information see coloured page A20/21

prices. From public opinion polls over the years, we can be sure of one thing: if the housewives of Britain think of the Community at all, they do so as they pay their food bills at the supermarket, the butcher, the fishmonger, the fruiterer, or the baker. And their thoughts are far from benevolent.

They are also far from well-based. The question of food prices is little less complex than that of agriculture itself. A few facts, however, should be put on record.

• Over the past six years, food prices have risen by less than the retail price index.

• The greatest price rises in the average food basket since 1973 have been in respect of coffee and potatoes; neither is covered by the CAP.

• We spend more of our disposable income nowadays than we did in 1973 on cars, gambling, alcohol and holidays; but we spend less on food.

• In real terms (i.e. the number of minutes worked to earn a pound of steak, fish or butter, a pint of milk, a loaf of bread, a bottle of beer, or whatever) food and drink are actually cheaper now than they were when we joined the Community.

And although it is obvious in the window of every food shop, we might occasionally remind ourselves of the extraordinary difference in the range of choice available to the housewife today as compared with that of 1972.

The anti-Marketeers extract the maximum possible advantage out of the amount of fruit and vegetables destroyed in Europe. 'Do you know,' they thunder on every television programme on which they appear, 'that 41 cauliflowers are destroyed in the EC *every minute?*'

Well, that's one way of putting it. You could argue with equal truth that 3959 are sold or given away in the EC every minute; that 98 per cent of all cauliflowers produced in Europe are now actually eaten; and that this is perhaps the highest percentage in the history of the farming trade. It is probable (though difficult to prove) that *less* food is now destroyed in Community countries than before the CAP was established.

* * * *

Many economists argue that Britain, outside the CAP, would be able to buy food more cheaply than it can as a Community member State.

Beyond doubt this would be true for the products of dairy farms. The situation in the case of other food is less clear. The sudden arrival on the world market of a nation of 50 million people importing half of its food would have a dramatic effect on the price of 'parcels' of food in surplus which float around the world at various

For detailed information see coloured page A21

time in various places.

Few of the opponents of British membership of the Community have attempted to assess the impact on the pound, inward investment, and employment in Britain if the UK were to pull out of the CAP and therefore, effectively, the Community. They would presumably be dramatic.

Christopher Tugendhat, when Budget Commissioner, estimated that returning to our old system of farm support (or something resembling it) would cost around £1,500 million a year. The TUC in a similar estimate made the figure less, but still more than Britain has ever subscribed in net terms to the Community. (At present, of course, our agricultural price support system and a good deal else besides is paid for by our subscription to the Community.) There would almost certainly be a saving 'across the exchanges' – in terms of balance of payments; but it would not look too impressive to the taxpayer or the housewife shopping for food, who would have to foot the bill in one way or another.

There is, however, one aspect of food in which the Community has not only failed, but failed disgracefully. This is in its attitude to the Third World.

We do not give anything like enough in food aid or skilled help to assist the developing countries to produce their own food. Over-fed and over-caloried ourselves, we are far from generous in our farm trading relations with the poorer countries. We are considerably better in these respects than the Soviet Union, Japan, and in some respects America; but that makes our behaviour no whit the less selfish or stupid.

FISHERIES

Fishing commands loyalties of a fiercer and deeper kind than any other industry. Although there are only about 260,000 fishermen in the Community (compared with 9.5 million in agriculture) the industry is crucial to many areas, where entire communities depend upon it. The first Common Fisheries Policy was established in 1970, though very soon after, negotiations over UK, Danish, Norwegian and Irish membership of the EC were begun. It was not until January 1983 that a revised fisheries policy was introduced.

This consists, in essence, of common-sense arrangements for conservation and management of stocks in the waters of member States, and the laying down of total allowable catches. These are agreed anually at the Council level for all species threatened by over-fishing. They are then divided into national quotas on a complex but flexible basis agreed in the final settlement.

Zones are established around coasts to protect the interests of inshore fishermen and to safeguard traditional rights. There is help

For detailed information see coloured page A21

for marketing organisations when prices fall, and money for the improvement of boats, harbours and the food-processing industry.

Each nation must declare its catches, and in addition to national monitoring the Commission now employs a corps of inspectors from Community countries who are independent of their own governments and form transnational inspection teams.

A common marketing organisation, administered by the producing organisations themselves, is responsible for guaranteeing fishermen a living when prices collapse.

Both the UK government and the fisheries organisations declared their satisfaction with the 1983 agreement, and it seems to be working well. The share-out of fish stocks for 1984, 1985 and 1986 were agreed on time and in relative harmony.

When Spain and Portugal joined the Community at the beginning of 1986 they brought with them a fishing fleet larger than that of the other 10 members, and increased the total catch by nearly 30 per cent. Not surprisingly, the argument about accession in the fisheries sector was as prolonged and difficult as any. It was necessary to preserve progress to date yet get the new balance right. It proved easiest to get agreement on conservation measures in the Atlantic: since 1 January 1986 both Spain and Portugal are pledged to obey Community rules.

On marketing, there are transitional arrangements to help the two newcomers overcome the problem of accepting the disciplines of the CAP: market support for certain species of particular interest to the two states, gradual alignment of anchovy and sardine prices, progressive abolition of customs duties and other barriers to trade, all spread over a period of around seven years.

Most troublesome (in negotiation and no doubt in the years to come) proved the problem of access to Community waters. Complex transitional rules govern the rights which new and old member States must afford each other in the years until 1996. They attempt to take into account traditional rights, and offer mutual access to several fishing zones. This will be monitored regularly, and reviewed in 1995 at latest. There are limits on the catches permitted, and on the number of boats fishing in these zones at any one time.

The stormy scenes which characterised the early years of the Common Fisheries Policy may not yet be over. To imagine that it will be easy to double the Community's fishing fleet overnight and do so smoothly or easily would be to forget that fishermen are the last active hunters on this difficult planet.

At the international level, the Commission has been concerned to maintain the traditional activity of European fishermen in external waters and to keep an eye on developing resources. It has now concluded international agreements with Norway, Sweden, the Faeroes, the US and Canada, together with certain developing

For detailed information see page A21

countries, particularly in Africa. The Council is the repository body of NASCO (the North Atlantic Salmon Convention) which was established during 1984 in Edinburgh.

In December 1984 the Commission proposed that RDF help for economic regeneration in areas of particular difficulty should be extended to traditional fishing areas – in the UK, around Hull and Grimsby. Around £9 million (out of a Community total of £24 million) would come to Britain. The money would go towards improvement of the environment, the development of SMEs and craft activities, and the stimulation of industry, including tourism. The DTI issued an explanatory memorandum on the scheme on 21 December 1984; the government welcomed the idea in principle but suggested possible extension of the areas.

During 1986 two important agreements were reached. The first was a package of technical measures to conserve fish stocks in Community waters, largely by increasing the mesh size of nets from 80mm to 90mm over a three-year period. The second approved a 10-year structural policy for the Community as a whole, including help for the building and maintenance of fishing boats more generous and extensive than in the past, particularly in areas of particular difficulty such as the West of Scotland, Orkney and Shetland, and Ireland.

SPAIN AND PORTUGAL

The Community now embraces more than 320 million Europeans (almost twice as many as there were when the Community was established in 1957) the Ten having become Twelve on 1 January 1986 with the accession of Spain and Portugal. This happened after eight years of intense and often difficult negotiations and is a cause for real pride on the part of the Council and of all twelve governments. Spanish and Portuguese entry strengthens the Community's voice in world affairs and enriches Europe culturally. Above all, it should reinforce the spine of democracy in two nations which have recently emerged from periods of dictatorship.

The problems of enlargement are real, particularly in respect of Spain. Before considering the agricultural impact of Spanish membership of the EC, one must not forget that Spain is the tenth major industrial nation in the world. It is especially competitive in the steel, textiles, and shipbuilding industries. The Community, already with the makings of an olive oil lake, must in future absorb Spanish production equalling half that of Italy and a third of that in France. One Spaniard in six works on the land – in the case of Portugal the figure is one in four. Although it will be 10 years before the new entrants are full members of the Common Agricultural Policy, there is already growing pressure for more farm support

For detailed information see coloured page A21

spending, at the very time the Community is trying to cut back. The detailed arrangements for the gradual entry of the Spanish fishing fleet into the Common Fisheries Policy will require careful policing, patience and cool tempers.

The impact on the institutions will be considerable – if only because it is more difficult to get 12 governments to agree in Council than 10. At a more workaday level, there are simply not enough translators and interpreters who can speak Portuguese and Greek, or Spanish and Danish.

Problems aplenty, certainly. But they must be surmounted. The Community cannot refuse membership to any European democracy which wishes to join. A regional policy for Western Europe which excluded Portugal was a sham; the industrial protectionism which ruled in Spain for almost 50 years was as bad for that country itself as it was for Europe as a whole.

The Institutions

The Council of Ministers now has 12 members. In terms of voting, Spain has eight votes and Portugal five when a qualified majority is called for (compared with 10 votes for Germany, France, Italy and the United Kingdom, five votes for Belgium, Greece and the Netherlands, three votes for Denmark and Ireland, and two for Luxembourg). Spain now has two members of the Commission (one a Vice-President) and Portugal one, bringing the total to 17. Spain currently (June 1989) holds the Presidency of the Council of Ministers.

The European Parliament has 518 members, including 60 from Spain and 24 from Portugal, and the Court of Justice has 13 judges instead of 11, Portugal and Spain each sending one. There are six advocates-general, Spain and Portugal filling the sixth seat in turns. The Economic and Social Committee has 189 members, including 21 from Spain and 12 from Portugal.

The Common Market

Spain is abolishing customs duties over seven years and aligning its customs tariff with the Community over the same period. It is already subject to competition rules, and has introduced VAT and abolished quantitative restrictions to trade. There are special provisions for motor vehicles, textiles, steel and certain national monopolies.

Portugal is abolishing internal customs duties over seven years and simultaneously aligning tariffs with those of the Community. It is introducing VAT and abolishing quantitative restrictions to trade at a slower rate than Spain, and also has special provisions in respect of motor vehicles, textiles and some national monopolies.

For detailed information see coloured page A21

Agriculture

The entry of Spain increased the Community's agricultural land area by 30 per cent and the farm labour force by 25 per cent; Portugal brought in another 12.8 per cent of farm workers. The enlarged Community is now around 90 per cent self-sufficient in terms of citrus fruit and completely so in respect of most other fresh fruit and vegetables. This has made for difficult and detailed transitional arrangements to protect the produce of other Community countries:

In *Spain:* progressive application of the machinery of the common organisation of the markets and establishment of the free circulation of goods after transitional periods, varying according to the products. General or 'classic' arrangements will apply to most agricultural products over a seven-year period, with progressive alignment of prices and aids, accession compensatory amounts, the gradual implementation of the customs union and Spain's progressive application of the Community's preferential arrangements. There are special arrangements for wine, vegetable oils and fresh fruit and vegetables, and a surveillance system for imports of sensitive products (fruit and vegetables, milk, butter, cheese, beef/veal, common wheat, milk-powder, potatoes and table wine).

In *Portugal:* the same general principles as for Spain, with 'classic' transitional arrangements which will apply to processed fruit and vegetables, sugar and isoglucose, and vegetable oils, in general over a seven-year period (10 years for vegetable oils). Specific transitional arrangements cover 85 per cent of Portuguese production (cereals, rice, milk and milk products, beef/veal, pigmeat, eggs and poultry, fresh fruit and vegetables, and wine); there is a surveillance system for imports, a specific development programme, and production rules for tomato concentrates, canned tomatoes, sunflowers, colza and rapeseed. Special arrangements are made for sugar, and the same arrangements as for Spain in the case of vegetable oils.

Spanish accession to the Community posed particular problems for the US, and what was known as 'the pasta war' filled the pages of the press in most Community countries during the first half of the 1986. At time of writing agreement has been reached; it will doubtless be monitored with great care.

★ ★ ★ ★

It is too early to judge the impact of this third enlargement on the earlier Community and on the Iberian states themselves.

The two countries themselves have, of course, had long standing disagreements and difficulties, particularly in terms of immigration, trade, fishing and communication. Nonetheless, during 1986 trade between the two increased greatly, and during October there was a meeting between the Prime Ministers of both countries which was,

For detailed information see coloured page A21

on all accounts, considerably more *simpatico* than previous meetings at summit level.

Britain and Spain too have their problems, particularly over Gibraltar. But even during the first year of membership tension has eased, and the warmth of the welcome accorded to the Spanish Royal Family during their visit to Britain (and the equally warm words of both the King and Queen Elizabeth on the value of Community membership) was encouraging.

A PEOPLE'S EUROPE

For some years it has been accepted wisdom that the Community should be made more real to its peoples, and that ways should be explored of encouraging them to identify with it. In 1984 a Committee of senior civil servants was appointed to explore the possibilities; it reported to the European Council in June 1985, in a two-part document entitled 'A People's Europe', quickly approved.

The report is based on the well expressed premise that 'what has been achieved until now in Europe has been the work of those who experienced the horrors and destruction of war. Continuation of the venture rests on the assumption that future generations will also understand and appreciate one another across borders, and will realise the benefits to be derived from closer cooperation and solidarity'.

The first part of the report concentrates, appropriately, on the general need to abolish frontiers of all kinds. The second makes more novel proposals: for the wider recognition of the special rights of Community citizens, both politically and in practical terms; cooperation in culture, communication and information, with particular emphasis on the visual; the establishment of a European Academy of Science, Technology and Art; more exchanges of young people and young ideas, perhaps involving joint sports teams and a European scheme on the VSO lines; cooperation in the health field, and action to combat drug abuse; more town twinning and easier travel; a strengthening of the Community's 'image' (flag, anthem, emblems, postage stamps, etc). A Community ombudsman, and a lottery to finance cultural projects are suggested. Perhaps the most important conclusion is on the need for information campaigns designed to explain the importance of the Community to the peoples of member States, and the cost to these States (and the peace of the world) were the Community to cease to exist.

A fair amount has been achieved since June 1985. We now have a European flag and a European Community passport. Many of the agreements reached on tourism, youth, education and travelling and working in Europe, touched on earlier in the book, have been carefully crafted to encourage people to think across frontiers. Some

For detailed information see coloured page A21

progress has been made on mutual recognition of diplomas and freer travel. Anti-cancer and anti-AIDS campaigns have been agreed, together with a European emergency health card. A Cultural Foundation is establishing itself in Paris and hammering on the fund doors. Duty-free allowances have been raised again, and it is easier to send presents by post. Yachting, cycling, swimming and marathon races are now established at Community level.

But several good ideas for visits and cooperation between young people (the ERASMUS and YES programmes mentioned earlier), schemes for improving the environment, restoring monuments, creating a voluntary service organisation, etc, have so far failed to win anything like enough money from the Council. The immediate need is to mobilise young people themselves to start demanding these things, at which point politicians will sit up and listen.

And the authors profoundly hope that this will be the last edition of this book written at a time when it still costs more to travel by air from London to Brussels than from New York to Los Angeles.

For detailed information see coloured page A21/22

PART VII
GETTING MONEY FROM EUROPE

Far more information is available on how to get grants and loans from Europe than on any other Community policy. There are leaflets, booklets, and indeed bulky books on the subject, available from industry departments, quangos, banks, local authorities, solicitors, commercial advisers, and the Commission itself. Some of the more important of these are listed in Part IX.

It would be foolish to try to duplicate all of this well-researched effort. What follows summarises Community aid, but concentrates disproportionately on three aspects of it:

(a) what other sources of information are coy about;
(b) recent changes in the European Regional Development Fund and the Social Fund;
(c) smaller and lesser-known funds.

See also the important entries on funding in the Chapters in Part V entitled Employment and Social Policy, The Troubled Industries, Small and Medium-sized Enterprises, The New Technologies, and Youth and Education.

Loans and grants from the Community are essentially concerned with work. They are there to provide and maintain jobs, to train people to fill them, and to provide infrastructure to support them. Such exceptions as there are to this rule are interesting, but under-financed and often deployed on an *ad hoc* basis. The reason for this is that member states have not yet managed to agree that there should be adequate funding for them in the Community budget, despite repeated and eloquent pleas from the Commission, the Parliament and the Economic and Social Committee.

Community aid has nothing to do with charity or the 'begging-bowl'. A policy for the regions is important to the aims of the Community, not only to level up the differences in employment, prosperity and opportunity between the various areas of Europe, but to make the Common Market work properly. Help for small firms is not merely a salute to courage and entrepreneurship; it is based upon a belief (supported by much hard evidence) that the key to pulling

For detailed information see coloured page A21-23

out of the recession may lie with small enterprises. Aid for inventiveness in the new technologies may go to learned research teams, but there must be a workforce and a saleable product pretty clearly in view.

Social policy is shaped partly by the decent, idealistic reasoning of the preamble to the Treaty of Rome, partly by economic realism. The Social Fund helps the handicapped, working women who deserve a fairer deal, and migrant workers. Otherwise, it has virtually nothing to offer for what we in Britain think of as social work. It is a training and retraining fund, aimed at filling jobs and where possible helping to create them. It is an attack upon unemployment (particularly among the young and the unskilled), launched for hard-nosed political reasons.

In nine cases out of ten, it is pointless to apply for any form of Community grant without the blessing of the British government or one of its agencies. In ten cases out of ten it is *better* to have it, whether it is essential or not. Those who seek grants from the Community have everything to gain by keeping in touch with Commission officials. But there is no short-circuiting government channels; there is not going to be for the foreseeable future; and you would be foolish to try.

(There is, however, a difference between approaching a national civil servant dealing with loans and grants and his counterpart in the Commission. The former, by training and by nature, is circumspect. The latter will often be frank and informative in a fashion which is astonishing the first time you encounter it.)

Another point to be made forcibly and in general is that Community aid policies are far from static. Priorities change, sometimes suddenly, and terms and conditions can be flexible. Knowing *when* to ask for money can be as important as knowing whether it's worth asking for it at all. Here, personal contact with UK or Commission officials and MEPs (or paid professional advice) can pay real dividends.

Lastly, IF NECESSARY, ASK AGAIN. This is one of the most important and least appreciated aspects of Community aid.

If you ask a government department for a grant or a loan and are turned down, you can be reasonably sure that only a major shift of policy is likely to make any difference to your future chances. In the case of the Community, you can be turned down three times and get your money at the fourth attempt. Many have done so.

To sum up: if you seek money from Europe in the forms of grants, remember:

(a) all Community grants are work-related in one way or another;
(b) you must normally have a UK department on your side;
(c) by all means make and maintain contacts in the Commission

For detailed information see coloured page A21-23

and among MEPs – but don't try to upstage British civil servants, who know the game better than you;

(d) remember the importance of timing; take advice (the European Information Service, MEPs on the relevant committees, Commission offices and professional consultants can all be helpful here);

(e) don't give up at first refusal.

'ADDITIONALITY'

The question of 'additionality' has been aired at length in the press and television of Britain but less illuminated. The word is shorthand for the assumption, implicit in Community regional policy, that aid from the various Community sources should be additional to that given by the government of the country concerned. It should be 'new' money, creating jobs, or training opportunities, or roads or bridges or dams, which that government would otherwise have been unable to afford.

This is extremely difficult to prove or disprove. The government gives £10 million to a new electronics factory and successfully claims £3 million of it from the RDF. 'Is anyone trying to pretend' thunders an editorial next day 'that the factory would not have been built without Brussels money?' This quite misses the point. £3 million pounds were thereby released for the government to use to support a number of smaller but equally important industrial projects.

A publicist for Community aid would clearly be delighted if Community grants went direct to companies in particular areas for a clearly identifiable purpose which would create a quantifiable number of jobs. But would this be sensible, or even feasible? The staff of the Regional Development Fund, covering 12 nations, hundreds of regions, and thousands of different problems, would fit comfortably into one corner of one floor of one building of the UK Department of Industry. How could a few officials based in Brussels possibly adjudicate between the thousands of very different claims upon Community funds – between say, a water scheme in Fife, a gas pipeline in France, or a roadbridge in Italy – without relying upon expert local and governmental advice? But priorities will very often coincide. The Community therefore puts its money into those projects which national and local administrators and experts consider to be particularly important and timely.

The most commonly voiced complaint about RDF aid is that local authorities, when they get a grant, have their public sector borrowing right reduced by a like amount. This is true, and is a British, not a Community rule. But RDF grants are nonetheless of direct help. They save ratepayers considerable sums in interest charges, and they

For detailed information see coloured page A21-23

can often mean that it is easier to get Community (and indeed public) assistance from other sources.

In Tayside Region, for example, planners have calculated that in recent years their accumulated debt was about £10½ million less than it would otherwise have been, because of RDF grants. Future savings should be even better. In all, this will represent a saving of between ½p and 1p on the rates.

It can be equally argued that Community grants (even small ones) have a very useful pump-priming effect. There are, to this writer's certain knowledge, several enterprise trusts and local initiatives which have managed to gather large resources of money, effort, time and equipment from private industry, local authorities, and quangos, for job creation and training, which would never have got off the ground without the initial backing of Community funds.

Two things are sure about the use of European money in the UK. The first is that the British government honours (and has honoured) the concept of 'additionality' in both the spirit and the letter as honestly and effectively as any other Community government, and better than many. The second is that even when the Treasury appears at its most acquisitive (in, for example, the use it makes of the Social Fund to finance ongoing training schemes), the end result is still of direct benefit to the British citizen.

This book is not the place to plug the value of Community aid to Britain. But it is surely unexceptionable to say that the United Kingdom has had at least its fair share of such aid, has paid more tribute to it than any other Community nation, and has earned international respect for the ways in which it has been used. (Which last is, after all, what Community aid is about.)

THE EUROPEAN REGIONAL DEVELOPMENT FUND

Much of what has been written about the ERDF is now out of date, since the Fund took on a new shape at the beginning of 1985 and was further revised in 1986. This note will therefore attempt a brief description of what will henceforth be called the RDF, and its activities, thereafter concentrating on recent changes.

A glance, first, at the philosophy behind the Fund. The RDF is emphatically *not* intended to reimburse governments, local authorities, or firms, for bits and pieces of their ongoing expenditure. It is there to help redistribute Community resources to the poorest regions.

This may seem a pernickety distinction, but local authorities, when drawing up their claims for submission, should keep it in mind. It could improve their chances, particularly under the recent rules.

* * * *

For detailed information see coloured page A21-23

Aid from the RDF comes in the form of non-repayable grants. The only way to get it is with the blessing of a government department. Its object is to stimulate development in the poorest areas of the Community (which the UK government has decreed should mean its own assisted areas). In practice this takes the form either of part-funding for industrial infrastructure – roads, water schemes, bridges, ferry terminals, telecommunications, ports, and so on – or the direct encouragement of job creation or maintenance in industry or the s′ ice sector.

Most money goes to infrastructure, which must be co-financed by a local authority or similar agency. Projects in industry, tourism and service activities must also receive UK government assistance, and create or preserve jobs. They must also have a choice of location.

Only the government can sumit applications to the Commission; these are then chosen on a strength of case basis. A local authority wishing to submit an infrastructure project for consideration should apply to the Department of the Environment (or Industry Department for Scotland). Individuals or companies cannot receive help direct, but if their plans for job creation, expansion, etc., fit in well with Community priorities, this may improve their chances of getting regional aid from the Department of Industry.

There is also special help from the RDF for what (until the end of 1984) were known as 'non-quota' activities (see below), and smallish amounts for feasibility studies and certain infrastructure projects linked with mountain and hill farming in remote areas.

THE NEW RULES

Prior to 1985, the RDF was distributed in the Community on a quota basis (Britain's share being just under a quarter). There was also a non-quota section (5 per cent of the total) subject to different rules, and directed to the very hardest-hit areas of the Community.

The distinction between the quota and non-quota sections of the Fund has been abolished since January 1985. The UK, instead of getting 23.8 per cent of the total fund, will now be able to bid for up to 19.3 per cent of it, but might manage only 14.5 per cent. (There are the upper and lower limits of a new system of 'quota ranges'.) There is every reason to hope that the UK will reach the top of the range (our record in submitting good projects, spending money as per the job description, and sticking to our time-scale is excellent) but it may be harder work. Our percentage has of course declined since the accession of Spain and Portugal. Whether it will remain the same in financial terms (a smaller slice of a larger cake) will depend upon whether the views of the Parliament and the Commission prevail over those of national Treasuries.

Quota ranges apart, there are several other important changes.

For detailed information see coloured page A21-23

First, grants for infrastructure projects are up from 30 per cent of total spending to 50 per cent (55 per cent in very special cases) and the money will be available earlier than in the past.

Secondly, the new Fund regulation talks a great deal of 'programmes' as well as 'projects'. For some years the Commission has tried to encourage the integrated use of Community funds: grants and loans from more than one source, to be used in a geographical or sectoral area rather than piecemeal. The new Fund therefore introduces 'programme financing' on an experimental basis. In the UK, at least 20 per cent of our share of the Fund must be spent on programmes by the end of 1987. These can be either *'Community programmes'*, or *'National programmes of Community interest'*.

Community programmes can be supported anywhere; like the old non-quota measures, they will not necessarily be confined to assisted areas, but in practice will probably be so by choice of the British government. There may well be an emphasis on cross-border projects (between Northern Ireland and Eire as far as the British Isles are concerned). Otherwise, programmes will probably follow the lines of the non-quota schemes introduced in Britain between 1980 and 1984. These gave special help for restructuring the steel and shipbuilding industries in certain regions of the UK, and help for textile areas. (In Scotland these were implemented not in the shape of help for the industries themselves, but by providing a special range of services for small and medium-sized businessmen, known as Better Business Services and Better Technical Services. Launched by the government and the local authorities concerned these have been immensely successful and are now available elsewhere in the UK. (Details from Industry Dept. for Scotland, Alhambra House, Glasgow.)

Community programmes must be endorsed by the Council of Ministers on the initiative of the Commission. Although the first three years are to be experimental, there is little doubt that all governments (including that of the UK) will hope to keep total control of the administration of RDF funds, within guidelines agreed by the Council.

National programmes of Community interest, the second category, apply only in assisted areas of member States (although a power station or a reservoir, say, might qualify for RDF grants even if located in a non-assisted area, provided a sizeable part of its output were to be made available to its less fortunate neighbourhood). Member States put together packages to submit to Brussels. They will be spread over several years, and must serve both national and Community objectives within the framework of the Community's Regional Policy. These can include infrastructure programmes, aid for industry, crafts and tourism, and local initiatives. Those which suggest use of other Community money (Social Fund, EIB, etc.) as

For detailed information see coloured page A21-23

well as the RDF will – contrary to widely help opinion – have a better chance of success, rather than a poorer one. Programme financing on an experimental basis will be possible – indeed, 20 per cent of a nation's possible RDF quota was devoted to this end during 1987. NPCIs will be drawn up in close consultation with local authorities, the various development agencies, ports authorities, etc.

The new Regulations spell out in Article 12 what they want in the way of a submission; this should be read with great care by local authorities in whose eyes glints the possibility of an NPCI. Applications must describe the aim of the programme, its objectives in quantifiable form, the area covered and what the money will, they hope, be spent on. But they must also include a timetable, a financial plan, a complete list of the authorities and agencies involved, a statement of priorities and how they were reached, and (hurrah!) details of publicity arrangements.

In its turn, the Commission has spelt out its own priorities:

- severity of economic imbalance;
- effect of employment;
- mobilisation of indigenous potential;
- economic development of the area;
- the situation in various economic sectors;
- peripherality;
- impact on national resources;
- integration with other Community funds.

Grants will still be available for individual projects and industries. These will probably cover requests from public sector bodies such as the electricity and gas boards, and British Rail, as well as being used as partial reimbursement for aid given to private firms.

For the first time there is a list of projects which are excluded from Fund support. This covers housing, hospitals, nurseries and old people's homes, educational establishments, fire stations, public administration buildings, coastal protection for agricultural purposes, land acquisition, and leisure facilities not connected with tourism. (Urban renewal – excluded in earlier drafts of the regulation – is however permitted.)

'Integration' is very much the buzz-word in Brussels these days, for excellent reasons. It clearly makes more sense, when distributing Community funds, to tackle a regional problem in the round and over a reasonable period of time, rather than stitch together hundreds of small individual grants, each approved separately. This allows for flexibility on the part of the recipient and makes life easier for both the initial assessors and the invigilators in the Commission. In the short term it is proving immensely taxing for those who are vetting the huge number of applications for help for NPCIs (six from Scotland alone); in the end it should prove more satisfactory for

For detailed information see coloured page A21-23

everyone concerned.

There are three more 'integrateds', the first two liable to confusion.

Integrated Development Operations (IDOs) are intended to bring together all relevant Community grants and loans in an area of particular difficulty, and accord them higher priority. Naples and Belfast were the first areas chosen. Despite initial difficulties the scheme has been extended, and some 60 submissions are rumoured to be in the process of consideration.

Not to be confused with these are *Integrated Development Programmes* (IDPs), which are essentially concerned with helping difficult agricultural areas (though tourism can be assisted) and are funded by FEOGA. One is in operation in the Western Isles of Scotland; others have been approved in principle and are being drawn up in detail.

Lastly, an *Integrated Mediterranean Programme*, begun to coincide with the accession of Spain and Portugal at the beginning of 1986, will once again coordinate aid from all available sources of cash – Community, national, regional and local – on the economic and social problems of France, Italy, Greece and, later, Spain and Portugal. It will cost £4½ billion over seven years in the first stage of its operations, apart from national and local contributions. In broad terms, two-fifths of it will come from existing funds, two-fifths in the form of European Investment Bank loans, and one-fifth in new money, which will have to be found somewhere. Monies under the Integrated Mediterranean Programmes are allocated to infrastructural projects, the development of food-processing industries, agricultural diversification schemes especially using irrigation water, the retirement and retraining of workers, and rural development projects.

★ ★ ★ ★

As before, the RDF will remain of principal interest to regional and district authorities, huge industries, and quangos. An excellent circular (ERDF No. 2/86) is available from the Department of the Environment or Industry Departments, entitled 'Quantified Objectives'. This gives a crisp summary of the type of information which should be supplied when RDF applications are submitted. It covers most principal areas in which aid is sought by public authorities – roads and bridges, water and sewerage, public transport, port and harbour facilities, industrial site servicing, workshop units, vocational training, tourist projects and energy schemes – and gives a brief note on the sort of supporting material which should be attached.

The new Regulations make changes in grant awards. 'Packaging' of small claims together to reach the minimum grant of about £30,000

For detailed information see coloured page A21-23

will still be permitted but the fund will now be able to contribute 50 per cent of the total expenditure by a public authority (compared with up to 30 per cent in the past). In the case of large applications (over about £10 million) the RDF will be able to pay between 30 per cent and 50 per cent; there is a strong implication that very large single grants are unlikely to qualify for the full 50 per cent. Projects deemed of particular importance within terms of Community priorities (as interpreted in the light of changing circumstances by the Commission) may receive 55 per cent.

As in the past there can be help for *feasibility studies* (50 per cent contribution to the cost, 70 per cent for studies of exceptional interest). These must be carried out in assisted areas, and there should be a real chance that they will result in direct requests for RDF or other Community aid.

Two new programmes (STAR and VALOREN) were agreed by the Council in October 1986. The first aims to improve telecommunications, the second development of indigenous energy potential, both in the least favoured areas of the Community. STAR will spend about £50 million over five years and VALOREN around £26 million over the same period. In the UK only Northern Ireland is likely to qualify.

HOW TO APPLY

Only governments can submit applications to the Fund. It is not possible for individuals or organisations to apply to Brussels directly; nor can European MPs apply for aid on behalf of their constituents.

As before, potential applicants should seek advice from the Department of Industry or equivalent departments in Scotland, Wales and Northern Ireland (see last pages). It is informally and readily given.

Those looking to the future can, I think, expect with confidence that the concentration of help for SMEs, craft industries and tourism in Britain will continue and intensify.

THE SOCIAL FUND

This is misnamed. There is virtually no Community money available for what we think of as social work. The Social Fund is concerned with training, retraining, resettlement and (more recently) job creation schemes. Once more there is a mass of available material on the Social Fund, its operations and its priorities. Much of this, too, is now somewhat out of date. A new version of the excellent booklet on the Social Fund prepared by the Department of Employment (01-213-7623) is now available. There is also a leaflet, 'The Social Fund – New Regulations' available from the Commission offices in Britain

For detailed information see coloured page A21-23

– where, of course, the regulations themselves and the current guidelines can be inspected.

★ ★ ★ ★

Social Fund money comes in the form of non-repayable grants. Its formal purpose is 'to improve employment opportunities for workers and to increase their geographical and occupational mobility'. In essence it helps to fund training and employment schemes, matching the financial contribution made by the government or other public authority.

The main recent change in the priorities of the Fund concerns the young unemployed, and 'black spots' (even those outside assisted areas) where unemployment is exceptionally high.

Under the new regulations, at least 75 per cent of the Fund's budget in any one year must go to schemes to help the under 25s to find stable employment. This may include basic vocational training for school leavers in special skills (particularly in the new technologies); and vocational training directly linked to obtaining a job of more than one year's duration. It therefore can not for example support the somewhat 'optical' training schemes in certain countries which are more concerned with keeping youngsters out of mischief than with finding real jobs for them. For the first time, the self-employed under 25 qualify for help.

Other priorities (in no fixed order) are training and retraining for:

(a) the long-term unemployed (on the dole for 12 months or more);
(b) women returning to work;
(c) handicapped people who are capable of working on the open labour market (now limited to certain regions);
(d) migrant workers and their families;
(e) those in small and medium-sized firms (employing not more than 500 people) who require training in new technologies.

There are special provisions for areas with particularly high and persistent unemployment or undergoing industrial restructuring. (Northern Ireland, for example, gets slightly more generous help than other regions of the UK.)

The Fund is invariably oversubscribed in every aspect of its work (except help for the handicapped), and since conditions in the labour market can change very rapidly it is essential for the Fund to be flexible. The Commission regularly revises its priorities and produces indicative guidelines. Certain rules, however, are unlikely to change:

(a) The Fund will support only the preparation and running costs of schemes; it cannot pay for capital costs, social security or unemployment benefits, medical expenses, depreciation costs of

For detailed information see coloured page A21-23

capital expenditure for which another Community grant has been given, or the costs of normal education;

(b) All schemes must be in receipt of financial support from a UK public authority;

(c) For schemes run by private organisations, the Fund's grant may equal but not exceed the grant from a public authority; a private applicant is expected to contribute at least 10 per cent of the programme cost;

(d) In the case of job creation schemes for under 25s, the Fund's contribution is limited to a maximum amount decided annually (around 15 per cent of the average gross wage of industrial workers in the UK).

How long schemes can be supported depends upon their nature. As a rule, aid is given for a year at a time, and a new application must be submitted in August for any subsequent year. Schemes accepted as being innovatory can, however, be funded for a three-year period.

Thirty per cent of a grant, once approved, is usually paid as soon as the scheme is under way, 30 per cent at the half-way stage, and the remainder on completion.

Pilot schemes and studies can be supported in certain cases; but amounts are small and heavily oversubscribed. They must be new in approach and of potential value at a Community as well as a local level. (No public authority input is essential here.)

THE CURRENT GUIDELINES

While retaining these general principles, the current guidelines narrow priority areas. Aid will be concentrated on projects to further employment opportunities in:

- the absolute priority regions (Greece, the French Overseas departments, Ireland, the Mezzogiorno and Northern Ireland);
- certain areas suffering from changes in the steel, shipbuilding, textile and fishing industries;
- areas of high and long-term unemployment drawn up by reference to unemployment rates and gross domestic product.

In the United Kingdom these last two areas cover the local authority areas of Central, Cheshire, Cleveland, Clwyd, Cornwall, Dumfries and Galloway, Durham, Dyfed, Fife, Greater Manchester, Gwent, Gwynedd, Hereford and Worcester, Highlands, Humberside, Isle of Wight, Lancashire, Merseyside, Mid Glamorgan, Northumberland, Nottinghamshire, Salop, South Glamorgan, South Yorkshire, Staffordshire, Strathclyde, Tayside, Tyne and Wear, West Glamorgan, West Midlands and West Yorkshire. In addition there are the travel-to-work areas (TTWA) of Workington (Cumbria), Coalville (Leicestershire), Corby (Northamptonshire) and

For detailed information see coloured page A21-23

Scunthorpe (Lincolnshire).

Preference, as in the recent past, will be given to training schemes for the young, but there is even more concentration on the hardest hit regions of the Community. Since there are currently few signs of the sort of increase in real terms demanded by the Parliament and the Commission (and since the Fund will now have to give special attention to the problems of much of Spain and all of Portugal) the available money will be concentrated on 59 per cent of the workforce of the Community, compared with 64 per cent in 1985. About 44 per cent of all commitments will go to 'absolute priority' regions listed above.

As before, preference will be given to training schemes which comprise a minimum of 200 hours of specific training, including 40 hours devoted to the new technologies. In the case of the under 18s priority will go to schemes of at least 800 hours training, including a minimum of 200 hours job experience, and with a definite job in view. (There are special exceptions for Spain and Portugal.) Again, small and medium-sized enterprises will be favoured clients.

The principal differences in the new guidelines concern the long-term unemployed (whose training should offer 'substantial prospects of employment'); training where companies must face structural change for technological reasons or because of changes in demand (this will in future only be available to industry); local employment initiatives and job creation schemes (no longer available for adults in non-priority regions); and schemes in the tourist industry (preference will be given to training necessary to modernise the industry or enable it to respond to change). There are minor changes in respect of self-employed workers, migrant workers, and the handicapped.

Linear Reduction

Because of the oversubscription of the Social Fund, 'linear reduction' has for some years become necessary. It is perhaps worth quoting the relevant paragraph in full:

> Applications will be approved by budget item. When appropri-
> ations are insufficient to cover priority operations, a linear
> reduction will be applied, calculated in proportion to the
> financial volume of remaining applications by each member
> State. This system will also apply to a surplus of non-priority
> operations.

Preference will be given to programmes involving help from other Community funds; training for SMEs in the new technologies; and operations 'particularly dependent on Fund assistance for their implementation'.

For detailed information see coloured page A21-23

It would be a great pity if such linear reduction should militate against those local authorities (Strathclyde Region being an example) which have put Social Fund money to extremely effective use merely because their very success has encouraged others to apply (in a Community as well as a local sense). There is reason to hope that ways will be found round this particular problem.

But there is little doubt that the UK's days as prime beneficiary (with Italy) from the fund are numbered. Indeed, the British share has fallen from about a third in 1984 to a quarter in 1985 and one-sixth during 1986. The solution, of course, is a bigger cake. Only the Council of Ministers can supply the ingredients.

APPLYING FOR HELP

Any organisation, public or private, can apply, but applications are not accepted from individuals. Public bodies include government departments and 'quangos', local authorities, and nationalised industries. Private bodies include, for example, companies, voluntary organisations, enterprise trusts etc. To be eligible, a private organisation must be receiving public authority funding and the relevant authority must guarantee completion of the scheme.

An excellent guide for applicant is contained in Briefing Note 11, 'The European Social Fund: a Review of Developments (1986)', produced for the Planning Exchange by Peter Aitken. Page 42 – on key points for applicants – is particularly recommended. Details on blue pages.

Before making formal applications, it is wise to consult the helpful Social Fund unit in the Department of Employment; a single letter or telephone call can save a great deal of time and trouble later. (01-213 7623 or 6998.) The address is Department of Employment, Overseas Division (OB2), Caxton House, Tothill St., London SW1 H 9NA. (In Northern Ireland consult the Department of Economic Development (ESF Branch), Massey Avenue, Belfast BT4 2JP.)

* * * *

THE EUROPEAN INVESTMENT BANK

Most of the voluminous material about the EIB is now out of date, thanks to a decision made on 18 July 1985 by HMG. This means, in effect, that loans to small and medium-sized enterprises in the UK are no longer available. More of this below.

The EIB is an unusal body. It has a gigantic operating budget, but is not allowed to make a profit. Although awarded triple A rating on the exchanges of the world, it works in some ways more like a friendly society than the powerful international finance corporation

For detailed information see coloured page A21-23

which it is assuredly is. Governed by finance ministers and chancellors of the exchequer, it has a miniscule staff.

The Bank borrows money on the world's capital markets on extremely favourable terms. Its capital is provided and guaranteed by Member States. For this reason it can on-lend at advantageous rates. There is no national, regional or other quota system for these loans; they go to areas where the need is greatest. There is often a useful 'grace' period before capital repayments begin, and anyone can apply if they are investing in industry, energy, infrastructure, tourism and some services. Projects may be eligible if they:

- stimulate the development of less prosperous regions; or
- serve the common interest of more than one Community state; or
- improve industrial cooperation or communications between member countries, develop new resources of energy (or more rational use there-of), expand the use of advanced technology, or protect the environment.

To date, roughly a third of EIB loans have gone to energy projects, around 20 per cent to water and sewerage, the same proportion to industry and services, 18 per cent to the rest – including agriculture and the advanced technologies. (The last of these can be expected to do a great deal better in future, particularly in 'problem' areas.)

The Bank loans both directly (in multi-million pound sums) and indirectly, through government departments, quangos, and (until recently) banks. The minimum loan is now about £1.5 million; there is no maximum.

Interest charges are very near to the EIB's cost of borrowing, and are not affected by the type or location of project. It is theoretically possible to borrow money from the EIB very cheaply indeed – a loan in Swiss francs, for example could probably be offered at time of writing at 7 per cent or less. But the loans must be repaid in the currencies in which they have been borrowed, and exchange rate movement can involve problems during repayment. Most loans in the UK are therefore paid in sterling and are only marginally cheaper than those available from government sources. (This, it should be stressed, is a British decision, not an EIB one.)

There are, however, other advantages. Interest is fixed for the period of the loan. Capital repayments are not usually required until between two and five years from the date on which the loan contract is signed, or until the project becomes operational. Variable rate loans may be repaid in advance without penalty. Formalities are few, and there are no fees or expenses. Although loans to industry are normally over periods of seven to twelve years, in the case of infrastructure projects the period can be up to twenty

For detailed information see coloured page A21-23

years.

EIB loans have been, and remain, useful to those wishing to borrow huge sums of money (and would become more useful still if the UK were to become a full member of the European Monetary System). But the Bank's attempts to make cheap loans available to small and medium-sized enterprises in Britain have, through no fault of its own, been frustrated.

From 1978 until July 1985, small firms could borrow EIB money from a variety of sources – government departments, ICFC, banks and quangos. These loans started at £15,000, and carried exchange risk cover so that the borrower received and repaid his loan in sterling. The Treasury took the risk, and duly charged for it. This meant that the loans were only just below the going rate: but they should have been easy to obtain and free from bureaucratic hassle.

By mid-1985, 500 of these smaller loans had been made, amounting to £300 million and creating or preserving about 35,000 jobs. More important: Britain's 13,000 bank managers had (sometimes reluctantly) come to terms with the scheme, and it was beginning to take off.

However, on 18 July 1985 the government announced that it was no longer willing to offer exchange risk guarantees for small loans. This means that the 'global' loans awarded to banks and other agencies and thus the EIB's accessibility to small businessmen has been ended at a stroke. (Loans to the public sector of over £1.5 million are unaffected, but these will still be at interest rates only 0.5 per cent less than the public sector borrowing rate, by decision of HMG.)

The Bank does, however, administer the New Community Instrument (sometimes known as NIC, or the Ortoli Facility). This makes loan money available to the Commission which is then deposited with the EIB and used for loans to projects to which the Commission attaches particular importance. These at present include loans for SMEs (for which £500 million was made available in December 1986), and activities in the energy, industry and infrastructure sectors, particularly where innovation is involved.

To apply: for loans of about £4 million or more, borrowers should apply directly to the EIB at 100 Boulevard Konrad Adenauer, Luxembourg. For smaller loans, take advice from the Bank's London office (23 Queen Anne's Gate, London SW1 – telephone 01-222 2933).

THE FARM FUND

The European Agricultural Guidance and Guarantee fund (usually known by its French acronym FEOGA) is in two parts. The first, and by far the largest, is the Guarantee section – the price support

For detailed information see coloured page A21-23

mechanism, which falls outside the scope of this book. The Guidance section is concerned with supporting schemes to improve agriculture and fisheries in a variety of ways.

Most FEOGA grants go to nationally supported schemes – agricultural and horticultural development, aid for small farmers, help for hill farming, infrastructure in difficult areas (Northern Ireland, the Western Isles), etc. But there are also grants (usually 25 per cent of eligible costs, but with certain exceptions in the fisheries field, negotiated in December 1986, which permit slightly higher grants in certain areas) for processing and marketing agricultural and fish products, for capital investment in buildings, plant, new machinery and equipment, fishing boats and fish farms. (These are not available for land purchase, working capital, or equipment leasing.)

Anyone can apply but projects must not relate to the retail trade. In all cases applications must be made on forms obtainable from the British agricultural departments. These are sometimes intimidating; but departments can give a good deal of help in their preparation. There are two rounds of applications per year, one closing at the end of February and the other at the end of October. Decisions take some 10 months to be made and approved.

Up-to-date information on FEOGA grants is available from a number of sources (see Part VIII). Broadly speaking, projects, in order to qualify, must contribute to improving the situation of the agricultural or fisheries sector in question; offer adequate guarantees that they will eventually be profitable; form part of a government-approved programme, vetted by the Commission; and be compatible with the Community's rules on fair competition and free trade. Any person or company submitting a project for consideration must contribute not less than half its total cost.

Priorities change, and should be monitored. Guidelines are published from time to time in the Official Journal. There are also useful newsletters published by the Commission, and a regular section in the magazine *British Business*. The journals of the National Farmers' Union and the SNFU are, however, probably the best and most up-to-date source of information.

In March 1985 the Council of farm ministers agreed on a package of structural aid to farmers. Over £3,000 million will be available over five years to modernise farms, improve land, and encourage efficiency, particularly in the poorest and least developed farm areas. These grants can be used for a wide range of purposes, thus enabling farmers to diversify – but *not* into products which are already in surplus. Grants for tourism and craft industries in less favoured areas have been increased, as have grants to young farmers. In 1988, 50 per cent of expenditure from the guidance fund went to particular projects in assisted areas, while a further 22 per cent went

For detailed information see coloured page A21-23

to particular projects in assisted areas, while a further 22 per cent went on improving farm size and layout in areas of the Community facing certain structural difficulties.

For Britain a key part of the package is that national grants can in future be paid to farmers to help to protect the environment of the countryside, and in certain cases to restore damage already done to hedges, forests, and flora and fauna in general. The plan has been greeted with moderate delight by conservation bodies.

The new structural programme for the fisheries sector is not to be financed by the FEOGA.

COAL AND STEEL

The European Coal and Steel Community, although 'fused' with other Community institutions in a treaty signed in 1967, still has funds and rules of its own. Its major activities are concerned with improving production, cost effectiveness and marketing within the coal and steel industries themselves by means of very cheap loans. It also offers (through the industries) loans at 1 per cent for the improvement, purchase or modernisation of houses for workers, and can contribute (in the form of reimbursement to the government, not directly) to redundancy payments. This lies outside the scope of this book. Information is available from the Iron and Steel Division of the Department of Industry (Room 819), Ashdown House, 123 Victoria St., London SW1 (01-212 6069).

★ ★ ★ ★

There are, however, funds available in two areas of more general interest. These are:

(a) extremely cheap loans for job creation or expansion in traditional coal and steel regions (but not necessarily *in* those industries);
(b) grants for research (technical, economic, social or medical) in the coal and steel industries.

Loans to investors in traditional coal and steel areas (often known as 'Conversion' or 'Article 56' loans) are among the cheapest ways of getting access to loan capital, but have been all too rarely taken up, despite determined efforts by the British government as well as the Community and its various on-lending agencies to publicise them. This is no doubt partly due to the recession, and partly because banks and other bodies are reluctant to lend large sums at 6 per cent or 7 per cent interest when their own money may cost twice as much or more! But it may also be in part due to a misunderstanding of the terms under which these loans are made. There are remarkably few restrictions. The most important is geographical. Loans are

For detailed information see coloured page A21-23

generally-speaking only available in certain areas defined by the British government, within a 'travel-to-work' radius of steel or coal works which have suffered redundancies. There is, however:

- no restriction on the type of jobs created;
- no need to employ a fixed proportion of ex-coal or steel workers – merely to offer jobs to those who would probably have been in such industries should they still exist in the area;
- no limit to the size of the loans, except that they may not exceed 50 per cent of total investment.

Anyone may apply. For loans of £1 million or more, application forms must be completed by prospective borrowers and the government, and then submitted directly to the Commission (advice: Departments of Industry).

For loans between £250,000 and £1 million, apply to the local office of the Industrial and Commercial Finance Corporation.

For loans under £250,000 several banks and the Scottish and Welsh Development Agencies can on-lend, on slightly less advantageous terms.

Funds for *research* in the coal and steel industries are awarded in the light of programmes drawn up by the Commision. These are publicised in the Official Journal. Applicants need not be directly connected with either industry, but projects must be of potential value to the industries of more than one Community country.

Grants are given for technical or economic research relating to the production and increased (and effective) use of coal and steel. On a separate budget they may go to research concerning health, safety, and the quality of life in either industry. In general the Community can pay between 60 per cent and 75 per cent of the total cost of approved projects.

No tenders are published; you must submit your project direct to the Commission. Information: any Commission office.

RESEARCH AND DEVELOPMENT

The subject of Community funding for R & D is covered generally in the section entitled 'The New Technologies' (p. 85). Several sources of information relating to grants in this sphere should, however, be mentioned here.

Two particularly useful guides to these funds can be consulted at any Commission office or EDC. The first, a 'Guide to Sectoral Grants in Sciences and Technology' lists those programmes falling under the DG for Science, Research and Development (DG XII and the Joint Research Centre). It gives detailed information about current programmes and their objectives, details on how to apply, and specimen application forms. Even more comprehensive (though

For detailed information see coloured page A21-23

marginally out of date) is Appendix II to the Information Report on New Technologies produced by the Economic and Social Committee: the document number is CES 732/85. A great number of other sources of information are listed in the blue pages.

An excellent booklet is available free from the Department of Industry. It is entitled 'Research and Development in the European Community', and apart from giving full details on the type and number of projects which are being supported or considered worthy of support it lists (with addresses and telephone numbers of UK members of advisory committees, and those British experts best equipped to give advice on the range of Community assistance available) the priorities under which it is awarded, means of obtaining information about work already done, and ways of applying for Community aid. It is available free from Industrial & Commercial Policy (A Division), Dept. of Industry, Room 144, Ashdown House, 123 Victoria St., London SW1E 6RB.

Those wishing to keep abreast of Community research programmes can, if they are employed in any institute of higher learning, be put on the distribution list for an 'early warning' sheet, issued by the Commission office in London. This advises subscribers:

- when a proposal for a research programme is drafted;
- when it is adopted;
- when a call for the submission of projects is published in the Official Journal.

In the third case a copy (or a summary) of the call for submission will sometimes be attached.

To be put on the mailing list, write to the Commission at 8 Storey's Gate, SW1P 3AT – but only one notice can be sent to each university or polytechnic.

VENTURE CAPITAL

The availability of venture capital in the Community is growing steadily. Around £3.6 billion was made available for investment during 1985 – 40 per cent up on the previous year. More was on offer during 1986. In terms of take-up, most money has gone into industrial production – about 20 per cent of the total – with 11 per cent into consumer-related products and about the same into computers and computer-related products. Britain is by far the biggest investor in venture capital, having put up over 40 per cent of the Community total to date.

In 1985 the Commission took part for the first time in a pilot scheme for venture capital, to be made available to small and medium-sized enterprises, particularly those in the new industries. The scheme, known as Venture Consort, has been operated by the

For detailed information see coloured page A14, A21-23

European Venture Capital Association, with headquarters in Brussels. During its first 18 months of operation Venture Consort invested virtually all of its initial capital, supporting some 20 joint enterprises between SMEs in two or more Community countries. The Commission contributed about one-tenth of the £16 million involved, the rest coming from the private sector.

The future of Venture Consort is in some doubt, since the larger sums asked for in future years by the Commission look like being cut out of the budget. This would be a pity, since the scheme was described by the chairman of ECVA as having proved its usefulness and value beyond doubt. Information: DG XIII in the Commission in Luxembourg.

MISCELLANEOUS FUNDS

The Community is committed to assisting member states in helping exchange experience and skills in a great number of fields: many branches of education, the cultural field, the preservation and fostering of the lesser-used languages, European studies, and human rights. Many admirable analyses of the problems in these fields have been prepared by the Commission and the Parliament, and duly presented to the Council of Ministers. They have been rewarded with approving words and inadequate resources.

What actually exists in the way of Community funding is something of a ragbag. Detailed advice is available from any Commission office; what follows is a summary only.

EDUCATION

There is no Community education fund. The new schemes (COMETT, ERASMUS, etc.) are described in the section 'Youth and Education' (p. 143). Such other money as is available is limited and can support:

(a) postgraduate studies at the joint Research Centres and into European integration.

(b) joint study programmes organised by higher educational institutes in two or more member states.

(c) pilot projects related to the transition from school to work and the education of children of migrant workers.

(d) exchange study visits to enable administrators in higher and secondary education and vocational training to study methods in other member states.

(e) scholarships under the Paul Finet foundation to help with the education of orphans of coalminers and steelworkers.

For detailed information see coloured pages A19, A21-23

Information: from the Coal Industry Social Welfare Organisation, 25 Huddersfield Rd., Barnsley (0226 43239) or the Iron and Steel Trades Confederation, 324 Gray's Inn Rd., London WC1X 8DD (01-837 6691).

(f) grants from the Kreyssig Fund, which can assist in promoting awareness of the Community and its activities among young people or in adult education. Information: from the London Office of the Commission.

(g) 'Robert Schuman scholarships' – offered by the European Parliament for students in higher education or young researchers for studying the Parliament. Worth around £250 a month for three months. Scholarship holders are based at the Secretariat of the Parliament in Luxembourg under the supervision of a senior official of the Directorate-General for Research. Applicants whose speciality is languages are not normally accepted for Robert Schuman scholarships but can apply to the Director of Translation and Terminology of the European Parliament in Luxembourg. Details from the DG for Research and Documentation, European Parliament, Batiment Robert Schuman, Plateau du Kirchberg, Luxembourg.

(h) exchanges of young workers. These begin with eight weeks of coaching in the language of the host country, followed by from four to ten months at work in various industries (these change from year to year). Host firms are encouraged to pay wages, the Commission pays the rest, including travel, subsistence and pocket-money. Details (in the UK): Central Bureau for Educational Visits and Exchanges, with offices in London and Edinburgh.

(i) scholarships to study in Japan are occasionally invited from young businessmen. Information: DG I (B/2) of the Commission.

(j) grants for Joint Study programme preparation & development to support cooperation between institutions of higher learning in different Member States; preparatory grants (worth £1000) to study possibilities; development grants (worth £2500 initially) to set up a joint study programme. Information: ERASMUS Bureau, 15 rue d'Arlon, B1040 Brussels.

(k) short study visits by teachers, researchers or administrators in higher education. Intended to extend knowledge of teaching in other member states (but not to extend academic research). Grants of £1000 for individual study visits, up to £5500 for organisation visits. Leaflets as at (j) above.

CULTURE

'If we were beginning the European Community all over again,' said

Jean Monnet, one of its founding fathers, 'we should begin with culture.' In fact, it took 25 years before Ministers of culture in the Community even had their first meeting. This (in 1982) resulted in a budget marker of £450,000 for culture in all its aspects, in all 10 nations of the Community!

To be fair, the Council of Europe has traditionally involved itself in cultural matters, and the EC has not wished to tread on any toes. Such minor contributions as the Community has been able to make to the performing arts (for example during European Music Year in 1985) have often been organised jointly with the Council of Europe. (It is also true that Community countries compete against each other in cultural exports almost as fiercely as in any other.).

The Community has, however, helped to create the European Community Youth Orchestra, one of the finest in the world at any age.

It offers 50 annual grants under which architects, townplanners and craftsmen study conservation and restoration. There have been small grants to help preserve architectural heritage and a pilot scheme (in its third year) on conservation. The EIB can also make loans for conservation – either to preserve monuments of major interest or to attract tourists to poorer regions.

A European Foundation with a cultural remit is in the process of establishment in Paris; so far it is recruiting staff but has little in the way of an operating budget. If Commission guidelines are followed, its initial activities will be concentrated on 'free trade' in cultural goods, improving the living and working conditions of cultural workers, enlarging audiences, and doing more for Europe's heritage by helping with preservation.

Early in 1983 a European Bureau for Lesser-used Languages was established with the aid of a tiny fund (about £60,000 for the entire Community). It has headquarters in Dublin (Gael—Linn, 26 Merrion Square) and committees in five Community nations including the UK. An information bulletin on the work of the Bureau is available free; it helps coordinate studies and exchange information and experience among the 40 million citizens of the Community whose native language is other than one of the working languages. It also advises the Commission on cultural policy in peripheral regions and on minority languages.

In the spring of 1985 the Commission tabled a draft Regulation for aiding non-documentary films and TV productions, involving at least three partners from different member States. This might come in the form of grants towards production and promotional costs, or loans (perhaps interest-free).

It also sent to the Council a note on taxation in the cultural field, suggesting that creative and performing artists should be able to spread their tax burden over several years; and that there should be

For detailed information see coloured page A19, A21-23

various tax concessions for cultural foundations, private architectural heritage, and investment in culture generally.

Each year a 'European City of Culture' is nominated: Amsterdam in 1987 (when a European Sculpture Competition will be inaugurated), Berlin in 1988 and Paris in 1989. The UK's turn will come in 1990: several cities indicated their interest, with Glasgow proving the winner (you could have got 5 to 1 against). All Community countries have agreed to give young people access at cut-price rates to museums, art galleries and cultural events without discrimination. In late 1985 the Council agreed to encourage transnational cooperation in creating 'cultural itineraries', to encourage better knowledge of Europe's history and culture; vague promises were made of financial help from 'existing Community instruments'. Other ideas being pursued concern a European Information Centre on stolen works of art, help with translation and circulation of books across frontiers, and aid for joint audiovisual productions in the cultural sphere.

★ ★ ★ ★

Two points cause confusion. The Community Foundation being established in Paris is unconnected with the European Cultural Foundation in Amsterdam, although it will doubtless enjoy excellent relations with it. The latter was founded in 1954 and can help promote cultural matters at the European level, as well as work in the fields of education, the environment, social affairs, international relations and the media. Its address is Jan van Goyenkade 5, 1075 HN Amsterdam.

It should also be noted that the much larger sums of money given by the RDF to cultural institutions such as the Plymouth Centre and Pitlochry Festival Theatre were given quite specifically for the preservation of jobs in areas of particular importance to the tourist industry.

POCKETS OF MONEY

This is a subtle subject, largely undocumented. I tread with appropriate decorum.

The Commission, the Parliament, and a number of Community-aided bodies in such fields as trade unions, education, information, research, science, social affairs, and relations with the developing world, have funds at their elbow. These are used largely to support worthwhile events with a major Community input: conferences, seminars, pilot projects, visits and exchanges, the preparation of reports, the commissioning of particular research, and the dissemination of thinking and effort on topics of Community interest and involvment.

For detailed information see coloured page A23

These various commissioning agencies have tiny staffs. They start out, when they prepare their budgets, with the best of intentions. Money and help is spread evenly by subject, nation, target group, and organising body, within guidelines laid down by the Council and the Commission, and which are flexible and responsive to change. All of this would work splendidly if all the organising bodies concerned were equally good, or equally well staffed. They are not.

One result is that in the latter part of a financial year it sometimes becomes apparent that money (sometimes a good deal of it) has been committed but will not be spent. If it is not used before 31 December, it will be lost. Cheques begin to flutter from the mast-head.

Granted that pockets of money turn up now and then, how do you get hold of them? With some trepidation, a few thoughts are offered.

First, to repeat advice offered earlier, don't hesitate to ask again. If you have failed with your appeal for funds in April, try again about October. This applies whether you are proposing to convert an old church into training workshops for the unemployed, whether you would like a few hundred pounds to organise a seminar on the Community and the developing world, or whether you would like to organise a teach-in on the new technologies.

Second, keep an eye on what you read in the press (and more particularly *European Information Service* and *British Business*) about Community targets and changing priorities. If you have an idea which seems to coincide, find out the name and number of the right man to tackle in the Commission, and telephone, particularly between September and December.

Third, try to cultivate contacts in UKREP and the civil service in Britain, particularly those on Brussels working groups, or who regularly 'commute' on Community business. They receive the odd nod and a wink if money in a particular budget seems likely to be underspent. So do Euro-MPs.

Lastly, be prepared to move fast. You are competing against eager claimants from 11 other countries, some of them a good deal nearer to Brussels than you are.

For detailed information see coloured page A23

BRUSSELS: MAKING CONTACT

There is a widely held belief that the European Commission is over-staffed. Not so. On many Community affairs there are only one or two officials directly concerned with specific matters, and only one of them may be able to discuss complicated matters in English. (You will not go wrong if you speak good French.)

If you have a question on the Commission:

(1) Seek advice from one of the UK Information Offices of the Commission. They are listed on page A24. They should be able to give you an answer on the telephone, or in response to a letter if the matter is complex.

(2) If you wish to approach the Commission direct, *write* if the matter is not urgent. If you are in a hurry, *telex,* directing your message to the appropriate Directorate-General. (You should be able to identify this from the tables which follow.)

Telephoning is expensive, and can be frustrating. Commission officials work far from gentlemanly hours: from 08.30 to 18.00, and often later. (Remember that for much of the year Brussels is one hour ahead in time from the UK.) But they spend a great deal of time in meetings: it's an inescapable part of the job. Even if you know whom to ask for you may find it difficult to get hold of him or her. Wednesday is a particularly bad day to telephone Brussels.

MEPs have excellent contacts in Brussels and Luxembourg, as well as in the Parliament itself. They can often offer excellent advice, as can members of the Economic and Social Committee. (See page A12 for how to get hold of their names and addresses.)

But in many ways your best approach to the Commission (and to Community affairs in general) may well be through UKREP – the office of the United Kingdom Permanent Representative to the European Community. The address is rond-point Robert Schuman 6, 1040 Brussels, the telephone number Brussels 230-62-05, and the telex 24312.

Apart from the Permanent Representative and his deputy, there are Ministers or Counsellors for agriculture; external relations; information, press and institutions; legal matters; industry; economics and finance; and social affairs, environment, regional policy and transport.

Most are supported by junior diplomatic staff, and there are also First Secretaries for the developing world, transport, energy, right of establishment, customs and excise, fisheries and food, the budget, industry and competition, commercial matters, the institutions, and administration.

On no account visit Brussels on Community matters without contacting UKREP. They can help greatly to ease your difficulties, and avoid wasting your time and that of others.

The Commission of the European Communities
Rue de la Loi 200, 1049 Brussels
Telephone: 010-322-235-1111
Telex: 21877 COMEU B

Secretariat-General

Legal Service

Spokesman's Service (Porte-Parole)

Joint Interpreting and Conference Service

Statistical Office Batiment Jean Monnet, Rue Alcide de Gasperi, 2920 Luxembourg. Telephone Luxembourg 43011

DG I: EXTERNAL RELATIONS

Directorate A: GATT, OECD, commercial questions on agriculture, fishing, services and high technology, relations with South Africa

Directorate B: Relations with North America, Australia, New Zealand; external relations in science, research and nuclear energy

Directorate C: Economic Policy

Directorate D: Textiles agreements; trade in industrial products

Directorate E: Relations with north and central Europe and State trading nations

Directorate F: Relations with Japan, China and the Far East

Directorate G: Mediterranean, Near and Middle East

Directorate H: Relations with developing countries in Latin America and Asia (except the Far East)

Directorate I: North — South relations

DG II: ECONOMIC AND FINANCIAL AFFAIRS

Directorate A: National economies

Directorate B: Economic structure and Community intervention

Directorate C: Macroeconomic analyses and policies

Directorate D: Monetary matters (EMS, national and international); European Investment Bank Liaison

DG III: INTERNAL MARKET AND INDUSTRIAL AFFAIRS

Directorate A: Industrial Affairs (removal of technical barriers in mechanical engineering, foodstuffs, pharmaceuticals, electricity, chemicals, transport)

Directorate B: Non-tariff barriers, and obstacles to trade in textiles, paper, miscellaneous industries, public contracts and distribution

Directorate C: Approximation of laws, freedom of establishment, freedom to provide services

Directorate D: Steel

Directorate E: Industrial restructuring, non-member countries, raw materials; SMEs, Business Cooperation Centre

Task Force: Small and Medium-sized Enterprises
Unit 1: Policy and coordination
Unit 2: Relations with Community institutions
Unit 3: Implementation of Commmunity projects (including Business Cooperation Centre)

DG IV: COMPETITION

Directorate A: General competition policy

Directorate B: Restrictive practices and abuse of dominant positions (1) – manufacturers, textiles, service industries

Directorate C: Restrictive practices and abuse of dominant positions (2) – steel, coal, transport, energy, agriculture and food, metals, minerals, construction, wood and paper

Directorate D: Coordination of decisions on fair competition

Directorate E: State aids

DG V: EMPLOYMENT, SOCIAL AFFAIRS AND EDUCATION

Directorate A: Employment (including social aspects and equal treatment for women)

Directorate B: Living and working conditions and welfare

Directorate C: Education, vocational training, youth and the disabled

Directorate D: The European Social Fund

Directorate E: Health and safety at work

DG VI: AGRICULTURE

Directorate A: General matters (analysis, studies, relations with NGOs)

Directorate B: Agricultural legislation (including veterinary regulations)

Directorate C: Markets in crops (cereals, rice, sugar, olives, oil seeds, protein and textile plants)

Directorate D: Markets (livestock): milk, beef, veal and sheepmeat, animal feed, pigmeat, poultry

Directorate E: Markets in specialised crops: fruit, vegetables, alcohol, tobacco, hops, potatoes etc

Directorate F-1: Agricultural structure and forestry

Directorate F-2: FEOGA Guidance Fund and research

Directorate G: FEOGA Guarantee Fund

Directorate H: International affairs

DG VII: TRANSPORT

Directorate A: Maritime transport legislation, economics

Directorate B: Inland transport (including safety and research)

Directorate C: Air transport, infrastructure, social and ecological matters

DG VIII: DEVELOPMENT

Directorate A: Development activities (including food aid, energy, mining and industry, commercial development and primary products)

Directorate B: West and Central Africa

Directorate C: East and Southern Africa, the Indian Ocean

Directorate D: Mediterranean (south and east), the Caribbean and Pacific

Directorate E: Finance (including emergency aid); the EDF

DG IX: PERSONNEL AND ADMINISTRATION

Directorate A: Personnel (including recruitment, training and the Stagiaire system)

DG X: INFORMATION, COMMUNICATION AND CULTURE

(See page A24 for UK information offices)

Directorate A: Information (including decentralised information and documentation, development, trade union and social affairs, and higher education)

Directorate B: Communication (including campaigns and exhibitions, women, youth and sport, audiovisual production, radio and TV studios, publications and public relations)

DG XI: ENVIRONMENT, CONSUMER PROTECTION AND NUCLEAR SAFETY

Directorate A: Protection and improvement of the environment

Directorate B: Protection and promotion of consumer interests

DG XII: SCIENCE, RESEARCH AND DEVELOPMENT

Directorate A: Scientific and technical coordination, cooperation with non-member countries, COST, FAST, CREST

Directorate B: Means of action: budget policy, research, contracts

Directorate C: Technical research (new technologies, steel)

Directorate D: Nuclear research, and safety

Directorate E: Alternative energy, conservation, and energy R & D

Directorate F: Biology, radiation protection, medical research

Directorate G: Environment, raw materials and materials technology (including waste)

JOINT RESEARCH CENTRE

21020 Ispra, Italy. Telephone 78-91-11.

DG XIII: TELECOMMUNICATIONS, INFORMATION INDUSTRY AND INNOVATION

Directorate A: New Technologies

Directorate B: Information management

Task Force: Information and telecommunications technologies:

Directorate A: Information technology – ESPRIT

Directorate B: Telecommunications

DG XIV: FISHERIES

Directorate A: Markets and international questions

Directorate B: Internal resources and monitoring

Directorate C: Structural policy

DG XV: FINANCIAL INSTITUTIONS AND TAXATION

Directorate A: Financial institutions (banks, insurance, stock exchanges, etc)

Directorate B: Company law, taxation, capital movements

DG XVI: REGIONAL POLICY

Directorate A: Guidelines and priorities

Directorate B: Preparation and assessment of operations, including ECSC loans

Directorate C: Development operations, including implementation of ERDF integrated operations and programmes

DG XVII: ENERGY

Directorate A: Energy policy, analysis, forecasts and contracts

Directorate B: Coal

Directorate C: Oil and natural gas

Directorate D: Nuclear energy policy

Directorate E: Energy saving and alternative energy sources, electricity and heat

Directorate F: Euratom Safeguards

DG XVIII: CREDIT AND INVESTMENTS

(Batiment Jean Monnet, Rue Alcide de Gasperi, 2920 Luxembourg. Telephone: 430 11.)

Directorate A: Borrowing and administration of funds

Directorate B: Investments and loans

DG XIX: BUDGETS

Directorate A: Expenditure

Directorate B: Resources

Directorate C: Budget execution

DG XX: FINANCIAL CONTROL

Directorate A: Internal control of operating, research and cooperation expenditure

Directorate B: Control of revenue, agricultural, Regional and Social Fund expenditure

DG XXI: CUSTOMS UNION AND INDIRECT TAXATION

Directorate A: External tariff matters

Directorate B: Customs union legislation

Directorate C: Indirect taxation, including VAT

DG XXII: COORDINATION OF STRUCTURAL INSTRUMENTS

OFFICE FOR OFFICIAL PUBLICATIONS OF THE EUROPEAN COMMUNITIES (OOPEC)

(5 rue de Commerce, 2985 Luxembourg. Telephone 49 00 81. Telex 1324, PUBOFLU)

COMMISSION INFORMATION OFFICES IN EUROPE

Belgium

Bruxelles/Brussels
Rue Archimède 73,
1040 Bruxelles
Tel. 235 11 11
Telex 26657 COMINF B

Denmark
Kobenhavn
Hojbrohus
Ostergrade 61
Postbox 144
1004 Kobenhavn K
Tel. 14 41 40
Telex 16402 COMEUR DK

France
Paris
61, rue des Belles Feuilles
75782 Paris Cedex 16
Tel. 501 58 85
Telex Paris 630176 F COMEUR

Marseille
(sub office attached to
Paris office)
C.M.C.I. Bureau 320
2, rue Henri Barbusse
F-13241 Marseille CEDEX 01
Tel. abbreviated code 8467

Federal Republic Germany
Bonn
Zitelmannstraß 22
5300 Bonn
Tel. 23 80 41
Telex 886648 EUROP D

Berlin (sub office attached to
Bonn office)
Kurfürstendamm 102
1000 Berlin 31
Tel. 8924028
Telex 184015

Munich
(sub office attached to
Bonn office)
Erhardstraße 27
8000 München
Tel. 23 99 29 00
Telex 52 18 135

Greece
2, Vassilissis Sofias
T.K. 1602
Athens 134
Tel. 724 39 82/724 39 83/
724 39 84
Telex 219324 ECAT GR

Ireland
Dublin
39 Molesworth Street
Dublin 2
Tel. 71 22 44
Telex 2551 EUCO EI

Italy
Roma
Via Poli 29
00187 Roma
Tel. 678 97 22
Telex 610184 EUROMAI

Milano (sub office attached to
Roma office)
Corso Magenta 61
20123 Milano
Tel. 80 15 05/6/7/8
Telex 316002 EURMIL I

Luxembourg
Luxembourg
Bâtiment Jean Monnet
Rue Alcide de Gasperi
2920 Luxembourg
Tel. 430 11
Telex 3423/3446/
3476 COMEUR LU

Netherlands
Den Haag
Lange Voorhout 29
Den Haag
Tel. 46 93 26
Telex 31094 EURCO NL

Portugal
Lisboa
Rua do Sacramento à Lapa 35
1200 Lisboa
Tel. 60 21 99
Telex 18810 COMEUR P

Spain
Madrid
Calle de Serrano 41
5a Planta
Madrid 1
Tel. 435 17 00/435 15 28
Telex 46818 OIPE E

Switzerland
Genève
Case postale 195
37-39, rue de Vermont 1211
Geneve 20
Tel. 34 97 50
Telex 28261 and
28262 ECOM CH

Turkey
Ankara
Kuleli Sokak 15
Gazi Osman Paça
Ankara
Tel. 27 61 45/27 61 46
Telex 42819 ATBE TR

COMMISSION OFFICES IN THIRD COUNTRIES
A list of Commission offices in third countries is given in the Commission Directory (available in any Commission office or EDC).

PART VIII

SOURCES OF INFORMATION

CONTENTS

★ ★ ★ ★ ★

REFERENCES TO MAIN TEXT:

INTRODUCTION

The first section (pages A5 to A11) lists general sources of reference. The second (pages A11 to A23) follows the main text of the book.

If no symbol appears before separate references, the pamphlets or booklets mentioned are *free*. You can get them from any Commission office (addresses: page A24) or the source indicated.

The symbol ★ means that the source of reference can normally be consulted at any Commission office or European Documentation Centre (listed on page A23).

Two contractions are used repeatedly: EF means European File, and ED means European Documentation. A complete list of the booklets or pamphlets in these free series is given on pages A6/7.

Several publications (in particular the *European Information Service* and *British Business)* are mentioned so often that it has not always seemed necessary to refer back to them. They are described (with prices and sources) on page A6.

A Basic Library about the Community
is available free from any Commission office
Here it is

1 *Working Together* by Emile Noël, Secretary-General of the Commission. A 40-page guide to the Institutions of the Community and how they work.
2 *Steps to European Unity.* A chronological account of the Community's origins and development.
3 *Britain in the EC – the Impact of Membership.* A detailed summary of developments since 1972. Covers most areas of policy; particularly strong on trade, industry, agriculture and legislation. *Regional versions* for Northern Ireland, Scotland, Wales, and the major English regions are available and contain much additional detailed material. *Note:* stocks of the current editions of these dossiers are dwindling, but you may be lucky. They can be consulted at any Commission office. All are being revised.
4 *One Parliament for Ten.* The European Parliament – its powers, groupings, committees, etc. Colour.
5 *About Europe.* A substantial, illustrated booklet examining many Community policies.
6 *Finance from Europe.* Detailed guide to Community funds.
7 *The EC as a Publisher.* 80-page pocket catalogue of material about the Community, by subject.
8 *Europe at a Glance* – a brief guide to the Community and Britain's share in its activities.
9 *Scotland in Europe and Questions and Answers (Wales)* are available free from the Commission's offices in Edinburgh and Cardiff respectively.
   NOTE: *Multiple copies of the last two series of pamphlets may be available for seminars, etc.*

FOR SCHOOLS

10 The EEC – *Why? What? Who? How?* A brief guide to the Community and the UK's role in it, with suggested study subjects.
11 *The European Parliament* – 6 pages, colour, map with Euroconstituencies, list of MEPs, etc.
12 *Britain, Europe, the World.* (Big type, bright illustrations, for children in senior schools). And these may be free in a single copy for classrooms.
13 *Wallchart:* The European Community: What it is, How it works. Brightly illustrated, covering many Community policies.
14 *Learning About the European Community.* (Two volumes.) Designed for work with 14–16 year olds, this consists of an Information Booklet and Teacher's Guide (Part I) and a Pupils' Workbook to accompany this (Part II). Free from any Commission office.
15 *Map:* The European Community. 42 x 25cm, colour, useful facts and figures.
16 *A Journey through the EC.* 60pp, colour, with facts, figures and illustrations relating to all 12 Community countries, a brief introduction to the Community and its institutions, and an excellent chronological table. (Single copy may be available free; on sale at HMSO, price £1.40.)
17 *E12.* A 44-page booklet, illustrating in maps, graphs and coloured tables, the Community's place in the world in terms of demography, industry, commerce, employment, wealth, etc. Attractive for classroom projects.

HOW TO KEEP UP TO DATE

Read the *Financial Times* and *The Independent* (plus the *Aberdeen Press and Journal* if you have a particular interest in agriculture or fisheries).

Get on the list for the *newsletters* published by the Commission Offices in Cardiff and Belfast, and anything published by your *local* MEP.

Ditto for *Background Reports* from the London Office of the Commission, which offer useful updates on Community policies as they affect Britain.

Ditto for EP *News,* a free monthly tabloid about the work of the Parliament, written for the UK. Free from 2 Queen Anne's Gate, SW1H 9AA.

Ditto for *The Kangaroo News,* an admirable tabloid newspaper published by a ginger group, headed (in the UK) by Basil de Ferranti, MEP, and available from Millbank Tower, London SW1.

Ditto (if you live in Ireland) for *Community Report* published by the Commission Office in Dublin and available from 39 Molesworth Street, Dublin 2.

★Subscribe to *European Information Service,* the bulletin of the International Union of Local Authorities. This is designed primarily for local authorities, but is perhaps the best regular summary of developments in Community policies published in the UK, containing material which appears nowhere else. (10 times per annum, £30 post free, from 12 Old Queen Street, SW1H 9HP.)

★Read *British Business,* the weekly magazine published by the DTI. The best running source of information about EC policies from the point of view of HMG; indispensable for businessmen and industrialists. (£75pa post-free, from HMSO, PO Box 276, SW8 5DT.)

★Subscribe to the papers produced by *The Planning Exchange,* 186 Bath St, Glasgow. Written or edited by Peter Aitken, these are intended primarily for local authorities, but are excellently detailed and again contain material available nowhere else.

Get on the list for the EC *Briefs* produced by Barclays Bank European Community Unit, 54 Lombard St., EC3P 3AH, the series 'Doing Business in the European Community' produced by National Westminster Bank, Office of EEC Affairs, 41 Lothbury, London EC2P 2BP, the Touche Ross European Commentary, which has a useful 'Brussels Update', and everything produced by the Midland Bank.

Get the magazine FACTS free with membership of the European Movement – full of useful information and authoritative articles. 1A Whitehall Place, London SW1.

Get on the list for SCAD NEWS, published several times a year and updating the catalogue. 'The EC as a Publisher' – see Basic library. Free from OOPEC.

Keep in touch with your nearest *Commission office* or *European Documentation Centre.* List: page A23/24.

THE EUROPEAN FILE (EF) SERIES

This series (free in single copies from any Commission Office) builds into an excellent brief guide to the Community's policies and their progress. Regularly updated, and 8–12 pages long on average, they are written for readers in the Community as a whole and not only for those in Britain. The following titles should be in stock and can certainly be photo-copied on request. (An asterisk indicates that they are shortly to be updated.)

EUROPEAN FILE:
CHRONOLOGICAL INDEX
1980

11/80 Tomorrow's bio-society★
12/80 A future for Europe's wine
17–18/80 The Community of Ten: welcome to Greece

1981

9/81 Generalized preferences for the Third World
18/81 Towards the European patent and trade mark

1982

9/82 The European Community and state aids to industry
11/82 Europe against poverty
14/82 The European Community and world hunger★
18/82 Euronet-Diane: towards a common information market★

1983

6/83 The Community and small and medium-sized enterprises

7/83 Social security: a Europe-wide debate

9/83 The Europe – United States – Japan trade controversy

13/83 European political cooperation

17/83 The enlargement of the European Community

1984

1/84 New rights for the citizens of Europe

3/84 Young people in the EC

4/84 Equal opportunity for women

5–6/84 The EC: some questions and answers

7/84 FAST: Where does Europe's future lie?

8/84 The EC and new technologies

9/84 Workers' rights in industry

10/84 Tax harmonization

13/84 Recognition of diplomas and professional qualifications

15/84 The regions of Europe

16/84 The Community and the car industry

1985

1/85 European Community borrowing and lending

2/85 The European steel policy

3/85 The EC and education

4/85 Company Law

5/85 The EC and environmental protection

6/85 European competition policy

7/85 European regional policy

8/85 The European internal market

9/85 The EC and the Third World

10/85 The Community and transport

11/85 Tourism and the EC

12/85 The EC and consumers

13/85 Migrants in the European Community

14/85 The EC and research policy

15/85 European research policy

16/85 The Nuclear industries in the EC

17/85 A Community of Twelve: welcome to Spain and Portugal

19/85 The EC and the textile industry

20/85 European File: Catalogue 1979–85

1986

1/86 The integrated Mediterranean programmes

2/86 Europe's common agriculture policy

3/86 Towards a people's Europe

4/86 An industrial strategy for Europe

5–6/86 EUR12: diagrams of the enlarged Community

7/86 European demonstration projects in the energy field

8/86 The social policy of the European Community

9/86 Towards a Europe without Frontiers: The approximation of European tax systems

10/86 The common fisheries policy

11/86 The institutions of the EC

12/86 The EC and Latin America

13/86 Telecommunications and Europe's future

14/86 Television and the audio-visual sector: towards a European policy

15/86 The European Monetary system

16/86 The European Community in the world

17/86 The EC budget

18/86 The Sprint Programme

1987

1/87 The external trade of the EC

2/87 The European energy policy

THE EUROPEAN DOCUMENTATION (ED) SERIES

Individual policies covered in more detail. Single copies free from any Commission office. Usually from 30 to 80 pages long and occasionally amusingly illustrated, they have statistical tables and a bibliography. For those who want to learn more than is contained in the European File. Because of their comprehensiveness, they become out of date relatively quickly. Current titles include:

4/79 25 Years of EC external relations

5/79 The second enlargement of the EC

1/80 The Community and its regions

3/80 Cultural action in the EC

6/80 The EC and vocational training

4/81 The Economic and Monetary Union

3/82 Freedom of movement
4/82 An education policy for Europe
5/82 The EC's industrial strategy
6/82 The agricultural policy of the EC
1/83 The EC and the energy problem
2/83 Wine in the EC
5/83 The Social policy of the EC
6/83 The Customs Union
1/84 The EC's environment policy
3/84 The EC's transport policy
4/84 Women in the EC
5/84 The EC's legal system
6/84 The ECU
7/84 The economy of the EC
1/85 The EC's fishery policy
2/85 The EC's research policy
3/85 Grants and loans from the EC
4/85 The EC and the Mediterranean
5/85 Nuclear safety in the EC
1/86 The EC's budget
2/86 The ABC of Community law
3/86 European unification
4/86 Europe as seen by Europeans
5/86 The Court of Justice of the EC

STATISTICS

A mass of statistical information of every
kind is available in the EUROSTAT series,
published by OOPEC (see page A24) and
held by Commission Offices and EDCs. (Get
the annual free catalogue of publications –
see *Basic Library* – for an indication of what
it contains.)

There is also a free quarterly, *Eurostat
News*.

★ The *Eurostat Review*, published
annually, covers the previous ten years in
statistical terms for all Community
countries. It includes economic, industrial,
social, agricultural, trade and other matters
and is broken down in immense detail.
(£7.50 from sales agents – see page A25 – for
250 crammed pages.)

★ There are two digests: a pocket-book,
Basic Statistics of the Community, available
from sales agents at £3.40, and a free leaflet,
Statistical Panorama, from OOPEC.

POLITICAL OPINION

★ The best source of information about
government and opposition views on
Community matters is, of course, *Hansard.*
House of Lords debates on Europe are
particularly well informed. Lists of
documents produced by the Scrutiny

committees of both Houses are published
regularly in the *London Gazette,* and
occasionally featured in *British Business.*
Speeches by Ministers and shadow
spokesmen on Community matters are
often much fuller (and more balanced) than
newspaper or TV reports indicate; party
headquarters will often supply full texts.

An excellent 60-page booklet, *Britain in
the European Community,* is published by
the COI as No. 73/86 in its reference
pamphlet series. It summarises the
Community's institutions, policies and
principles from the point of view of the
government, includes an excellent
chronology from 1946 to June 1986, and
demonstrates a degree of commitment
unusual in an official publication.

★ A good resumé of Parliamentary
Scrutiny of Community business is
contained in *European Community
Information – its use and users* (see page
A9).

The Financial Times and *The
Independent* are indispensable, and many
of the heavy dailies, nationally and
regionally, report Community affairs in
detail.

BUSINESS AND
INDUSTRY

Although there is much Community
material on all aspects of trade and
industry, it is largely written from a very
general point of view, and is listed later
under subject headings. Material for British
businessmen and others trading with
Europe is very largely national in origin,
and the appropriate bodies (the DTI and the
British Overseas Trade Board, the CBI,
Customs and Excise, various quangos, and
many commercial organisations) have
produced useful guides.

★*British Business* is indispensable. Other
useful addresses for those concerned in
investing and exporting to Europe are given
on pages A25/27. In general, there will be
an enquiry point – in most cases the
simplest approach is to ask for 'enquiries'
rather than to be specific with the operator.
Commission information offices will
usually be able to give you a name and a
telephone number.

Detailed advice for potential exporters to
EEC countries is contained in a series
produced by the National Westminster

Bank, called *Doing Business in the EEC*. Free from the Bank's Office of EEC Affairs, 41 Lothbury, EC2P 2BP.

Chambers of Commerce can often be useful.

A guide for exporters, *Selling to Western Europe* is free from BOTB, 1 Victoria Street, SW1H 0ET.

Both *Official Sources of Finance and Aid for Industry in the UK*, published by Natwest, and *The EEC – A Guide to Finance, Trade and Investment* from the Midland have useful sections for businessmen and exporters.

The City and Europe, a brief by Stephen Hugh-Jones, looks at British financial services in the EC; it is now somewhat out of date, but copies may still be available at Commission offices.

★ World Trade Intelligence publishes a series: *Exporting to France, Exporting to Germany*, and so on, for all Community Countries. Details: FREEPOST London EC2B 2LA.

Those interested in competing for *contracts* (both inside the Community and in areas benefitting from Community aid) should get:

(a) The brief *Opportunities for Contracts under EEC Aid Programmes*, produced by UKREP and available from Rond-Point Schuman 6, 1040 Brussels. This gives not only the facts, but the essential names and telephone numbers.

(b) Two pamphlets from the EIB: *Financing under the Lomé Convention*, and *Financing outside the Lomé Community: Mediterranean Countries:*

(c) *The TED Action Pack* – your key to the public tenders market, a useful guide to tendering (and, in particular learning about tenders in good time). Free from any Commission office.

★ GENERAL REFERENCE

All Commission Offices, all EDCs, and most public libraries will have a range of reference books and other material; it is impossible to quote them all. The list which follows is based upon those most often consulted in the Commission offices of the UK.

The *Official Journal* – the Community's running record of virtually all its activities (see page A10).

Commission Documents (COMDOCS). Even more detailed (and not all published in the OJ). There is an excellent Index to COMDOCS, written by Giancarlo Pau, and available (£19.50) from Eurofi, the Old Rectory, Northill, Beds (SG18 9HA.)

European Information Service, British Business, and Britain in the European Community are all invaluable.

Annual Reports cover policies by sector, and *Monthly Bulletins* give a brief running record of developments. Both are published by the Commission.

A Directory of Community Legislation in Force is published annually in Brussels by the Commission.

A free leaflet available from OOPEC entitled *Focus on Europe* lists some of the booklets and periodicals which are available for sale from HMSO, Alan & Armstrong, or direct from Luxembourg. The *European Perspectives* series is particularly useful, covering such subjects as Community law, finance, trade, the professions, and the new technologies.

★PUBLISHED BOOKS

There are so many published books about the Community that it would be impossible to quote them all here. The selection below is a personal and empirical one; they are selected as much for their value as a guide to further reading as for their own excellent qualities. Between them they cover a great deal of ground.

The European Community – the Practical Guide for Business and Government, by Brian Morris, Peggy Crane and Klaus Boehm (Macmillan). In alphabetical form, with useful appendices and an additional index. Detailed, particularly sound on references to source material.

The Common Market and How It Works, by Anthony J C Kerr (Pergamon Press). Comprehensive, well written, much inside information, excellent bibliography. In process of reprinting with revisions.

European Communities Information – its use and users (edited Michael Hopkins, Mansell Publishing Ltd). Up to date, of particular interest to librarians.

Making Sense of Europe, by Christopher Tugendhat (Viking), written for the 'Community-watcher' rather than the layman, is particularly vivid in its account of the way the Commission goes about its task, and the difficulties of reconciling national loyalties with a sense of common purpose.

Common Market Digest (David Overton, the Library Association). Admirably arranged (typically each subject is covered under 'Basic Information', 'Purpose and Method' and 'Further Information'). Excellent Index.

Doing Business in the European Community (John Drew, for Touche Ross International). Indispensable for the businessman and industrialist, but also has good short summaries of policies. Excellent bibliography.

FILMS AND AUDIOVISUAL MATERIAL

A number of *films and video-cassettes* are available on loan, free of charge, to schools, universities, professional associations, etc. A list of these is available from both the Commission and Parliament Offices in London. (Waiting lists tend to be long – apply well in advance.)

Most are general; but there are also films on particular problems – equal opportunities, accident prevention, a guide for businessmen (Europe of Opportunities), agriculture, ESPRIT, the environment, research and development, help for SMEs, etc.

Two films are particularly designed for use in schools: *Decision Time,* for sixth forms, in which students simulate the working of the Community, and *Europe, Why?* a general introduction to the Community for senior pupils.

There is also a tape/slide presentation with accompanying handbook, entitled *The European Economic Community, Past, Present and Future,* available on loan from Commission offices. This is intended for fourth to sixth form pupils following social science and liberal studies courses.

From the European Parliament you can borrow *The European Parliament in 20 Slides, together with explanatory notes.* A film on the work of the Parliament with a commentary by Peter Ustinov, 'Our Europe' (20 mins) is also available on cassette. There are also attractive *wallcharts* and a series of *posters* describing the work of the Parliament and its various committees.

★ THE FULLEST DETAIL

It is widely believed that all the secrets of the Community lie buried in the *Official Journal,* and that if only someone had time to read it, all would become clear. This is nearly true.

The OJ is indeed the Community's running record of its activities. It contains all proposed and actual legislation and a great deal else besides, and its text is precise. It can be bought from official agents (see page A25) by the single copy (although popular issues sometimes sell out very quickly) or by annual subscription which costs £121 per annum on paper. (It is also available on microfiche at £110 per annum.) And it can, of course be consulted at any Commission office or EDC.

Finding the right issue is not always easy; the index takes a bit of getting used to. Your best method is to consult the monthly *Bulletin,* which, although brief, covers most of the Community's work and gives reference numbers for the appropriate copies of the OJ.

But there is much that the OJ does not contain. For this you must turn to *Commission Documents,* or COMDOCS.

These are the vehicles through which the Commission communicates with the Council. They contain all proposals for new legislation, new policy initiatives, action reports and 'state of play' papers. In the case of proposals for legislation, the text will indeed be carried by the OJ. But the COMDOC will often have a lengthy explanatory memorandum, with a summary, which will not be printed in the OJ.

You cannot buy a single COMDOC (although you can consult it in Commission offices or EDCs). You can, however, subscribe to the whole series, or by individual subjects (agriculture, law, transport, competition etc), up to a total of five subjects. Prices range from £130.50 per annum for papers on agriculture to £6.50 for papers on regional policy. The whole series is available on paper at £522, or on microfiches at £91.25 – this last a remarkable bargain. (Details: OOPEC.)

There are also similar papers produced by the *European Parliament,* and the detailed *Opinions of the Economic and Social Committee.* Both are obtainable from OOPEC in the same way.

Government Departments often issue *explanatory memoranda* when they are incorporating Community legislation in national law. These are particularly valuable when, as is often the case, there is a considerable interval between agreement in the Council of Ministers and actual application of the new legislation in individual countries. For example, although the UK is not yet required fully to implement Community legislation on the quality of drinking water, a full memorandum by the Department of the Environment, explaining in detail the implications of the new rules, was available as early as 19 August 1982.

It is scarcely necessary to remind anyone who has got this far in the book of the excellence of *British Business,* the *European Information Service,* the notes produced by the Planning Exchange, and the various publications of *Eurofi.*

But two publications have not been mentioned and yet are, in fact, the fullest of all. These are *Agence Europe* and *European Report.* Both appear daily in English as well as other languages; both have 'hot' news, detailed background material, and inside information not available from any other source. They differ in presentation but not in excellence. Read either daily, and you will be magnificently informed on every aspect of the Community's activities. Addresses: any Commission Office.

Agence Europe costs 36,000 Belgian francs per annum, post free, and *European report* 29,900 BF, post free.

There is, lastly, an immense amount of detailed material in commissioned *Reports* and *Studies.* It would be impossible to list these here. To take a single example by way of illustration: Study No. 23 in the Regional Policy Series (1984) is entitled 'The effects of new information technology on the less-favoured regions of the Community'. It was prepared for the Commission, and directed and coordinated by the University of Newcastle. Experts from all Community countries contributed to it. Its detailed conclusions (oversimplified) were that not only were peripheral and less favoured regions of the Community lagging behind the central regions and falling to share in the benefits of new information technology, but the gap shows signs of widening rather than narrowing. The study proposed a regional policy for information technology.

A few of these studies are mentioned in the pocket catalogue (see *Basic Library*), but many are listed only in the fuller catalogue of publications available from OOPEC, and some cannot be bought at all. They can, however, be consulted at all Commission offices and EDCs.

THE EUROPEAN COMMUNITY AND ITS PURPOSES

In the *Basic Library* (page A5), numbers 1, 2, 4, 5, and 8, are all relevant, as is European File (EF) 5/84, and 3/86 in the European Documentation (ED) series. For *schools,* nos. 10–17 in the *Basic Library* are available.

Audio-visual material is listed on page A10. There are very many *published books,* among the best those by Richard Mayne. Anthony J C Kerr (page A9) has an excellent bibliography.

The *Programme of the Commission* (Bulletin Supplement 1/86) lays out in detail what the current Commission sees as the Community's objectives and how it proposes to pursue them.

★ *Working for Europe* is a record of the ambitions, achievements and failures of the Commission between 1981 and 1984.

★ *The Community Today,* though very out of date, is still an excellent assessment, by young European civil servants, of what they believe in and why they work for it. Good bibliography.

★ *Making Sense of Europe* by Christopher Tugendhat (page A10) gives an insiders view on the recent scene.

THE UK IN THE COMMUNITY

In the *Basic Library,* No. 3 (and its regional versions) are essential reading. 1, 2, 4 and 8 are also relevant.

★ *Hansard,* the *European Information Service, British Business* and the *Financial Times* are the best sources of information on government and opposition views on membership and policy.

Background Reports produced by the Commission's London office are free and helpful. All *published books* listed (page A10) are useful, particularly *Doing Business in the European Community*.

★A particularly good article, 'Getting Business from the EC' was published in the 26 July 1985 edition of *British Business*. Apart from many useful addresses and telephone numbers, it lists free publications on Western Europe available from the British Overseas Trade Board.

Three excellent recent publications are mentioned in the main text. They are *Britain in the European Community*, from COI, the British Business *DTI Guide*, and *The EEC: A Guide to Finance, Trade and Investment*, available from the Midland Bank.

THE WAY THE EUROPEAN COMMUNITY WORKS

In the *Basic Library*, nos 1, 4 and 8 are particularly useful. 10 and 11 are specifically designed for use in schools. EF 11/86 is short and factual.

Audio-visual material on the institutions and the way they work is listed on page A10.

Background Report 4/85 gives a list of the new members of the Commission and their responsibilities.

★The *Directory of the Commission* gives a complete breakdown of the Directorates-General and other agencies, by subject, with names.

★The *Guide to the Council* does the same for the Council of Ministers, and also includes information on working parties, special committees, foreign representation in Brussels etc. (Pub. twice yearly by the Council.)

★*Council and Commission Committees*, a Bulletin Supplement (2/80) is self-explanatory, but also includes references to the OJs which set up the committees and their terms of reference.

The Economic and Social Committee is a free booklet which describe the work of that body and the ways in which it exerts influence. There is also a ★*Directory* of the Committee, broken down by country and by group, with names, and monthly and annual *Reports*, and detailed *Opinions* are available for consultation. A free *Catalogue of Publications* is available from Commission offices.

The Court of Justice of the EC and *The ABC of Community Law* are both available free in the ED series, and together form an excellent layman's guide to the work of the Court.

The EC's Legal System, in the same series, is for those with some legal knowledge.

Do you Know Your Rights? is a pack of leaflets covering social rights, industry, business and the environment in the light of Court judgements.

★'The functioning of the Community' a paper in Issue 1 of *Government and Industry*, published by Kluwer gives a detailed insider's guide to the institutions, the way in which they work together, and Britain's approach to the process. Written by Bill Nicoll, ex-Deputy Permanent Representative and now Director-General in the Council Secretariat, it is particularly interesting in its detailed account of the workings of the Council and the Commission on a day-to-day basis.

THE UNCOMMON MARKET — POLICIES AND PEOPLE

In the *Basic Library*, nos. 2, 3, 4 and 5 are relevant. In the EF series, see in particular 9/82, 19/83, 4/86 and 9/86.

There are useful *Background Reports:* 18/84 (on *Expanding the internal market – removal of internal barriers to trade); 14/84 (A new commercial protection policy); 2/84 (The City and Europe); 20/85 (Completing the Internal Market); 9/85 (Harmonisation: a New Approach)* and 15/85 *(The British Presidency).*

The Customs Union (6/83 in the ED series) is a good general introduction.

The *White Paper on completing the internal market* (the 'Cockfield White Paper') is available in a free off-print from any Commission office. An excellent abridgement with a detailed introduction is available from Touche Ross International.

★The abridged edition of the *Treaties* establishing the European Communities is available in pocket-book form at £4.90 – a bargain.

DECISION-MAKING AND HOW IT IS INFLUENCED

In the *Basic Library,* 1, 4 and 8 are relevant. EF 11/86 outlines the decision-making process briefly. *Background Report* 24/82 outlines Community *voting* procedures. *The Directory of the European Commission* and the *Guide to the Council* break down these institutions by area of work, with names. The latter also lists the specialists in UKREP.

European Information Service and British Business are good at reporting progress on draft legislation. *Anthony Kerr* (page A9) gives an insider's view, provocatively and interestingly.

Parliamentary Questions (published in the OJ) often elicit a great deal of information on subjects being considered, and the *Reports* of Committees can also be consulted or bought. Committees of the Parliament and their members are listed in the EP Bulletin available from EP or Commission offices.

A list of trade, professional and other bodies which 'lobby' Brussels on behalf of their members is given in *'The European Community – the practical guide'* (page A9).

Three other books are helpful. *Who's who in the European Committees* (pub. Brussels, Delta), EEC *Contacts* by Jim Hogan (pub. Eurofi, Northill, Biggleswade, Beds.,) and in particular *Doing Business in the European Community* (page A10).

*Bill Nicoll's paper on 'The Functioning of the Community' (see page A12) is of particular value in its account of decision-making and how it can be influenced.

EMPLOYMENT

(See also 'Social Policy', 'The Troubled Industries', 'SMEs', 'The New Technologies', and Part VII.)

Basic Library: 3, 5 and 6. *European Files* 6/83 and 4/86. Current *employment strategy* is outlined in The Commission Programme (Bulletin Supplement 1/86) and subsequent papers; *Background Reports* 26/85, 27/85, 10/86 and 12/86 are relevant.

*The *Annual Economic Report* gives facts and figures about employment and industry in the Community and elsewhere.

Commission plans for the *'radical solutions'* though summarised in the EFs and Background Reports listed above, are best read in COMDOCS: 83/543 on overtime, 81/775, 81/779 and 82/830 on flexible retirement and part-time work. Council recommendations on retirement are in OJ L357.

Background Reports 27/83 and 1/85 look at work sharing and part-time and temporary work respectively. On temporary work, the draft directive is in COM 84/159.

*All the above are updated regularly in the periodical *'Social Europe'*, available from HMSO and consultable at any Commission office or EDC.

*A report, *'Activities for the Unemployed'* is available from the European Foundation for the Improvement of Living and Working Conditions, Loughlinstown House, Shankhill, Co. Dublin, which also produces a variety of studies covering the field its title suggests.

The *Summit Communique* of December 1986 and the *Council Resolution* of 11 December on an action programme on *employment growth* have not, at time of writing, been printed, but can be consulted at any Commission office. The Commission proposals are summarised in Information note P(86) 515.

The series *Economic Papers* published by DG II in the Commission, examines economic aspects of employment. (Issue 42, for example, is entitled *Work sharing: Why? How? How not...)* These cannot be bought but can be consulted at Commission offices and EDCs.

The Commission basic strategy paper on *Technological Change and Social Adjustment in Industry* is in COMDOC 84/6 of January 1984.

SOCIAL POLICY

(See also Part VII.)

Basic Library: Nos 3, 5 and 6. *European Files*: 11/82, 13/85 and 8/86. In the *ED* series, 6/80, 5/83 and 4/84.

Background Reports 1/85 (on social developments) 10/86 (on the disabled) and 12/86 (equal opportunity for women) are all relevant.

*The periodical *Social Europe,* from

HMSO or available at Commission offices and EDCs, examines social trends and employment generally, and has a series of detailed supplements. No.1 of 1986, for example, covered 'New Technology and Social Change – Manufacturing Automation'.

Trade Union Information Bulletin, published quarterly, looks at Community policy from the TU point of view. Issue No. 2 of 1986, for example, contains a summary of steps towards a reduction in working time taken in six Community countries. The Bulletin is free from DG X in the Commission (TU Division).

The Council *Recommendation on the employment of disabled people* is in OJ L 225/43, of 12 August 1986.

A free *newsletter* on projects for the disabled, *Interact News* is available from Ambiorix Square 32, Box 47, B 1040 Brussels. There is also an occasional *Newsheet* from the Commission Bureau for Action in Favour of Disabled People, DG V C-3 in the Commission.

There are two *free newsletters* for women. The first is *Women of Europe,* available from the Women's Information Service in DG X. (Some detailed supplements on equal opportunities, Community law and women, women at work, etc. are still in print.) From the London Office of the Commission comes *Women in Europe,* directed specifically at the UK.

Copies of the Commission's action plan, *Equal Opportunities for Women – 1986–90* are available from DG V A-4 in the Commission.

A leaflet, *Women and the European Social Fund,* is free from Equal Opportunities Commission offices.

The *Model Code for the Disabled* is in COMDOC 86/9 of 24 January 1986.

Material in Braille: information from Christopher Smith, RNIB, 338 Goswell Road, London EC1, or Playback Service, 276 St. Vincent St., Glasgow G2 5RP.

The *Charter for the Aged* is discussed in European Parliament Report A 2-7/86, of 1 April 1986.

A leaflet on the *European Foundation for the Improvement of Living and Working Conditions* is available from any Commission office. There is also an occasional newsletter, *EF News,* available free from Loughlinstown House,

Shankhill, Co. Dublin.

The *Poverty Action Programme* is considered in *Background Report* 10/84.

THE TROUBLED INDUSTRIES

See *European Files* 9/82, 19/85 and 4/86, *Background Reports* 3/85 (on steel) and 5/86 (on shipbuilding) are relevant, as is ED 5/82.

For the rest, the reader must rely on COMDOCS, of which there are a multitude, since the situation in all three industries changes so rapidly. Consult any Commission office.

Community aid for steel, shipbuilding and textiles is covered in Part VII.

SMALL AND MEDIUM-SIZED ENTERPRISES

The basic document is *EF 6/83.*

The *Summit Communiqué* of December 1986 can be consulted at any Commission office.

Commission proposals for help for SMEs are in COMDOC 86/C 287; the plan for Information Centres in COMDOC 86/445.

A note on the *Business Cooperation Centre* and the *Business Cooperation Network* is available from the Task Force (see main text).

Perhaps the best booklets on *Business Improvement Services* and *Better Technical Services* are available from Industry Department for Scotland, Alhambra House, 45 Waterloo St., Glasgow G2 6AT.

★A *Guide to Small Firms Assistance in Europe* covers 17 countries in Western Europe. It is available from Gower House, Croft Rd., Aldershot, GU11 3HR.

A video film and handbook entitled *European Community Activities of Interest to SMEs* are available on loan from Commission offices.

A document entitled '*Microcomputers in the Administration and Management Processes in Smaller Business'* can be consulted at any Commission office.

Help for financing *Innovation in SMEs* is summarised in Supplement to Euroabstracts No. 0806 of July 1985.

Elise News (see text) is a free bulletin on local employment initiatives of interest to SMEs.

THE NEW TECHNOLOGIES

The most comprehensive source of information known to the writer is *Appendix II to the Information Report On New Technologies,* prepared by the Studies and Research Division of the Economic and Social Committee. The reference number is CES 32/85 final. This covers Community programmes such as ESPRIT, RACE, INSIS, CADDIA, CD, EUROTRA, COMETT, BRITE, energy programmes, biotechnology, FAST, CODEST, COST, the 'Stimulation' Programme, the Framework Programme, and multilateral programmes such as the European Space Agency, EUTELSTAT, EUMESTAT, APOLLO, CERN, SUPER-PHENIX-NERSA, AIRBUS INDUSTRIE and EUREKA. Published on 12 February 1986, it is already somewhat out of date, but there are grounds for hope that it will be updated. (Push for this with your Economic and Social Committee member and your MEP!)

It is difficult to purchase or get hold of (even some EDCs seem not to have it) but can be consulted at any Commission office. The presentation is particularly concise and it lends itself well to photocopying.

⋆A hefty booklet, *Industrial Innovation: a Guide to Community Action,* written by Giles Merritt, can be bought from sales agents or consulted.

The important *European Files* are 8/84, 18/82, 11/80, 7/84, 15/85, 4/86, 13/86, 14/86 and 18/86. In the ED series 5/82 and 2/85 are useful, as are *Background Reports* 32/83 (biotechnology), 33/82 (information technology), 31/82 (innovation), 11/82 (living with the new technologies), 1/86 (ESPRIT), 8/86 (industrial technologies), 17/86 (television) and 21/86 (The EC and Chernobyl).

A good brief summary of the *Community R & D Framework Programme, 1987–91* is obtainable from any Commission office. It is dated 28 October 1986. The Programme itself is available for consultation (COM 430/86).

A guide for UK participants in EC programmes, entitled *Scientific Research and Development in the European Community* was produced by the Cabinet Office, 40 Whitehall, London SW1 during 1986. It may be available from that Office

and can be consulted in Commission offices. It has a particularly comprehensive list of useful addresses and telephone numbers and is the perfect adjunct to the summary mentioned above.

Euronet DIANE News is a regular leaflet available free: telephone Luxembourg (352) 4301 2879.

⋆*The Green Paper on Broadcasting,* a very lengthy document, can be consulted at Commission offices, and the *proposed Directive* 'The Community's Broadcasting Policy' is available as Supplement 5 of 1986 to the Bulletin.

⋆A good summary of the EUREKA proposals was published in *British Business* on 4 October 1985.

⋆Much detailed material is available. It is listed in the *Catalogue* (Basic Library No. 7).

To keep up to date, subscribe to the free *Newsletter on New Technologies and Innovation Policy,* available from DG XIII in the Commission. There are also two commercial newsletters: ⋆*Tech-Europe,* available from 46 avenue Albert Elisabeth, 1040 Brussels, and (on biotechnology) ⋆*EBIP News,* from The British Library, 9 Kean St., London WC28 4AT.

Individual Programmes

The following documents are available free from Commission offices:

Research Programme in the field of *Environmental Protection* – an information file (sample tender, explanatory notes, guidance, application forms).

Proposal for a Council Regulation on *RACE,* (COMDOC 86/547 in booklet form).

An information pack on *BRITE,* and a booklet describing *Projects Supported* under the first call for proposals.

A leaflet on *Biotechnology,* with details of how to participate and a list of relevant publications.

A 'Guide to *Sectoral Grants* in Sciences and Technology'.

A 'Vade-mecum of *Contract Research'.*

A booklet on the *'Research Action Programme* – Materials'.

A guide for applicants under the Community *Stimulation Action* scheme.

A note (IP(86) 592) on *'Promoting Non-polluting Technologies'.*

A package on *ESPRIT,* and a report on Esprit Technical Week held in Brussels in September 1985.

A coloured booklet, '*Innovations* from Community Research'.

A Publications Bulletin on *Energy projects.*

WORKERS' PARTICIPATION AND COMPANY LAW

The indispensable document is the Price, Waterhouse Bulletin mentioned in the main text. This lists all the relevant COMDOCS and proposals.

In the EF *series:* see 9/84 and 4/85 *Background Report 1/85,* 'Social Developments', summarises recent thinking.

Background Report 29/83 is on *Worker Participation in Decision-making,* and 24/83 on *The Employee's Right to Know.*

★The Green Paper, '*Employee Participation and Company Structure'* is Supplement 8 of 1975 to the Bulletin of the EC.

★The EP *Resolution on Company Structure* is in OJ C149 of 14 June 1982.

★The Committee *Report on 'Vredeling'* is number 1–324/82. The many subsequent amendments to the *Vredeling proposals* are available for consultation. The latest *Council Conclusions* are in OJ C203/1 of 12 August 1986.

★Proposals on *Company Structure* are in COMDOC 83/185.

A booklet on the *European Trade Union Confederation* is available free from DG X in the Commission.

CONTRACTS AND TENDERS

The Commission proposals on *public procurement* in the Community are described in two COMDOCS: 86/375 of 19 June, and 86/297 of the same date. There is a *Background Report:* B20/86, of 9 October, and a later *Information Memo* (P-105) of 17 December.

Two brochures for businessmen are available. They are *Public Supply contracts in the EC* and *Government procurement in Japan: the way in.* Both are in the ED series.

Doing business in the EEC — *public contracts* is available, free from Nat-West, 41 Lothbury, EC2P 2BP.

Two free booklets come from the EIB: *Financing under the Lome Convention,* and *Financing outside the Community — the Mediterranean countries.* Much other material is available (consult the EIB office in London).

An excellent (and very frank) leaflet entitled *Opportunities for contracts under EEC aid programmes* is available from UKREP.

★*British Business* and the occasional pamphlets of the British Overseas Trade Board are helpful.

★A list of *Community delegates to third countries* (with telephone and telex numbers) is given in the Commission Directory.

A useful pack on TED (*Tenders Electronic Daily)* is free from any Commission Office.

TRANSPORT

For background: *European Files* 10/85 and 11/85 , ED 3/84 and *Basic Library* 3. There are *Background Reports* on transport barriers to trade (29/82), shipping (18/85), air freight (22/85) and civil aviation (19/86).

The Commission proposals on a *Transport Infrastructure Programme* are in COMDOC 86/340, and on *funding* the programme in COMDOC 86/674. The programme is summarised in an *Information Memo* – P-55 of June 1986.

Proposals for a Regulation on competition in *air transport* are in OJ C324 of 17 December 1986.

★Agreements already achieved, and proposed legislation in the field of transport are listed in a booklet available from the Department of Transport (£5.50 from 2 Marsham St., SW1P 3EB).

ENERGY

Policy on Energy is outlined briefly in EF 2/87, and ED 1/83. These are updated by regular reports on all aspects of energy, listed in the free SCAD *News* available free from OOPEC.

Other relevant *European Files* are 7/86 (on energy demonstration projects) 16/85 and 4/86.

A free *newsletter, Entech,* appears occasionally, covering in some detail the Community's non-nuclear energy R & D programmes. It is available from DG XII-E in the Commission.

There is a free booklet on the JET *project*, available at any Commission office.

★Details of support for *energy demonstration projects* are given in the OJ. An *Evaluation of Community Demonstration Programmes in the Energy Sector* is available free from DG XVII in the Commission.

★To keep up to date on all aspects of Community energy policy, subscribe to the new magazine *Energy in Europe,* published three times a year and available from OOPEC.

On funds, see also the section on the New Technologies.

THE ENVIRONMENT

A general introduction is given in EF 5/85 and ED 1/84. Two others in the EF series are being updated: *The EC and waste recycling,* and *The EC and water.* (The earlier versions can be consulted and photocopied.)

Background Reports 4/84 *(control of industrial pollution)* 21/83 *(Acid rain and other poisons),* and 22/86 *(the quality of life)* are relevant.

★*European Information Service* and *British Business* are as usual the best sources of information on the progress of proposed legislation.

Those interested in Community *help to the Third World* in the environmental field should subscribe to the free magazine *Courier* (page A20).

The *Environmental Impact Assessment Directive,* agreed by the Council on 8 March 1985, is in OJ L175 of 5 July 1985.

★An excellent *paper on its probable impact* is available from Peter Aitken of the Planning Exchange, 186 Bath St, Glasgow. An *explanatory memorandum* is available from the Dept. of the Environment.

A Note entitled *Research Programme in the Field of Environmental Protection* (1986–90) gives a detailed description of actual and proposed areas of research. Available free from DG XII in the Commission.

The aims of European Year of the Environment are laid out in *Background Report* B22/86 *(The Quality of Life),* available from any Commission office.

★During 1987 the *European Environmental Yearbook* will be published

by the Docter Institute. In around 800 pages it will study environmental law in EEC member countries in depth. Details from Peter Byron, 15 Kensington Court, London w8 (01-937 3660).

Try to get on the list for *press releases* sent out by the European Centre for Environmental Communication, 55 rue de Varenne, F-75341 Paris. The Centre, with help from the European Cultural Foundation in Amsterdam, will be organising a variety of events during 1987 and later.

The Commission's *Draft Resolution* on the Fourth Environmental Action Programme (1987-1992) is in COMDOC 86/485.

★*EEC Environmental Policy and Britain,* by Nigel Haigh (£12.95 from EDS Ltd., Unit 24, 40 Bowling Green Lane, London EC1R ONE) is in three sections. The first examines differences between national and Community policies on the environment; the second looks at actual and proposed legislation; and the third at its possible impact on the UK. Comprehensive and authoritative. EDS also publishes excellent periodic reports.

MONEY

The 'British problem' (budgetary contributions and refunds) is considered in detail in *Britain in the EC* and its regional companions (see *Basic Library*).

The UK Government's point of view is well laid out in the CO1 reference pamphlet 73/86 'Britain in the European Community'.

★A good summary of the *Fontainebleu agreement* is given in *British Business* of 6 July 1984, and in *Bulletin* No. 6 of 1984.

On the Budget in its broader aspects, see *Basic Library,* (3, 4 and 8), EF 17/86 and *Your Parliament in Europe* by George Clark. In the ED series, *The EC's financial system* and *The EC's budget* are both relevant.

A European Parliament paper, *Counting the Cost* deals with parliamentary control of community finances. Free from any Parliament office, as is *EP News,* a useful monthly, particularly full on budgetary matters.

Background Report 13/86, *The Community's Budget: Facts and Difficulties* is available free from any

Commission office, as is *The European Community Budget: The Facts* in more detail.

EF 9/86 deals with the approximation of European *tax systems.*

All the principal *banks* publish helpful material on the EMS, usually free. A simply written note on the ECU is available from the National Westminster Bank, and there is much useful detail in *The EEC – a Guide to Finance, Trade and Investment* published by Midland Bank International.

The twenty-seventh *Report of the Monetary Committee* of the EC (September 1986, available from OOPEC) summarises recent moves on monetary policy generally and the EMS in particular.

There is an introduction to the *European Monetary System* in EF 15/86 of that title; ED 6/84 and 4/81 are relevant. *Background Report* 5/85, *Developing the Community Monetary system* brings matters up to date.

★ Economic *statistical* material is covered in voluminous detail in the EUROSTAT series (page A8), and updated in a monthly supplement *European Economy,* produced by DG 11 in the Commission.

CONSUMERS

The basic document in EF 12/85.

★ *British Business* keeps a particularly careful eye on proposed legislation, listing the basic COMDOCS and OJ entries. The individual *directives* are summarised in the *European File* above, and available for consultation.

Two useful booklets can be consulted at Commission offices and EDCs. The first, *Consumer Redress* is Bulletin Supplement 2 of 1985. The second, *A New Impetus for Consumer Protection Policy* is an off-print of a communication from the Commission to the Council in early 1986.

Background Report 11/84 deals with proposed *Curbs on Misleading Advertising,* and 11/85 with *House Purchase.*

A variety of excellent pamphlets (many of them free) are produced by the *Consumers in the European Community Group,* 24 Tufton St, SW1P 3RB, from whence a list is available. They cover almost all aspects of Community consumer policy, with special leaflets on lobbying, air fares, protectionism, the CAP, and the role of the

European Parliament.

★ The magazine *Which?* is particularly well informed on EEC legislation.

★ UK *Trading Standards Legislation* is a running account of progress in this field with some commentary on possible implications for Britain. (Pub: Institute of Trading Standards Administration, 37 Victoria Ave., Southend on Sea, SS2 6DA.)

YOUTH

EF 3/84 is useful.

★ *The Young Europeans,* a study of 15–24 year olds in EC countries, is available at Commission Offices and EDCs.

★ A report on *Youth Initiatives* in the European Community is available in Supplement 5/86 of the periodical *Social Europe* – £2.50 from OOPEC.

A free leaflet on funding for youth initiatives on transition from school to working life is available from DG V in the Commission. It is entitled *Young People's Projects.*

★ The Community's survey of public opinion, *Eurobarometre,* is interesting in its breakdown of attitudes among the young.

For details of COMETT, ERASMUS and YES see below.

EDUCATION

An Education Policy for Europe (ED 4/82) looks at the education systems of the Community and the embryo Community policy for education. See also EF 3/85. A free pamphlet on EURYDICE (the Education Information Network in the EEC) is available from Commission offices.

A 14-page pamphlet, *Resources for Teaching About Europe,* is available from the UK Centre for European Education, University of London Institute of Education, 18 Woburn Square, London WC1H ONS.

Details of *grants for exchanges, joint study programmes, and short study visits* are given in the booklet *Finance from Europe* (*Basic Library* No. 6). There is also a fuller leaflet, *Higher Education Cooperation,* available from the Office for Cooperation in Education, 51 rue de la Concorde, B 1050 Brussels.

★ Commission proposals for the extension of *Language teaching* are in COMDOC 78/222. *Parliament and*

ECOSOC *reports* are also available at Commission Offices and EDCs.

The best summary of the COMETT, ERASMUS and YES schemes is in the magazine *Community Report,* published by the Commission Office in Dublin. Photocopies available from any Commission office. (Irish readers should get on the list for this excellent free magazine: available from the CEC, 39 Molesworth St., Dublin 2).

★ A new publication, *The Joint Study Programme Newsletter of the Commission,* is full of news about the various Community initiatives in the field of education. Available from the usual sources.

★ Two detailed guides are available from the Commission. *The Student Handbook* gives basic information for students intending to study in other Community countries. The booklet *Postgraduate Degrees in European Integration* covers the ground indicated (in the UK as well as other countries).

TRAVELLING AND WORKING IN EUROPE

See first EF 1/84, 13/84, 8/85 and 17/85 plus ED 3/82. There are useful *Background Reports:* 18/83 *(jobs for young people),* 15/83 *(Protecting travellers' interests),* and *16/82 (Working in the EC),* together with a paper called *Notes for Holiday-makers: medical care and duty-free allowances.*

Community action in the field of tourism is a Supplement (4/86) to the Bulletin. It can be consulted at any Commission office or EDC.

★ A guide, entitled *Working in the European Communities,* together with a supplement and continuation, by A J Raban of the University of Cambridge Careers Service, is available from Hobsons Ltd., Bateman St., Cambridge CB2 1LZ.

Government forms and leaflets about *travelling, medical treatment, etc.,* can usually be obtained from travel agents. The important ones are *Form* E111 and *leaflets* SA 29, SA 30 and SA 36.

★ Commission proposals on *road safety* are available in COMDOC (84) 170.

Background Report 5/84 looks at *compensation for victims of traffic accidents.*

From Jobcentres you can obtain the free leaflets *Working Abroad* and *Your Social Security and Pension Rights in the EC.*

★ A detailed guide, *Freedom of Movement for Persons in the EC* is available from HMSO. Individual countries have, of course, different rules; embassies can be helpful.

See also the note on COMETT, ERASMUS and YES mentioned above.

A leaflet on *Jobs with the Community* (including the Stagiaire system) is available free from any Commission office.

POLITICAL COOPERATION

The background to recent developments is laid out in *Working for Europe* (page A11). Most pamphlets in the *Basic Library* are relevant, though now out of date, as is ★ the Economist Schools Brief *Europe's fledgling foreign policy,* available in off-print from the 4 December 1982 issue.

★ A good summary of the decisions taken on *Political Cooperation* is in Bulletin No. 2 of 1986.

★ The *Single European Act* is given in full in Bulletin Supplement 2/86 (there may be some spare copies in Commission offices). The *House of Lords Report* on the Act is available from HMSO, price £2.10.

Commission proposals on *Overseas Representation* are in COMDOC 86/227.

EXTERNAL RELATIONS AND TRADE

The background is well laid out in ED 4/79 (*25 Years of EC External Relations* by Edmund Wellenstein).

The relevant *European Files* are 1/87, 16/86, 1/86 and 9/85.

A *Background Report* on *The EC and Japan* (B11/86) is available from any Commission office. A note on the *Executive Training Programme* in Japan can also be consulted; the number is IP (86) 99.

Documents on *Relations between the EC and the US* are listed in the main text. There is also a report of the same title by the Economic and Social Committee.

European Files 9/83, 19/83, 12/86 and 16/86 are relevant.

The whole gamut of the Community's external relations is covered in the series *Europe Information.* Some 70 titles detail the main agreements with third countries and groupings of countries, cooperation, aid, etc. Many of these are available free from the Documentation Service of DG X in the Commission; all can be consulted in Commission Offices or EDCs. A partial list of the series is given in the *Pocket Catalogue (Basic Library)*.

THE DEVELOPING WORLD

A dossier, *Europe-South Dialogue* contains four pamphlets and two maps, and covers the Community's relations with the Third World generally. It has a useful bibliography listing some of the hundreds of other books and pamphlets available.

These are the relevant European Files: 9/81, 14/82, and 16/86.

Background Report 16 and 17 of 1984 (on *Attitudes to aid,* and *Industrial developments in the Third World* respectively) are useful. 13/84 updates the *Generalised system of preferences,* 10/85 is on *Food Aid,* and 7/86 deals with *Halting the Advance of the Deserts.*

An Information note (P (86) 78), entitled *Science and Technology for Development* can be consulted at Commission offices.

An attractive illustrated booklet, *Ten Years of Lomé,* is available from Commission offices.

A free magazine, *The Courier,* is published six times per year and deals in depth with Community affairs in the context of *aid and development overseas.* It can be obtained by writing to the Commission in Brussels, or phoning Brussels 235 6367.

★ *The Brandt Report* is essential reading. It is available in an ultra-cheap pocket book published by Pan Books.

A study, *the EEC's Trade Relations with the Developing Countries,* was published in 1985 as No. DE 48 in the Europe Information (Development) Series.

AGRICULTURE

There is no really fast way of keeping track of the Community agricultural policy except by reading the daily press (coverage in the *Aberdeen Press and Journal* is the most detailed in the UK) and the journals of the various farmers' unions, or keeping in touch with your nearest Commission office.

The *Information Memo* series, produced in Brussels by the Spokesman's Service, probably offers the quickest detailed summary of CAP proposals and agreements which is available in Commission offices for photocopying. *Background Reports* produced by the Commission's London office, and the newsletter *Green Europe* and its occasional *Newsflash* supplements, issued by the Agricultural Information Service of DG X in the Commission are prompt and useful. All three will usually list the relevant COMDOCS.

The December 1986 *Farm Council agreement* is available in all three sources. The most important background papers are:
- the *Council agreement* of March 1984 (available with much supplementary material in *Green Europe Newsflash* 27 April 1984);
- the Green Paper entitled *A Future for Community Agriculture* (COMDOC 85/750), which incorporates views on its earlier Green Paper, *Perspective for the CAP* (COMDOC 85/350).

There are two useful *Background Reports:* 18/86 *(Helping the Farmers)* and 9/86 *(Reform of the CAP),* which is a shorter version of *Information Memo* P/12 of the same title.

Most other Commission material is unavoidably out of date before it appears, but EF 2/86 gives a good background summary of the CAP. There is also a free leaflet, *Agriculture in the European Community – Facts and Figures.*

Many banks produce material on the CAP.

Virtually every aspect of the CAP is dealt with in general in the *Green Europe* series; back numbers may be available from OOPEC, and any issue has a list of the full series.

Lastly, DG VI sponsors a massive programme of printed research, conclusions of working parties, summaries of conferences, etc., on every aspect of the farming industry. A few of these are listed in the *Pocket Catalogue (Basic Library)* but it is necessary to consult the full OOPEC catalogue to keep track of the remainder.

FOOD

The best record of food price movements and comparative prices related to the cost of living is published annually by HMG. Tables are given in *Hansard*.

Since the UK is unique in believing that the CAP is responsible for 'high' food prices, there is virtually no material available outside the British Press. See, however, *Basic Library* No. 3, and the COI reference pamphlet *Britain in the European Community*. On surpluses, *Background Report* 23/5 and *Green Europe* 205 (on fruit and vegetables) and 215 (on disposal for welfare purposes) are useful.

On *food aid*, EF 14/82, 10/85 and 2/86 are relevant. Current Commission proposals on food aid for the developing world are in COMDOC 86/418, and are summarised in *Information Memo* P-63 of July 1986.

Two *illustrated booklets,* 'Sudan and the European Community' and 'Operation Flood', dealing with aid for India, may be available free from Commission offices. There is also a *free dossier,* 'Europe-South Dialogue'.

FISHERIES

The lengthy tale of the agreement on a *Common Fisheries Policy* is told in ED 1/85 and EF 10/86.

★ A *Yearbook of Fisheries Statistics* is published annually, with quarterly updates.

The impact of *Spain and Portugal* on the CFP was the subject of a Communication to the Council dated June 1986 (COMDOC 86/302), backed by statistics on fishing in the Ten and the Twelve (COMDOC 86/975). This was revised as a result of discussion in Council and resubmitted as COMDOC 86/474.

The agreement on *technical measures on conservation* agreed in September 1986 is published in OJ L288 of 11 October.

The agreement of December 1986 on *structural policy* was reached on the basis of Commission proposals put forward in June 1986 (COMDOC 86/302) and published in their final form in OJ C279 of 5 November 1986.

The Commission's proposals for *economic regeneration* in fishing areas are in COMDOC 84/715.

SPAIN AND PORTUGAL

European File 17-18/85 gives a good summary of the negotiations for *Spanish*

and Portuguese accession, and the terms agreed. There is also a *Background Report* (17/85).

EF 5/6/86 shows the enlarged Community in diagrammatic form.

Most Community pamphlets and booklets have been, or are being, revised to take into account the 1986 enlargement.

★ On agriculture, the newsletter *Green Europe,* available from DG X, devoted issue 214 to 'Agricultural aspects of Community Enlargement'.

★ An assessment of 'The Economic and Industrial Impact of Spain's accession to the EEC' by Thierry Paccoud is available from Bureau d'Informations Europeennes, Rue Leys 8, 1040 Brussels.

Barclays, National Westminster and Midland banks all have useful free material.

A PEOPLE'S EUROPE

EF 3/86, *Towards a People's Europe* gives an excellent introduction to the subject.

The *Report of the People's Europe Committee* is in Bulletin Supplement 7 of 1985. The Commission's view is in COMDOC 85/640.

See also the sections on the Environment, Television, Culture, Youth and Education, and Travelling and Working in Europe.

MONEY FROM EUROPE
General

Finance from Europe (No. 6, *Basic Library*) gives a good general introduction and essential contacts.

In the *EF series*, 8/86, 8/85, 1/85 and 15/84 are relevant. ED 3/85, *Grants and Loans,* give the wider Community picture. Recent *Background Reports* include 13/85 and 7/85 on *The Social Fund* and *Encouraging Small Businesses* respectively.

Some of the very best material is now produced by British banks. Particularly recommended are:

– *The EEC – a Guide to Finance, Trade and Investment,* produced by Midland Bank International – a guide not only to funds but to the whole Community, and very readable to boot;

– *Official Sources of Finance and Aid for Industry in the UK,* produced by the National Westminster Bank – even more comprehensive in its coverage of loans and grants, broken down regionally, and with many useful addresses and telephone numbers; NatWest also produce an excellent series of leaflets, by subject and by country;

– *Finance for Farmers and Growers,* from Barclays Bank, which has a detailed section on funds for agriculture.

* Among a number of books are *Grants from Europe* by Ann Davison (£5.25 from Macdonald & Evans, Estover Rd., Plymouth PL6 7PZ); *Attracting Money from Europe* (£4.50 from the Association of District Councils, 9 Buckingham Gate, London SW1E 6LE); and *Finding Money in Brussels* (£6.50 from CBI Publication Sales, Centre Point, 103 Oxford St., London WC1A 1DU).

* Of particular value to local authorities is a series edited or written by Peter Aitken of the Planning Exchange, entitled *Briefing Notes.* Recent issues cover changes in Community funding policy relating to the RDF, rural areas, the Social Fund, and aid to traditional industries. A list of the notes with prices is available from The Planning Exchange at 186 Bath St., Glasgow G2 4HG.

* *Promoting Local Authorities in the EC,* edited by Colin Mellors is authoritative and wide in scope; from IULA (who produce *European Information Service)* at 38 Great Smith St., London SW1P 3BJ.

* *Regions in the European Community* looks at the problems of obtaining and using Community funds in England, Scotland, and Wales, Ireland North and South and other areas; edited by Michael Keating and Barry Jones, and available from Clarendon Press for OUP.

Several government departments produce leaflets and guides to Community funds. (Addresses: last pages). and those of the DoE, the Environment being particularly helpful (Addresses: last pages).

A handbook, *Government and EEC Grants and Assistance to Businesses in the UK* is free from Hacker Young, 2 Fore St., London EC2Y 5DH.

* Several professional guides, regularly updated, are available. Particularly recommended: *A Guide to European Community Grants and Loans,* compiled by Gay Scott for Eurofi (Northill, Biggleswade, Beds.) and the weekly monitoring service *Update on EEC Grants,* produced by Ceres and available from Newcastle-upon-Tyne Polytechnic, Library Building, Ellison

Place, NE1 8ST.

Specialised Funds

(See also text, and entries under various individual sections – particularly The New Technologies, The Troubled Industries, Employment and Social Policy, SMEs, Energy, the Environment, Youth and Education, and Fisheries.)

The better known funds (ERDF, ESF, ECSC, EIB, FEOGA and the NIC or Ortoli Facility) are all dealt with in the material listed above.

Wider in scope than the title suggests is a handbook, *Operations of the European Community concerning SMEs and Craft Industry,* of which Commission offices may still have a few copies. This remarkable compilation was produced as long ago as July 1984, but is still worth consulting for its wealth of detail – particularly in the form of contact points in the Commission.

There is an EF (1/86) on the *Integrated Mediterranean Programmes.*

The 1987/9 Guidelines for the *Social Fund* are in OJ L 153/59, of 7 June 1986. See also the *Briefing Note* mentioned in the text.

The EIB publishes a great variety of reports and pamphlets. Most are summarised in *'100 Questions and Answers',* available free direct from the Bank or its London Office (see page A24).

Perhaps the best summary of FEOGA grants and other Community assistance is contained in *Finance for Farmers and Growers,* published by Barclays Bank and free from 94 St. Paul's Churchyard, EC4M 8EH. There are also useful leaflets from MAFF (and DAFS in Scotland – see last pages).

Apart from re-adaptation, or 'Article 56' grants from the ECSC, covered in the General section (and in detail in recent articles in the magazine *Social Europe)* there are several specialised funds. Grants for *technical steel research* are summarised in OJ 294/3 of 16 November 1985. A Commission Memorandum on *pilot and demonstration projects* in the steel industry is COMDOC 336/86; this was agreed in July of that year. A Community *coal research programme* was agreed in May; details are in OJ C122/86. There are also Commission Memoranda – 85/652 on *coal research,* 1986–90, and 86/134, which records progress on the implementation of the Community's *iron and steel research* programme.

A note on *cheap loans* to help miners and steelworkers buy their own homes is given in *Finance from Europe – Basic Library No. 6.*

★ A *Yearbook on Venture Capital* is published by VUGA, PO Box 16400, NL 2500 BK, The Hague, Netherlands.

On the *cultural* front there is a *European File* (14/85). Four Resolutions (on *architectural heritage, business sponsorship, conservation,* and *European cinema and television year*) are all published in OJ C320 of 13 December 1986.

★ *Bulletin* 12/85 lists references to previous proposals and agreements, including *access to museums and cultural events* for young people, the *'City of Culture'* scheme, progress on establishing the *European Foundation,* the establishment of *transnational cultural itineraries,* schemes for *cinema and TV co-productions,* and proposals on *copyright, translation and taxation* in the cultural sector.

EUROPEAN DOCUMENTATION CENTRES AND DEPOSITORY LIBRARIES

EDCs contain all important documents relating to the Community in its various aspects, plus published books. The practice is that in return for receiving this free service from the Commission such libraries should be open to the public.

There are EDCs at the following Universities and Polytechnics:

Aberdeen, Bath, Belfast, Birmingham, Bradford, Brighton, Bristol, Cambridge, Canterbury, Cardiff, Coleraine, Coventry, Dundee, Durham, Edinburgh, Essex, Exeter, Glasgow, Guildford, Hull, Keele, Lancaster, Leeds (University and Polytechnic), Leicester, London (University, LSE, Polytechnic of North London and Chatham House), Loughborough, Manchester, Newcastle, Norwich, Nottingham, Oxford, Portsmouth, Reading, Salford, Sheffield, Southampton, Wolverhampton, Wye.

There are similar collections at Depository Libraries in:

Boston Spa (EC Liaison Officer, British Library), Liverpool and District Scientific Industrial and Research Library. London – British Library Reference Division; City of Westminster Libraries.

SUGGESTED FURTHER READING

Cohen, C.D. (1983) The Common Market – 10 Years After. Philip Allan.

Fennell, R. (1988) The Common Agricultural Policy. Granada.

Freestone, D.A.C. and Davidson, J.S. (1988) The Institutional Framework of the European Communities. Croom Helm.

Harrop, J. (1989) The Political Economy of Integration in the EC. Edward Elgar.

Hill, B.E. (1984) The CAP – Past, Present and Future. Methuen.

Hine, R.C. (1985) The Political Economy of European Trade. Wheatsheaf.

Keating, M. and Jones, B. (1985) Regions in the Community. Clarendon.

Lodge, J. (1983) Institutions and Policies of the European Community. Frances Pinter.

Lodge, J. (ed) (1986) European Union: The European Community in Search of a Future. Macmillan.

Pryce, R. (ed.) (1987) The Dynamics of European Union. Croom Helm.

Seers, D. and Vaitsos, C. (1982) The Second Enlargement of the EEC. Macmillan.

Taylor, P. (1983) The Limits of European Integration. Croom Helm.

Tsoukalis, L. (1986) Europe, America and the World Economy. Basil Blackwell.

Wallace, H. (1985) The Challenge of Diversity. Routledge and Kegan Paul.

Williams, A. (ed.) (1984) Southern Europe Transformed. Croom Helm.

I would also suggest that those interested in particular issues relating to the EC should consult the periodical 'Journal of Common Market Studies'.

SOME ESSENTIAL ADDRESSES

The admirable 'EEC Contacts' by Jim Hogan lists pretty well every address in the Community as a whole as well as the UK which the reader is likely to need. It is revised regularly and published by Eurofi (UK) Ltd. the Old Rectory, Northill, Biggleswade, SG18 9AH.

The list which follows, though short, may be helpful.

COMMUNITY ORGANISATIONS
UK Permanent Representation

6 Rond Point Schuman,
1040 Brussels,
Belgium.
Tel: 230 6205

Commission of the European Communities

Brussels Office,
Rue de la Loi 200,
1049 Brussels
010 322 235 1111
Telex 21877

Luxembourg Office,
Bâtiment Jean Monnet,
Rue Alcide de Gasperi,
Kirchberg, Luxembourg,
010 352 43011
Telex 3423

London Office,
8 Storey's Gate,
London SW1P 3AT.
01-222 8122
Telex 23208

Belfast Office,
Windsor House,
9/15 Bedford Street,
Belfast.
0232 240708
Telex 74117

Cardiff Office,
4 Cathedral Road,
Cardiff CF1 9SG.
0222 371631
Telex 497727

Edinburgh Office,
7 Alva Street,
Edinburgh EH2 4PH.
031-225 2058
Telex 727420

European Investment Bank

Head Office,
100 bd Konrad Adenauer,
2950 Luxembourg.
010 352 43791
TELEX 3530

Liaison Office for the UK,
23 Queen Anne's Gate,
London SW1H 9BU,
01-222 2933
Telex 919159

Publications

The Office of Official Publications (OOPEC) is at
5 rue de Commerce
2985 Luxembourg.
Lux. 490081 or 490191

The Official Journal of the European Communities and other EC publications can be obtained from:

Her Majesty's Stationery Office (HMSO),
PO Box 276,
London SW8 9DT.
01-622 3316

or

Alan Armstrong and Associates,
Sussex Place,
Regents Park,
London NW1 4SA.
01-258 3740

The European Parliament

London Information Office,
2 Queen Anne's Gate,
London SW1H 9AA,
01-222 0411.

Administration:
Centre European,
Plateau du Kirchberg,
PO Box 1601,
Luxembourg,
Luxembourg 43001.

Plenary sessions:
Palais de L'Europe,
67006 Strasbourg,
France,
Strasbourg 374001.

Brussels Office:
97 rue Belliard,
1040 Brussels,
Belgium,
234 2000.

Names and addresses of Members of the European Parliament can be obtained from any Parliament or Commission Office

Council of Ministers

Secretariat,
170 rue de la Loi,
1040 Brussels,
234 6422

Economic & Social Committee,

2 Rue Ravenstein,
1000 Brussels,
512 3920.

Names and addresses of Members of the Committee can be obtained from any Commission Office.

European Atomic Energy Community (Euratom)

European Commission,
DG XVII,
rue de la Loi 200,
1049 Brussels,
235 1111.

European Court of Auditors

29 rue Aldringen,
118 Luxembourg,
Tel: 4773–1.

European Court of Justice

BP 96
Plateau du Kirchberg,
Luxembourg,
Tel: 43031.

TRADE & INDUSTRY

An excellent 'DTI guide' is published annually as a supplement to 'British Business.' It is also available as an offprint, price £1.25. It lists offices, names and addresses and telephone numbers of those Departments most concerned with Community matters. From DTI, Millbank Tower, London SW1 4QU.

OTHER ADDRESSES:

Department of Industry,
Kingsgate House,
66 Victoria St.
London SW1E 6SI,
01-212 0400.

These are the addresses of the regional offices of the Departments of Industry in England:

Northern Region,
Stanegate House,
Groat Market,
Newcastle-upon-Tyne
NE1 1YN.
0632 24722
Telex 53178

North West Region,
Sunley Building,
Piccadilly Plaza,
Manchester M1 3BA.
061 236 2171
Telex 667104

Merseyside Region
1 Old Hall Street,
Liverpool L3 9HJ.
051 236 5756

Yorkshire and Humberside Region,
Priestley House,
1 Park Road,
Leeds LS1 5LF.
0532 443171
Telex 557925

West Midlands Region,
Ladywood House,
Stephenson Street,
Birmingham B2 4DT.
021-632 4111
Telex 337919

East Midlands Region,
Severns House,
20 Middle Pavement,
Nottingham NG1 7DW.
0602 56181
Telex 37143

South Eastern Region
Charles House,
375 Kensington High St,
London W14 8QH.
01-603 2060
Telex 25991

South West Region
The Pithay,
Bristol BS1 2PB.
0272 291071
Telex 44214

**South West Industrial
Development Office,**
Phoenix House,
Notte Street,
Plymouth PL1 2HF.
0752 21891
Telex 45494

Northern Ireland

Department of Economic
Development,
Netherleigh,
Massey Avenue,
Belfast BT4 2JP.
0232 63244

Scotland

Industry Department for Scotland,
Alhambra House,
45 Waterloo Street,
Glasgow G2 6AT.
041 248 2855
Telex 7778839

Wales

Welsh Office,
Industry Department,
Government Buildings,
Gabalfa, Cardiff CF4 4YL.
0222 62131
Telex 4982679

North Wales District Office,
Government Buildings,
Dinerth Road,
Colwyn Bay,
Clwyd LL28 4UL.
0492 44261

OTHER ORGANISATIONS

Industrial and Commercial
Finance Corporation
(now known as Investors in Industry),
91 Waterloo Road,
London SE1.
01-928 7822
Telex 917844 9

Northern Ireland
Development Agency,
100 Belfast Road,
Holywood,
Co. Down. 02317 4232
Telex 7471729

Scottish Development Agency,
120 Bothwell St,
Glasgow G2 7JP.
041 248 2700
Telex 7776009

Welsh Development Agency,
Treforest,
Pontypridd,
Mid-Glamorgan,
044 385 2666
Telex 4975169

AGRICULTURE DEPARTMENTS

The addresses of the national
Agriculture Departments are:

Ministry of Agriculture
Fisheries and Food,
Whitehall Place,
London SW1.
01-233 3000
Telex 8893519

Dept of Agriculture
for Northern Ireland,
Dundonald House,
Upper Newtownwards Road,
Belfast BT4 3SB.
0232 650111

Welsh Office, Agriculture Dept,
Pearl Assurance House,
Greyfriars Road,
Cardiff.
0222 44151
Telex 4982039

Dept of Agriculture
and Fisheries for Scotland,
Chesser House, Gorgie Road,
Edinburgh EH11 3AW,
031-443 4020
Telex 7274789

Other organisations:

Central Council for Agricultural &
Horticultural Cooperation, Market
Towers, New Covent Garden Market,
1 Nine Elms Lane, London SW8.
01-720 2144

Agricultural Training Board,
Bourne House,
32 Beckenham Road,
Beckenham, Kent.
01-650 4890

The Agricultural Development and
Advisory Service can be contacted
through the local office of the national
Agriculture Department.

OTHER GOVERNMENT DEPARTMENTS

British Overseas Trade Board
Exports to Europe Branch
1 Victoria St.
London SW1H 0ET,
01-215 7877.

Industrial Development Board for
Northern Ireland
LDB House
64 Chichester St.
Belfast BT1 4JX.

Scottish Office
Alhambra House
45 Waterloo St.
Glasgow G2 6AT
041-248 2855

Welsh Office
New Crown Building
Cathay's Park
Cardiff CF1 3NQ
0222-825111

Department of Employment

Caxton House
Tothill St.
London SW1H 9NA
01-213 3832

Department of Energy

Community Research matters;
Room 1297
Thames House South
Millbank
London SW1P 4OJ

Department of the Environment:

2 Marsham Street
London Sw1P 3EB
01-212 3434

HM Custom & Excise

King's Beam House
39 Mark Lane
London EC3R 7HE
01-626 1515 ext. 2081

INDEX